THE RED AND THE WHITE

THE RED AND THE WHITE

THE STORY OF ENGLAND v WALES RUGBY

HUW RICHARDS

First published in Great Britain in 2009 by Aurum Press Ltd
7 Greenland Street, London NW1 0ND
www.aurumpress.co.uk

ISBN 978 1 84513 405 1

10 9 8 7 6 5 4 3 2 1
2013 2012 2011 2010 2009

Typeset in Spectrum by SX Composing DTP, Essex.
Printed and bound by MPG Books Ltd, Bodmin, Cornwall

To Gethin Rhys John Charles, born 17 November 2008 and qualified to play for both England and Wales, his big sister Carys and my godson Matthew Finn 'Finny' Wittstock McDonald

CONTENTS

	INTRODUCTION	1
ONE	OPENING SHOTS, 1881–90	12
TWO	THE GOULD STANDARD, 1891–98	32
THREE	THE MOST BEAUTIFUL GAME, 1899–1909	46
FOUR	THE TWICKENHAM EFFECT, 1910–22	62
FIVE	REVENGE OF THE FORSYTES, 1923–32	79
SIX	POETRY AND PARITY, 1933–39	96
SEVEN	WAR AND PEACE, 1940–51	109
EIGHT	ONLY TWO CAN PLAY, 1952–58	125
NINE	WRESTLING IN THE MUD, 1959–68	140
TEN	THE DRAGON THAT SLEW ST GEORGE, 1969–79	160
ELEVEN	RECESSION, 1980–89	184
TWELVE	ANGLO-SAXON ALTITUDE, 1990–2003	205
THIRTEEN	MODERN TIMES, 2004 AND BEYOND	234
	RESULTS	246
	ACKNOWLEDGEMENTS	250
	SOURCES AND BIBLIOGRAPHY	252
	INDEX	257

INTRODUCTION

They're physically bigger, socially superior and often formidably accomplished. And they live next door!

Dai Smith

It is the one match, this Welsh one, which every Englishman wants to be part of, which just has got to be won . . . nothing really compares to the atmosphere of this Welsh match. It's a confrontation, it's history.

Dean Richards

This is the moment. It comes once a year, alternately at Twickenham and the Millennium Stadium, Cardiff. The anthems have been sung, the band is trooping off, the teams are poised for kick-off. The referee consults both his watch and the official from the host broadcaster as he prepares to blow his whistle.

It is a moment of both anticipation and apprehension, of relish for the spectacle that is to come and fear that it might presage twelve months of crowing by the old enemy. There is a pause, an automatic intake of breath in preparation for a roar that will greet the whistle and the moment when one of the thirty players in the arena, fifteen in red and fifteen in white, propels the ball towards the opposing goal-line and the battle for its possession commences.

It is also a moment when it is almost impossible not to think back to earlier games and players. For the hundreds of former internationals from both teams in attendance, those memories will be of matches they played in and of old colleagues and adversaries. For the rest of us, they are of the games and players we have seen, and those we have read, or been told, about.

In that moment those thirty young men become not only their

nation's chosen representatives on the day, but successors to great traditions. Just as Isaac Newton saw himself as standing on the shoulders of the thinkers who had come before him, an international rugby player stands in the boots and shirt of the men who previously held the same position. As we look at the Wales scrum-half, the mind's eye also sees Robert Jones, Gareth Edwards, Haydn Tanner and Dickie Owen. England's centres stand in a place once occupied by Jeremy Guscott and Will Carling, Jeff Butterfield and Phil Davies, Ronnie Poulton and J.G.G. Birkett.

The players themselves are, or at least should be, concentrated wholly on the here and now. Nobody on the red side wants to lose a line-out because a lock forward was pondering his historical relationship to Rhys Williams and Bob Norster. The whites want their full-back to concentrate on catching the up and under hoisted his way by the Welsh outside-half, rather than trying to decide whether he would rather be Alastair Hignell or Herbert Gamlin.

At the same time those memories are highly relevant to the players. Their accumulation and the passion they generate are the reason why today's players are being well paid to perform before huge crowds in modern, state-of-the-art stadiums, rather than changing in a pub before running out on to a roped-off playing area to perform in front of a crowd perhaps three-deep around the touch-line, like their predecessors in the first England v Wales match, at Richardson's Field, Blackheath on 19 February 1881. They evoke a rivalry which has no real parallel in rugby. This is not because it is the oldest fixture – England first played Scotland in 1871 and both countries had regular games against Ireland before Wales entered the fray. It is not because they have often been the strongest countries in the world – for most of the past century, the likeliest de facto world champions were New Zealand or South Africa.

It is, though, by far the most closely and evenly contested of all great rugby rivalries. There have been 117 meetings in the 127 years since that Victorian afternoon in south-east London. The overall result of all those matches spread over three centuries, thirteen decades and seven royal reigns is close to a dead heat. England lead by fifty-three wins to fifty-two, with twelve drawn. No other rivalry is nearly as well-balanced.

This means that the memories are evenly shared. If the Welshman awaiting the kick-off is thinking fondly of Gavin Henson's goal in 2005,

Scott Gibbs's triumphant charge in 1999 and the years in the 1970s when either J.P.R. Williams or Gareth Edwards routinely put England to the sword, the man next to him in the white shirt has his own happy thoughts of Will Greenwood's hat-trick at Cardiff in 2001, Bill Beaumont saluting the crowd in 1980 and matches in the 1990s and early 2000s when Carling and Martin Johnson's teams wreaked revenge for the hammerings of the 1970s. That balance goes back beyond living memory – to golden ages associated with Wavell Wakefield and Tom Voyce for England in the 1920s, and Gwyn Nicholls and Dickie Owen for Wales two decades before that.

That long-term competitiveness adds an edge to what in any case would be a charged and deeply felt rivalry. Christopher Wordsworth wrote in 1989: 'This never was, and never will be, just another international match.' As Dean Richards realised, it is about history – the expression via an annual contest of a relationship which long predates organised sport. The emotional pull of international competition comes from identity. It expresses who we are, or at least who we think we are, and how we relate to other peoples. It helps create and define those identities, imposing clear delineations on what, in reality, is rather blurred. Few of us doubt who we are or which side we are on when the teams in the red and the white run out at Twickenham or the Millennium Stadium. The elementally physical nature of rugby deepens that sense.

Yet there are many people who have a foot in both camps. With a Welsh father and an English mother, I am equally eligible to play for either country and am prevented from doing so only by a complete absence of talent for rugby. I chose to support Wales so early in life that I cannot remember why. My younger brother, who does have sporting ability, took the opposite decision at an equally young age. Part of the genesis of this book is in the fraught international match days of our childhood.

This blurring is a consequence of the peculiarities of Britishness. Other international sporting teams represent nation states. French teams have French passports. Players' roots may be Cameroonian, Burkinabe or Georgian, but they are citizens of the French Republic. Subsets within states, even those as self-conscious as Spain's Basques and Catalans, don't get to play full internationals. Britain is different. Its subsets do play, because they got there first in numerous sports, football and rugby among them. Yet nobody carries a Welsh or English passport. As Billy Bragg, the songwriter and political activist, points out: 'The only time you'll need an official document to prove you are English is if you are chosen to represent the country at sport.' The same goes for Wales, at least since it discovered that the assertions of New Zealanders about Welsh ancestry needed checking.

All British national identities are entwined with others, but none more than England's with Wales and vice versa. Scotland was a separate state until 1707, and afterwards retained its legal and educational systems. Ireland joined the United Kingdom in 1801, but remained apart by virtue of geography and the profound desire of the majority of its citizens to secede. England and Wales are different. 'England and Wales' was the administrative unit recognised for much of their history. As Jeremy Paxman has written in his thoughtful analysis of Englishness: 'It has never remotely looked a relationship of equals.' Wales was subjugated in the thirteenth century, and its legal system – which conceded some rights to women – suppressed. It was formally incorporated between 1536 and 1543 in Acts of Union a psychiatrist might interpret as Henry VIII's Oedipal revenge on a father born in Pembroke. Its incorporation within the United Kingdom is crisply delineated by historian Robert Colls in *The Identity of England*: 'The English sought union for reasons of security, the Scots for economic advantage, some Irish joined with it in the hope that it might yield to them what it had yielded to others. The Welsh were not consulted.' Though crassly insensitive, the listing in the 1888 edition of *Encyclopaedia Britannica* was, in strictly administrative terms, correct: 'For Wales, see England.'

There remained people who saw themselves, and were recognised, as Welsh. Shakespeare's Fluellen, in *Henry V*, is the prototypical stage Welshman – emotional, emotive and wordy. There was a boundary, more or less corresponding to the dyke constructed by King Offa of Mercia, 'a man of sense and discernment' in the view of journalist T.W.H. Crosland. Yet even the border was blurred. Though usually regarded as Welsh, Monmouthshire was not formally a part of Wales until 1968.

This process left Wales without the institutions and symbols of nationhood. This also applied to England, but since most United Kingdom symbols and institutions had English roots and, as James Bryce put it in 1887, 'An Englishman has only one patriotism because England and the United Kingdom are to him practically the same thing', was scarcely noticed.

If nations are imagined communities, Wales has needed more imagination than most. It had no parliament, no separate legal or educational system, nor a capital city. Its language had no official standing. Nor did its flag.

Not that this occasioned great discontent. When the Prince of Wales watched Wales play England in Swansea – always more self-consciously Welsh than Cardiff – in 1932 he received 'a cheer the likes of which was never heard before at St Helen's'. At the end the crowd, headed for the exits, froze for the playing of 'God Save the King' then mobbed the Prince's car. The Prince's reception expressed, wrote the local paper, 'a nation's pride and loyalty'. The same paper had noted after the 1928 match that: 'Of all the singing at St Helen's on Saturday, that of "God Save the King" was the heartiest of any. Which is as it should be.'

Welsh nationalism has been a comparatively mild affair. Painting road signs green and burning the occasional holiday home is as violent as it has ever got. The leader of Plaid Cymru launched its first national assembly campaign in 1999 by denying it had ever advocated independence. But being more comfortable with Britishness than Scotland or most of Ireland is exactly why Wales has needed some means of asserting a distinct identity, showing it as more than, as Pope Benedict XV claimed in a far from infallible encyclical of 1916, 'a particular part of England'.

This is not about disliking England, although that has played its part. Small nations define themselves by reference to larger neighbours: Canadians are not American, the Portuguese are not Spanish. The converse also applies, but it is less important to larger nations. Not being English is central to Welsh identity. Not being Welsh rarely bothers the English; they are defined far more by their attitude towards France and, to some extent, Scotland. Sport is ideal for self-assertion. As Eric Hobsbawm wrote: 'The imagined community seems more real as a team of eleven (or fifteen) named people.' Football coach Ondino Viera said: 'Other countries have history, Uruguay has football.' Wales has history, but it also has rugby union.

The irony is that rugby is, by origin, an English game, devised in its public schools and brought into Wales by their alumni. The genius of the

Victorian English was for codification, not invention. Nobody invents activities as elemental as kicking a ball or running with it, but somebody has to give these folk-games a shape and an agreed set of rules that allow them to be played elsewhere. It has been England's fate that so many recipients – Australian, Indian and West Indian cricketers, footballers the world over, Welsh and New Zealand rugby players – took their games, transformed them into something distinctly their own and then returned to beat the English at them.

Why rugby has exerted such appeal for Welshmen is a matter of debate. Gareth Williams, the leading historian of the game, argues that: 'We should never lose sight of the central appeal for an industrial population of a physically vigorous sport; its theatricality, its opportunity for self-expression as well as for entertainment, its affirmation of life after work, of a sense of wholeness denied elsewhere.' As journalist John Morgan wrote in 1958: 'Picking the rugby team is the nearest Wales gets to self-government.' Gerald Davies, both a great Wales player in his time and a perceptive observer of the game, has recalled walking through Cardiff with his team-mates and hearing passers-by talking of 'the "Welsh team" as if there were only one Welsh team in sport'. England derives sporting satisfaction and frustration from a wider range of sources. Any reference to 'the England team' is more likely to mean football or cricket, even though its rugby players have won a World Cup.

If I seem to have concentrated largely on Wales so far, there is a reason. It is because Wales has put so much of itself into rugby union that the rivalry with England, as results over 117 years show, is a true relationship of equals. It is almost the only field in which Wales has been able not merely to ask for recognition and respect – those eternal needs of the small nation – but demand it. English rugby and its players have been defined by Wales just as much as has been the case in reverse. For more than a century, until the coming of leagues produced a more introverted approach, Anglo-Welsh fixtures were among the highlights of the club season. Welsh opponents were often more familiar than England team-mates from other parts of the country. London Welsh straddle the divide, while matches pairing off the British unions for centenaries and other landmarks have invariably been England and Wales v Scotland and Ireland. British and Irish Lions tours have provided a further common cause between the countries.

Few English rugby clubs lack a resident Welshman. Teachers, along with coal and steel, have been the third of Wales's historic holy trinity of exports and Adrian Smith argues that Welsh migration, bringing an influx of teachers into the city's schools, helped turn Coventry into England's leading club between the late 1950s and early 1970s.

It is not, though, an easy relationship. There was considerable truth in the jest of an English official, who described Anglo-Welsh relations as being 'based on trust and understanding. They don't trust us, and we don't understand them.'

History is compounded by class. Once the English game had split into amateur and professional in 1895, Wales's wider social base moved it further away from the overwhelmingly middle and upper-class game that prevailed in England. Fundamental to Wales's ability to compete, the class issue was also a source of tension – and not only with England. In 1903, Ireland allotted a smaller budget for entertaining Wales after a match because 'champagne was given to the Scotsmen and beer only (but plenty of it) to the Welshmen ... The Scotsmen were gentlemen and appreciated a dinner when it was given to them. Not so the Welshmen.' In the same year a Scottish referee told a middle-class Welsh player of his surprise that 'Wales selected miners, steelworkers and policemen for their international teams and suggested that these players should join the Northern Union [the professional game in the north of England]'. The Rugby Football Union has an honoured place in Welsh demonology, but it often showed more understanding of, and flexibility towards, the different circumstances of the Welsh game than did the Scots or Irish.

Tensions have sometimes spilled on to the field. Alan Watkins wrote after a particularly rough contest in 1987 that 'this has traditionally been a bad-tempered and vicious fixture'. Player eligibility has been a consistent source of debate. Rules were, until recently at least, more a matter of custom and a certain amount of trust than of precisely delineated legislation. Birth, descent and residence – particularly the last – have all played their part. There was a certain irony in Wales being caught playing ineligible New Zealanders at the end of the twentieth century, since for most of it controversy had surrounded England's partiality for young men who were unquestionably New Zealanders, South African or Australian, but had been studying at an English university or medical school. Wales, like the Duke of Dorset in *Zuleika Dobson*, had no objection to these young men existing, but regretted 'that Mr Rhodes had enabled them to do so in Oxford'.

Far more numerous have been those who qualified for both sides. Wales picked Arthur Evanson, an Oxford student born in Llansoy, Monmouthshire, for the very first meeting. Evanson, whose elder brother Wyndham had already been capped by England, preferred to wait for a chance to wear the white shirt, which came the following year at Swansea. John Robins even played for both, although his England caps were in wartime service internationals. Many players ended up 'on the wrong side' because of wider population movements. Late nineteenth-century migration from depressed rural England meant that many Wales players answered to Gareth Williams's felicitous description of Gwyn Nicholls as 'a West Countryman by birth, but Welsh by adoption, inclination and location'.

More than eighty Wales players – around eight per cent of the total – were born in England. The number of Welsh-born England internationals is smaller but not insignificant. Indeed, the town or city to have produced the most players in one England team is Cardiff, which boasted three of its sons in the XVs that played France and Ireland in 1922. Such exchanges reached a Pythoneseque peak in 1993 with the spectacle of Dewi Morris, from Crickhowell, playing scrum-half for England while the Welsh No. 9 shirt was occupied by Rupert Henry St John Barker Moon, born in Walsall. Comic though it was, each exemplified a significant stream. Morris, like W.J.A. Davies and Bev Risman, had played all his serious rugby in England. Moon's years with Abertillery and Llanelli made him Welsh by adoption and affinity. Morris points out that no choice was involved on his part – nobody had asked him to play for Wales, or was likely to. Others, like Risman, Gwyn Rowlands and Geoff Windsor Lewis, had to make a choice. Some selections, such as Stanley Williams playing for England in 1911, struck the other nation as sharp practice.

There were still more players who, while always clear in their allegiance, were eligible for the other side. One reason why Dean Richards was so aware of the fixture's meaning is that his father was born in Treorchy. J.P.R. Williams, the hammer of the English during the 1970s, could have played for them, since his mother came from Rochdale. Three of England's 2003 World Cup-winning squad have Welsh qualifications. Dorian West was born in Wrexham and raised in Ynysybwl, while both Josh Lewsey (first name, Owen) and Martin Corry qualify through their mothers. Nationality is neither as simple nor as clear-cut as it looks.

The Wales v England fixture also took part of its character for nearly a century from its place in the rugby calendar. Until fixtures began to be rotated in 1974 it was usually both teams' first match. Playing in January made foul conditions – particularly at Cardiff, where the River Taff made regular attempts to reclaim the Arms Park – a recurring theme. The earliness of the fixture meant that it was rarely a title decider. Instead it was the launch-pad for the season, unveiling fresh talent and new line-ups. More than half of the Englishmen capped between 1881 and 1973 made their debuts against Wales, appearing at the scarcely credible rate of nearly six per match. Wales were usually less prone to wholesale renewal, averaging four new caps per match. Both teams averaged a little under two new caps per match against other opponents.

More recently fixture rotation has meant that the game has sometimes been the season's climax, most famously with Wales's unexpected win at Wembley in 1999. While the fixture has been moved around, it has not been devalued. Part of its continued appeal is that once-a-year rhythm, sacrificed only in World Cup years. South Africa and New Zealand have gone from playing each other in a series only once or twice a decade to playing twice and now three times a year, scarcity giving way to over-familiarity. With England v Wales there is always next year, but there is no risk of surfeit.

One side's golden memory is unavoidably the other's nightmare. If a Welsh fan has only to think of J.P.R. Williams smashing through white-shirted tacklers to be transported back to a happier place, for his English counterpart that image has something of George Orwell's boot crashing down repeatedly on a human face. Bob Hiller, the England full-back and Williams's opposite number on occasions, did put an amiably self-deprecating spin on it when he complained jokingly of seeing J.P.R. brushing him off on the way to the line around a dozen times in one international. 'I could understand them showing it on *Sportsnight* and *Grandstand*, and even *Newsnight*,' he said, 'but I thought putting it on *Jackanory* was a bit much.'

Debate has raged over the years as to why one side has enjoyed periods of supremacy over the other. Outstanding players, of course, can emerge at any time. There seems, though, to be some correlation between rugby fortunes and wider, social factors. Wales's best periods coincided with the peak of its coal industry and the relative prosperity of the 1970s; its worst came with the interwar depression and the ascendancy, politically and intellectually, of Thatcherism. Periods of dominance are also invariably attributed to superior organisation and tactics rather than greater innate talent. All of these factors appeared to play a part in 1970s Wales, but the precise order of cause and effect is harder to establish.

One thing is certain, the series has never lacked colour. The best sport needs a passionately committed audience. Observers from both nations have tended to ignore the role of the English supporters and concentrate on the antics, theatricality and singing of the Welsh. English fans have been travelling to Wales for as long as the Welsh have been making the opposite trip, but nobody has yet celebrated them in song as Max Boyce did the Welsh with 'Hymns and Arias', or through a film comedy like *A Run For Your Money*.

Central to it all are the men in the arena: enduring, era-defining giants like Wakefield and Edwards; those who became famous for one particular eighty minutes; and some who failed. Contemporary accounts recall their feats and foibles and show that even the greatest have limitations, critics and off-days, and not only on the pitch. Rugby players rarely do anything half-heartedly. The story of this fixture is a chronicle of lives lived to the full, if not invariably wisely. All of (male) human life is here – murderers and missionaries, trade unionists and Tory peers, miners and baronets, puritans and gamblers, war heroes and hippies, Test cricketers and Olympic sprinters. The matches have ranged between nail-biters and massacres, glorious displays of attacking rugby and afternoons of tedious ineptitude. But it has never, ever, not mattered.

A Note on Rugby Scoring

Until the late 1880s matches were decided by the number of goals scored, with tries as a tie-breaker if each team scored the same number. Agreed points systems came in from the 1890s and have changed as follows:

Season	Try	Conversion	Dropped Goal	Penalty	Goal from a Mark
1890–1	1	2	3	2	3
1891–2 to 1892–3	2	3	4	3	4
1893–4 to 1904–5	3	2	4	3	4
1905–6 to 1947–8	3	2	4	3	3
1948–9 to 1970–1	3	2	3	3	3
1971–2 to 1991–2	4	2	3	3	void
1992–3 to present	5	2	3	3	void

A Note on Terminology

Although the governing body for rugby in Wales was known until 1924 as the Welsh Football Union, it is referred to throughout as the Welsh Rugby Union (WRU).

CHAPTER ONE
OPENING SHOTS 1881–90

I affirm that Welsh nationality is as great a reality as English nationality.

William Gladstone, 1877

A journey of a thousand miles opens with a single step.

Lao-Tzu

This journey began with a kick, applied to the ball by England's captain Lennard Stokes, at Richardson's Field, Blackheath at 3.10 p.m. on Saturday, 19 February 1881. Wales had won the toss, so Stokes kicked off into 'a slight breeze'. In reality, the ball was caught and drop-kicked into touch by a Welsh player. But in another sense, it has never stopped rolling.

It was fitting that Stokes had been the player to kick things off. His elder brother Frederick had captained England a decade earlier in the first rugby international ever played. As a member of the Rugby Football Union committee, Lennard had proposed that England accept Wales's challenge. He joined RFU secretary Rowland Hill on the match arrangements sub-committee and helped select the team. Presumably someone else collected the gate money, fixed at 1/- with 'ladies to pay'.

If he was representative of a sport still confined to a limited social circle – a privately-educated medical student, one of six brothers who played for early giants Blackheath – he was far from typical as a player. He was winning his eleventh cap for England, a record, and was arguably the best player the game had yet seen. Match referee Arthur Guillemard recalled him as 'six feet in height and of sinewy frame . . . champion sprinter at the sports of the United Hospitals. He was a faultless catch and field, and a very quick starter . . . with his speed of foot, wonderful dodging powers and clever "shoving-off" . . . he was also for several seasons the longest drop in the three kingdoms.'

England fielded five Blackheath players and three from Richmond. Of the three northerners in the team two were from the gentlemanly Manchester club and the diversity represented by Charles Walker Luis Fernandes, from the Leeds club, was geographical and (presumably) ethnic rather than social: professionally, he was a landowner. They made up a formidable team. They had just recorded a thumping victory, by two goals and two tries to nil, over Ireland and the season before they had inflicted a record defeat, by two goals and three tries to a goal, on Scotland to become the first holders of the freshly minted Calcutta Cup.

If Stokes was the star, England had other players of substance. Temple Gurdon would eventually overtake Stokes as its most capped player. He was, recalled Guillemard, 'usually to be found in the heart of the scrummage', and was a superb dribbler, when this was one of a rugby forward's essential skills. The official history of the RFU recalls that these skills 'more than made up for his lack of weight'. His younger brother Charles also helped remedy any such deficiencies, being 15st – huge for a man of Victorian times – with power to match.

George Burton, another Blackheath forward, was described in that year's *Football Annual* as 'a splendid player when the ball gets loose, being a fine dribbler; and very difficult to stop when running, making the most of every opportunity'. England's two debutants included Harry Vassall, of Oxford University, 'a fine forward; very heavy and very fast, and difficult to stop'. They also fielded one player under a pseudonym. Arthur Budd, yet another RFU committee man, would become the most articulate spokesman for the fundamentalist amateur standpoint when the game split over making payments to players. In 1881 he was appearing in team lists and match reports as A.B. James, although given that 'James' was always in inverted commas the imposture was hardly subtle.

Like the best from any era, these players were not content merely to play the game as it had been handed down to them; they sought innovation. Rugby was still in its early stages of evolution. A proper set of rules had been agreed only a decade earlier, and it was less than five years since teams were reduced from twenty players to fifteen. How they lined up was still in flux. Some teams fielded ten forwards, and others nine. The use of two half-backs was reasonably standard, but there might be two or three threequarters and one or possibly two full-backs. Team play was in its infancy. The first recorded pass from a half-back to a threequarter would not occur until later that year. Blackheath enjoyed enormous success under Stokes's captaincy in the 1878-9 season by encouraging forwards to pass to each other, an idea that Vassall would introduce at Oxford with similarly spectacular results, particularly once they also decided to use their half-backs to link forwards and threequarters.

As well as evolving, rugby was also spreading. It had first reached Wales at Lampeter theological college, brought in 1850 by a new vice-principal who had studied alongside Old Rugbeians at Cambridge. Schools such as Llandovery, Brecon, Monmouth and Cowbridge Grammar echoed their English counterparts by developing their own forms of football in the 1850s and 1860s. The following decade saw the game spreading from schools and colleges into the wider community. Neath are the oldest major club, founded in 1871. By the end of the 1870s every significant community in South Wales had a rugby club. Newport, closest to the border, were the dominant early force and the first team to seek fixtures in England, playing Hereford three times in 1876-7.

There were early indications of the game's appeal in Wales. By 1880 listings in the *Football Annual* showed Welsh clubs with memberships comparable to longer-established English counterparts. Swansea claimed 120 members and Newport 300, compared to Blackheath's 98 and Richmond's 350. Matches in the South Wales Cup, begun in 1877, attracted substantial crowds. When Newport, emboldened by a four-year unbeaten run and their comprehensive retention of the South Wales Cup, challenged Blackheath, demonstrably the strongest team in an English game that rejected competition for clubs as the thin end of the professional wedge, they drew a crowd of 5,000. Their comeuppance was fearful. Blackheath won by four goals and eight tries to nil.

The same forces that had already impelled Englishmen, Scots and Irishmen to band together and find the best among them to challenge other nations inevitably worked upon Welshmen. While a leading churchman insisted in 1886 that Wales was merely 'a geographical expression', events were arguing otherwise as a new national consciousness began to evolve. Wales's rugby team was launched in the same year as the first specifically Welsh item of parliamentary legislation, the 1881 Sunday Closing Act that for decades dictated the distinctive, and not universally appreciated, character of the Welsh Sabbath.

Who the first Wales team really represented is debatable. The South Wales Football Union, successor to the South Wales Football Club that had fielded the first Welsh representative team, against Herefordshire in Hereford in 1875, played regularly against English counties. Yet the challenge that the RFU discussed and, after 'considerable discussion', accepted on Stokes's motion on 30 November 1880 came not from the SWFU but 'R Mullock of Newport, Monmouthshire'. It was essentially the private enterprise of an imaginative and ambitious official of a single club that also happened to be affiliated to the RFU. It also, though, reflected changes in Welsh outlook. Richard Mullock represented the renewed national awareness that wanted to place Wales on the same footing as the other three nations. The SWFU was, as Dai Smith and Gareth Williams wrote, 'content with being a provincial union, dealing amicably but unambitiously with its English and Irish counterparts, the Yorkshire County union, Gloucestershire, Munster.'

The match was initially scheduled for 8 January. It was moved to the 22nd, then further delayed by frost. On the 25th the RFU wrote to Mullock, 'informing him that at present it is impossible to fix a date for the proposed match with Wales as in the case of frost continuing it may be necessary to find fresh dates for the matches against Ireland and Scotland'. Left in little doubt as to where Wales stood among the RFU's priorities, Mullock was finally offered, at less than two weeks' notice, 19 February.

None of this helped the Welsh selection process. The 19th of February was peculiarly inconvenient. Swansea were playing Llanelli in a South Wales Cup replay. Since Swansea were the holders, and Llanelli were to be that season's runners-up, this was a problem, but Mullock had little alternative than to accept. So while in one sense the Wales team was more truly national than most that followed – with players from Bangor, Brecon, Chepstow and Haverfordwest alongside four each from Newport and Cardiff – it was scarcely representative of Wales's real strength. Years later a Swansea paper explained the defeat that followed by there 'not being a single Swansea man among the Cymru'.

The Welsh players were socially indistinguishable from their opponents. At least twelve were privately educated and eight had gone to Oxford or Cambridge, while Edward Treharne, not yet nineteen, would go on to Barts Hospital. One player, Edward Peake, came from a family with its own coat of arms. Three, including captain James Bevan, were destined for the church. Bevan, born in Melbourne and orphaned at eight when his parents were lost at sea, was described by the *Football Annual* as 'a very fast threequarter-back, dodges well, rather light'.

As later events showed, Mullock's entrepreneurial skills were not matched by administrative efficiency. Even so, it is possible that Welsh disarray has been overstated. Subsequent accounts have rested strongly on the memories of Wales player Richard Summers, interviewed years later after long service in the Indian army. He recalled: 'When we got to our changing rooms we discovered that we were two men short, their invitations apparently having gone astray. However, we picked up two Varsity men with Welsh qualifications, and they agreed to fill the vacancies on condition that they were allowed to play threequarter!'

It is an engaging story, but one contradicted by contemporary evidence. Wales did indeed suffer late withdrawals. Arthur Evanson, of Llansoy, Monmouthshire, J.A. Lewis, of Narberth, and Robert Knight, of Bridgend, were listed in Saturday morning's papers. None played, or ever would for Wales, but the Monmouthshire-born Evanson, inaugurating a long tradition of players pursued by both nations, did play for England, showing himself to be a serious loss to the Welsh. But the three replacements – Godfrey Darbishire, Edward Peake and Edward Treharne – were also listed as reserves in the *Sportsman*, so can hardly have been lucky touchline pick-ups. While Peake did play threequarter, Treharne and Darbishire were listed as forwards.

There is little doubt that the changes weakened Wales, in part by forcing players to play out of position. In the more representative team that faced England twenty-two months later, Treharne and Charles Newman, full-back at Blackheath, played at half-back. Nor did misfortune end there. They were down to thirteen men by half-time. Half-back Edward Lewis injured his ankle early on while Cardiff forward Bathyust Bellers Mann sprained his knee before the interval, leaving not only the match but – for more than a century – recorded history too. Mann is the only Wales player for whom the assiduous compilers of the

Welsh International Who's Who were unable to find any personal details. More recent researchers have found that he was born at the Curragh military camp in Ireland and educated at Uppingham School.

The choice of Blackheath as venue for that first match was also significant. It was the first time that England had played on a ground dedicated to rugby; previous games had been at the Oval cricket ground in Kennington, South London, a de facto national stadium in the 1870s as it also staged FA Cup finals and football internationals. It was the beginning of three decades in which the England rugby team was a wandering tribe before it came to rest at a purpose-built home in Twickenham in 1910. The thirteen meetings in England during that time were spread across nine grounds in seven towns and cities, with only the Rectory Field, Blackheath – the successor to Richardson's Field – visited more than once. While Blackheath were England's leading club, spectators were still a secondary consideration. Richardson's Field resembled much more an enclosure than a stadium. Summers recalled: 'The game was played before a small crowd of rugby enthusiasts, ranged perhaps three deep round the ground. There were no huge stands or terraced banks in those days.' The *Sportsman*, though, judged the attendance 'exceedingly large' in spite of 'dull and cheerless' conditions.

A fully representative, full strength Welsh team with luck on its side would have struggled to hold England in 1881. As Wales was neither representative, nor at full strength, what followed had a certain inevitability. One spectator later recalled that Wales, who had adopted red shirts with a Prince of Wales's feathers badge in place of the black shirts and white leek of the South Wales union, 'looked like pygmies' by comparison with opponents who wore England's well-established white shirt with a red rose. Wales also fielded nine forwards against England's ten. Early pressure forced Wales to minor – touching down behind their own line. The *Field* reported that 'this proved only the forerunner of a series of more serious disasters'. How long it took Blackheath half-back Henry Taylor to score England's first try is not clear – the *Field* reckoned five minutes and the *Sportsman* three. What is not in doubt is that Taylor was followed at regular intervals for the rest of the match. In total England scored thirteen tries, eight after the break when, with the wind behind them and a two-man advantage, they 'did much as they pleased'. Vassall became the first man to score three tries in an international, but was overtaken by Burton, living up to Guillemard's verdict that he had 'a happy knack of running in' by scoring four. It could have been even worse for Wales. Stokes's long line-out throw to full-back Robert Hunt, who was unmarked in midfield and crossed untouched, was deemed ungentlemanly conduct and the score disallowed. Even without this try, Stokes caused Wales quite enough trouble. Summers recalled: 'He had a most baffling, swerving run, and his left-footed kicking, which broke our players' hearts, astounded us all, for we had never seen a player who was able to kick with his left foot before.' Wales appear to have reached the England twenty-five-yard line once, during the first half.

Match reports at once established the tradition that Welsh and English newspapers rarely see the same game. Cardiff's *Western Mail* saw it as 'well-contested but withal one-sided' and felt that Wales 'proved themselves worthy of their formidable rivals' in a match of 'an interesting character'. The *Daily Telegraph*, by contrast, dismissed it as 'utterly devoid of interest' and England's win was 'ridiculously easy'. For the *Field,* it was 'impossible to congratulate the Welsh Rugby Union team on their first match with England, unless, indeed it be on their pluck in coming so far with the prospect of an almost certain defeat'. When a letter to the *Western Mail* queried the provenance of the Welsh team, the SWFU secretary cheerfully disowned it, referring the writer to Mullock. But the clubs who met in Neath in March to form the Welsh Rugby Union gave greater weight to Mullock's achievement in getting the match played than to any collateral mishaps and elected him their first secretary.

Ten of that first Welsh team never played international rugby again. Three emigrated within a year and several died in unlikely places – Darbishire in Florida, Leonard Watkins in Argentina, Barry Girling in Algeria, all before the age of fifty. Mann died in Los Angeles but proved much more durable, living until 1948, while Aneurin Rees broke his neck but survived for more than fifty years afterwards, thirty of them as town clerk in Merthyr Tydfil. Bevan became a clergyman of principles described as 'protestant fundamentalist' and had thirteen children, one of whom became a bishop in China. His, presumably numerous, grand-children remembered him as 'narrow and severe'. Peake's cap found a permanent resting home in the Welsh National History Museum at St Fagan's. Unlike their English counterparts, those players contributed little to rugby administration with the exception of W.D. Phillips of

Cardiff, who became a vice-president of the Welsh Rugby Union and served for twenty years on the International Rugby Board. He showed something of the sang-froid expected of survivors of great Victorian debacles when, while watching the Wales v England match of 1905, the ball struck him full in the face 'with a thud that resounded half-way to Newport'. The *Western Mail* reported that 'his pipe in his mouth was knocked yards away, but Mr Phillips never moved a hair. His only comment was a quick remark to Mr Arthur Gould that "I took that very well" and he nodded gratefully to the man who brought back the pipe'.

Neither Stokes nor Burton, who died in his mid-thirties, played against Wales again. Stokes's next match for England, against Scotland in Edinburgh, was his last, marked by a drop-goal, allegedly from eighty yards, which secured a draw. His six conversions against Wales contributed to an England career record of seventeen that survived for more than a century. He was, though, far from finished with rugby. He served as RFU president from 1886 to 1888 and was a committee man for half a century, with Temple Gurdon being a colleague for most of that time. He also enjoyed a long medical career and is credited by one Blackheath history with being Arthur Conan Doyle's original Dr Watson, although few other authorities agree on this.

The first England v Wales match passed into history but not, mercifully from a Welsh point of view, into the record books, even though it remains by far the biggest thrashing administered in the entire history of the Home International, Five Nations or Six Nations Championship. Under current scoring values it would have been 82–0, but in 1881 a points system had still to be devised. Matches were decided by the number of goals scored – either drops or conversions, as penalties had also yet to be introduced – with tries counted only as a tie-breaker.

In the circumstances it seems remarkable that Stokes said, at the after-match dinner: 'I have seen enough of you Welshmen to know that you will be hard to beat in a few years' time.' He did, of course, have to say something to opponents who had been beaten to the point of mutual embarrassment. Perhaps he thought back two years to that day in Newport and remembered not the similar thrashing his team inflicted, but the potential implicit in the size of the crowd. Rather more pressing for Wales was the task of persuading the RFU that they were worth playing the following year. Mullock, by now writing as secretary of the

WRU, requested a fixture in the 1882-3 season, but in September the RFU committee resolved unanimously 'that an English team cannot be sent to play Wales, but that in all probability a match with either North or South will be arranged after a general meeting in October'.

That probability came to pass at Newport in January 1882. A North team containing five men who had played against the South – the biggest match outside internationals in English rugby – a month earlier, and three from the last England team to play Scotland, was held to a margin of a goal to the try scored by Treharne. A week later, again in Newport, a Midlands team was run ragged by Bill Evans, of Rhymney, who scored five tries. He later emigrated to Australia and became head of first Fremantle then Adelaide Grammar Schools before returning to live rough in the hills near Rhymney. Unsurprisingly, this earned him his first cap a week later when a team retaining only Newman, Phillips and the Irish-born Frank Purdon from the Blackheath pioneers went to Dublin and beat Ireland by a goal and three tries to nil. As Mullock reported: 'The style of play has much improved, and players seem to possess a far better knowledge of the rules of the game than they did last season, and are awakening to the fact that to play the Rugby game properly it must be played scientifically.'

Rowland Hill, the RFU secretary, was suitably impressed by Wales's performance against the North. 'This performance was highly creditable to the Welshmen,' he said. 'Not only on this occasion did Wales show great improvement.' On 4 April 1882 the RFU committee agreed to play Wales in Wales on 16 December.

This game, played at the St Helen's ground on Swansea's seafront, remains an anomaly: it is the only England v Wales match to have been played just before rather than just after Christmas. It also went into the history books as the first Home/Five/Six Nations Championship fixture, as it opened the first season in which all four home nations played each other. The first international in Wales, it established other enduring characteristics of rugby there. It rained 'from half past seven in the morning until the match was nearly over', and the day was also marked by high winds. If not quite as peripatetic as England, Wales too chose venues on a match-by-match basis in these early days, providing scope for future division given the vigour of inter-town rivalries. Four grounds were used in the first fifteen years, with trips being made to Newport (twice) and Llanelli before regular alternation between Swansea and Cardiff began in the late 1890s.

England arrived with eight new caps, an average maintained over their first ten visits to Wales. Stokes was gone, his place as chief tormentor taken by debutant three-quarter Gregory Wade – an Australian inaugurating another English tradition, that of recruiting overseas pupils studying at Oxford or Cambridge. Wade arrived at Oxford in 1881 and was, Vassall remembered, 'collared by the rowing enthusiasts' before 'letters then began to arrive from Parramatta asking what had become of their great threequarter back'. Persuaded to play rugby, Wade was 'at once recognised as a match-winner . . . especially by all those who tried to tackle him'. Wales might have wished the mail from Australia had been less reliable, and they also cursed the poor sense of direction shown by Philip Newton, an original choice in the team who reportedly got lost on the way to Swansea, so creating the vacancy that Wade filled. Stokes's successor as captain was Temple Gurdon, beginning a run of eight consecutive victories over the next three seasons. He and Vassall were England's only survivors from that first match at Blackheath.

Wales had marginally more continuity with three survivors – although only Purdon played in the same position, as Newman and Treharne switched from their previous posts to play at half-back. They were considerably more representative than they had been, with three players each from Swansea and Llanelli joining two from Cardiff and a quintet from Newport, including Tom Clapp. English-born but educated at Monmouth School, Clapp held the pack together for the rest of the 1880s before departing to join his brother as a fruit farmer in California. The captaincy passed with a certain logic to full-back Charles Lewis, who played for Llandovery, would later be its mayor and was already a WRU vice-president.

Wales were 'beaten as a matter of course, but far from disgraced' in the eyes of the *Cambrian*. Lest this be thought an echo of the *Western Mail's* optimistic view of the match at Blackheath, Arthur Budd later wrote that 'though the score was large, it was not a "runaway effort" for the Welshmen pressed their opponents on several occasions'. They were close to scoring first. Losing the toss forced them to play into 'a heavy driving wind and rain such as might have disheartened anyone'. As a spectator recalled years later: 'Dai Gwynn, securing near the touchline, dropped for goal. I can see the ball now. From a difficult angle Dai put in a screw kick – this was his forte – and a huge shout went up when it was thought the ball had passed between the uprights'. It was judged, though, to have gone over the post, and so missed. If England were shaken, it did not show. The *Cambrian* reported them regarding 'this bit of contre-attaque with indifference. It was now that the visitors began to play.' In a typical passage of play: 'The forwards broke loose and passed the ball to their backs, who here showed some splendid play. It was passed right and left, and the Welshmen could be seen rapidly retreating before the skilled tactics of their more dextrous opponents. Every opening left in the ranks of the home team was invaded, every weak point carefully tested . . . one thing was particularly noticeable, viz. the coolness which the visitors exhibited when they got possession of the leather.'

The reporter particularly admired Arthur Evanson, the man who got away from Wales in 1881 and one of seven Oxford University players in the England team. He was 'the man the Englishmen rested their hopes on. It would be impossible to enumerate the number of times the ball was passed to him, but never in vain, as always some ground was gained or some advantage taken.'

Nevertheless it was Wade who made the most spectacular impact, the 'powerful and dodgy running' recalled by Budd bringing him a hat-trick of tries before half-time. Wales made the odd incursion, but full-back Arthur Taylor – brother of the first try-scorer at Blackheath – invariably 'returned the leather with a kind of contempt for the intrusion'. The final difference was two goals and four tries to nil, England by the end 'passing the ball to one another with such rapidity that the Welshmen appeared almost awed, not apparently knowing where to meet the attack'.

Aside from the quality of players such as Gurdon, Evanson and Wade, England were praised by the *Cambrian* for 'the most unselfish and uniform way in which every man played – never for himself, but for his side'. The reporter's comment on 'the patient manner in which every man would gauge his distance when he had the ball, instead of running off at a tangent and not knowing where to go' was an implied comment on Wales, made explicit when the next paragraph detailed how the Welsh players were 'keeping their heads up in the scrimmage and not noticing the ball; the selfish play of most of the backs and the great lack of passing of the leather when they had the chance.' The lessons the reporter hoped would be drawn were also a comment on the Welsh game as a whole: 'Those pert youngsters who take an exaggerated and conceited view of their prowess and their matches, would do well to imitate the skilled players who have just been among us, and endeavouring to cheerfully obey the decisions of the umpires, instead of wrangling and disputing among themselves, and thus wasting fifteen or twenty minutes in a match.' The Welsh Rugby Union marked the occasion by nearly bankrupting themselves, devoting more than half of their annual income to the post-match banquet at the Mackworth Hotel.

It may not have been in the highly specific terms demanded by the *Cambrian*, but Wales evidently did take notice of the criticism. The surprise of the next few years was not that England continued to win – they were also beating everybody else; the victory at Swansea launched a run of ten consecutive wins, and they lost only once between 1878 and 1887. It was that massacres gave way so rapidly to seriously competitive matches.

England had had a decade's start and could call on players of the quality of the Gurdons, Wade, Evanson, Alan Rotherham – the first half-back to link backs and forwards – and another debutant at Swansea, giant wing Wilfred 'Baby' Bolton. His Sandhurst contemporary Philip Jordan, for many years the *Daily Telegraph*'s rugby writer, recalled Bolton as 'perhaps the strongest individual runner I have seen'. Over 6ft tall, 13st and a match for sprint champions, he also 'lifted his knees high as he ran and he could hand off in the most strenuous fashion without any visible loss of pace'.

With the game still being played by comparatively small numbers from a limited social range, the universities were an immense advantage to England. In later years it was sometimes seen as favouritism when England picked large contingents from Oxford and Cambridge, but in 1882 Oxford's seven was a simple reflection of strength – they were beginning an unbeaten four-year run. The universities were concentrations of young men from football-playing schools with energy and time to spare. Vassall recalled that Budd, who would be a fierce critic of demands for working men to be compensated for taking the time off work necessary to play at top level, 'demanded constant practice' when advising Oxford teams in the early 1880s, although little compulsion was needed as 'there were crowds of men willing to play six days a week if given a chance, the problem was to stop them playing too much'. Rugby's growth as a genuinely popular sport in Yorkshire worried the London-based rulers of the RFU. The game was no longer confined to the sort of people with whom they had gone to school and university, while the conjunction of growing gate-paying crowds and players who, as working men, could not afford time off work to train, travel or recover from injury inevitably created an impetus towards paying players. The RFU responded by bringing in the first systematic regulations on amateurism in 1886. At the same time this broadening of the social base brought in fresh streams of playing talent.

For Wales, recalled Townsend Collins, who was the most important chronicler of the early days of its rugby, the 1880s were a time of 'experimentation, learning from other countries, developing their own inventiveness'. Bill Gwynn, brother of the narrowly unsuccessful drop-kicker at Swansea, recalled some teams experimenting with eight forwards and seven backs as early as 1878. Cardiff made the decisive change in 1884, introducing a fourth threequarter to accommodate the gifts of Frank Hancock alongside three established players. It was equally typical of this period that Hancock was a transplanted West Countryman who eventually played for Wales, although the innovation was not deployed against England until 1890. There was a huge increase in the number of teams and players in Wales in the 1880s, and evidence that Welshmen were prepared to take the game seriously. John Gwilliam, captain of Wales in the early 1950s, recalled a great-uncle who had played for Llanelli in the 1880s telling him about Harry Bowen, a renowned kicker of drop-goals who would eat his lunchtime sandwiches rapidly in order to have time during the break to practise his skills.

Rugby's growing popularity was not to universal taste. In 1885 the Welsh language paper *Y Faner* lamented: 'The hankering for kicking "the black ball" has fallen like a plague on the boys of the South. Day and night, for the poor and the wealthy, the religious and the irreligious, football is the talking point . . . And several of the daily and weekly newspapers employ correspondents to cover it, and set aside long columns for the purpose of giving detailed reports of such bestial sports. Aren't things like this indisputable truth that this "Age of Light" is returning to the "Land of Darkness"?' The devil, it was feared, had some appealing new tunes.

They were being played increasingly in the North of England. The 1884 match was on Cardigan Fields, Leeds – England's first venture to Yorkshire, following a number of matches in Manchester. In the later 1880s the Leeds venue was sold off in lots, and one of those, number 17a, became the Headingley cricket and rugby grounds that are still used today.

The 1884 Welsh team arrived in Leeds to be told by the *Sportsman* that 'although victory cannot be expected, they will most assuredly give a good account of themselves' and duly did so. It rained heavily. Hill, reporting for the *Football Annual*, wrote that Wales 'seemed to like the wet, and generally held in the scrummage their much heavier opponents'. The RFU was less appreciative of the weather, which was blamed for the failure to attract the larger audience expected in the north, with only 2,000 attending.

England's edge was in turning possession into points. Tries by Wade and half-back Twynam, following a dribble from Temple Gurdon, bracketed a remarkable score created when Bolton 'made a magnificent run from near his own goal line into the Welsh twenty-five. Seeing he was then likely to be tackled, he passed to Rotherham who completed a most brilliant try.' Wales finally claimed a try of their own. Charles Allen, of Beaumaris, 'a sturdy threequarter back . . . but rather slow in starting', later the Liberal MP for Stroud, crossed after 'a brilliant rush'. Lewis added the goal. Since England failed to convert two of their own scores, another Welsh goal could have brought victory. In the first half Charles Taylor had dropped for goal. Taylor, only recently converted from football and also the Welsh pole vault champion, was recalled by the Rev. Frank Marshall as 'one of the most extraordinary players who ever played, as he retained much of his association style of play, he was one of the very few players who went in for the flying hack, and hardly ever failed to bring them off – a style of play then, much as now, much deprecated'. The *Sportsman* reckoned his shot 'a splendid drop', recording that 'the ball passed only a couple of feet wide of the post'.

Wales crossed for two tries the following year at Swansea through the diminutive debutant Martyn Jordan, but conceded five in a contest Budd, writing in the early 1890s, reckoned was 'the fastest that we ever recall seeing in an international match'. With half-backs Rotherham and Payne providing constant service, Wade 'never played so well in his life, and the Welshmen could make nothing of him. He ran and dodged just as he liked', scoring the last try. Rather less noticed were the debuts of England threequarter Andrew Stoddart and Wales full-back Arthur Gould, although the *Cambria Daily Leader* thought Gould 'did a lot of work and tackled the Englishmen in good style'. Much more would be heard of both.

Equally noted as a cricketer – he made four tours of Australia, two as England's captain and played sixteen Tests – Stoddart played the decisive role a year later when the fixture returned to Blackheath, albeit to the Rectory Field rather than Richardson's Field, which had been sold to a builder. Growing public interest was shown by the RFU's letter of complaint to the South Eastern Railway about the inadequacy of match-day services. This may explain why a match scheduled for 2.30 p.m. kicked off twenty minutes late. Again England scored more tries – two to one – but were lax in turning them into goals. Gould's conversion of William 'Buller' Stadden's late score might have stolen a victory for Wales on the 'most goals' rule but for the most debated incident of the match. England forward Charles Elliot caught a miscued clearance from Wales full-back Harry Bowen and, instead of taking what was described as a clear run to the line, called for a mark. This was reported as meeting 'an emphatic and forcible expression of disapproval from the England captain and the "finished" players of the side'. Since Elliot was a Sunderland player, one of four northerners in the team, it is not hard to detect metropolitan condescension. Contemporary reports say that he was anything from forty to fifty yards from the Wales line, so a score can hardly have been guaranteed – still less that the conversion would have been kicked. Much less questionable was his judgement in handing the ball to Stoddart (a kick from the mark could still be taken by any player). The cricketer had already made 'a grand run down the right wing, in the course of which his nether garment came to grief, enforcing his retreat for a few minutes'. Decency restored, he landed the decisive goal.

Wade had scored England's first try, although this was not his best performance. Indeed, he was criticised by the *Football Annual* for 'fumbling which cost three or four magnificent opportunities of scoring'. With his studies completed, Wade returned to Australia with the extraordinary

record of being on the winning side in all of the fifteen major matches –
internationals, Oxford v Cambridge and South v North – in which he
played. His six tries in four matches against Wales – scoring in each one –
out of seven tries in eight internationals, was a record not beaten for a
century and marked him out as the first in a long line of fine players
whose very best has been reserved for this fixture. Back home in Ausralia,
he rose to be Premier of New South Wales.

England had been shown in 1885 that it did not always rain in Wales, the
Football Annual commending St Helen's in Swansea as being 'one of the best
grounds in the United Kingdom . . . dry and level'. The 1887 match at
Llanelli made up for this – and more. Even the decision to play at the
West Wales venue had provoked a characteristically Welsh controversy,
Newport's representative calling it 'an out of the way place'. Out of the
way or not, excursion trains brought in 'thousands of people from
Cardiff, Swansea, Newport, Neath and Carmarthen' to make up a crowd
of almost 7,000. Unfortunately, the previous few days had been
ferociously cold and Stradey Park was frozen hard. England captain Alan
Rotherham refused to play on a surface consisting largely of rock-like
ridges. Mullock showed characteristic enterprise in inquiring about the
availability of Swansea, then equally typical disorganisation in failing to
send a further message once it was decided to use a neighbouring pitch in
Llanelli instead, leaving the ground authorities and several hundred
would-be spectators waiting fruitlessly at St Helen's. Since the alternative
pitch was behind the grandstand, disgruntled ticket-holders were
reduced to standing behind ropes around the touchline. The air of
improvisation was further enhanced when the cross-bar on one of the
rigged-up goals collapsed. Arthur Gould demonstrated how he had
acquired his nickname of 'Monkey' by shinning up the posts to effect
running repairs.

The watching Budd was profoundly unimpressed by what followed.
'The ground was not in a fit state for football,' he wrote. 'Not a player on
the field could keep his legs on the skating rink . . . Scientific football was
out of the question and the game, which consisted of slipping and
sliding, demands no serious comment.' This was not the Welsh point of
view – understandably, since they avoided defeat for the first time
against England through a scoreless draw, and felt that they might have
done even better. Their forwards were reported as 'greatly superior to

their opponents', the *Football Annual* noting a phenomenon that would recur often over the next century, that 'Welsh forwards who are well known in England, and whose powers are gauged to an inch, suddenly developed the most wonderfully improved form'. Most of the play took place inside the English twenty-five, but Wales failed to turn territory into points. Gould, rated the best Welsh back but criticised for over-using the drop-goal, came closest when one of his shots drifted only a few inches wide.

Of England's seven debutants, four – a distinct sign of changing times – came from the North. Among them was Swinton forward Bob Seddon, who drowned in the Maitland River the following year while leading the first British touring team to Australia. More noticeable in Llanelli was winger Dickie Lockwood, 5ft 4in and only nineteen years old, a working man from Dewsbury. The *Yorkshire Post's* report that he 'stood out in a bright and shining light' was not regional patriotism. His name cropped up consistently – on one occasion as 'the invaluable Lockwood' – in the *Cambria Daily Leader's* account. Some years later a Welsh writer would attribute England's survival that day entirely to Lockwood and Roberts, the full-back from Swinton.

Having avoided defeat at the sixth attempt, Wales keenly awaited its seventh shot at England, but had to wait three years. England would not play them, or anybody else apart from a single match against the touring New Zealand Natives, for the next two seasons.

The argument was one of rugby's growing pains, escalating from a dispute over England's winning try against Scotland in 1884. This and other disagreements led Ireland to propose the creation of an international body to set rules – matches had until then been played under the regulations of the host nation – and settle disputes. The Rugby Football Union rejected the suggestion that each member have three seats on the new body – a position informed both by the argument, echoed again over television money more than a century later, that it had more clubs and players than the rest combined and, it may be surmised, the belief that the game was their invention, and was merely on loan to the others. The Celts dug their heels in, although Wales offered England a match in 1889 'according to the laws of the game of the country in which the match should be played', before being dragged back into line by the others. England finally agreed to arbitration in December 1889 and was not displeased with the outcome – six seats out of twelve on the International Rugby Board, giving it a power of veto over rule changes that survived until 1948.

The arbitrators were still at work in January 1890 when England and Wales resumed their rivalry at Dewsbury. Nowadays identified as a rugby league town, the home of legendary commentator Eddie Waring, Dewsbury was still in 1890 part of a unified rugby game, but the North's wealth, voting power at RFU meetings and desire to ease the pressure on working-class players by offering compensation for time off work were increasingly regarded with fear and suspicion by the game's rulers in London.

Inevitably the playing cast showed numerous changes from the 1887 match, with only three Welshmen and not a single Englishman surviving. Wales had changed formation as well. The four threequarters line had taken time to win acceptance. It had an unhappy first international outing against Scotland in 1886, a heavy defeat that Budd argued 'had sounded the death-knell of the practice' and was resisted by Gould, who felt it cramped his own considerable style, but had gradually become common among Welsh clubs. Joe Warbrick, captain of the New Zealand Natives, noted that it enabled 'a succession of short passes with very little danger of their being intercepted'.

Local hero Lockwood, who had moved to Heckmondwike in 1889 under circumstances that provoked a Yorkshire Rugby Union inquiry and a three-day interrogation by witchfinder-general Rev. Frank Marshall, was cleared of professionalism only a week earlier (and after the team was picked) and so was absent. Yet Dewsbury was still represented. Stadden, forerunner of many Welshmen who 'went North' over the next century, had moved there, no less suspiciously, from Cardiff. Speculation that he might change international allegiance along with club and residence proved unfounded. Partnering him at half-back was the versatile Charles Thomas, who played for Wales at half-back, centre and wing as well as performing for Newport as full-back and a forward. Behind them could have been another Newport man, Tommy England. Picked for the previous match against Scotland, he had been injured the week before, forcing Wales to call up Swansea's Billy Bancroft to fill the vacancy, which would not recur for more than a decade as Bancroft played in every match until the end of

1901. Gould and Stoddart resumed their rivalry as centres and captains, Stoddart taking charge of eight new caps, including the Australian-born Cambridge student Sammy Woods, who had already played against England at cricket.

Anything Llanelli managed weather-wise, Yorkshire could match. Snow fell beforehand, and rain continued for most of the match. Nine tall English forwards failed to impose themselves on the smaller, stockier Welsh eight. The Welsh threequarters produced passing to 'beat anything previously seen on Crown Flatt', Budd noting that where England were flummoxed by the greasy ball, Wales 'by short, sharp passing kept the ball going from hand to hand and repeatedly gained ground' while Bancroft, 'a mere lad', fielded everything at full-back.

Stoddart was not amused, complaining at the after-match dinner, an event that earned more column inches in the *Dewsbury Chronicle* than the match itself, that the ground was 'really unfit for any ordinary player to play in and was an insult both to the English and Welsh teams to be asked to play on such a ground'. Greeted with applause and shouts of 'no, no', Stoddart was rebuked by Yorkshire president Mark Newsome, a Dewsbury official who was later RFU president, who said that he was 'cut to the quick' by Stoddart speaking 'of something he knew nothing about'. Mullock pointedly offered his congratulations to the Dewsbury club for their organisation.

There were reasons for Stoddart's gracelessness. He had a poor game – the *Chronicle* alleged that 'out of form he might be, but he evidently showed a little "funk" and a desire not to be "dirtied"' – and Wales had won. Taking advantage of inattention by opposite number James Wright, Stadden threw a short line-out to himself and dashed over for the only score.

Sporting triumphs rarely come more complete than scoring the winning try on your home ground in your nation's first victory over its defining enemy. It was, though, Stadden's last match for Wales. A grim fate was marked with poignant timing and brevity by the *Cambria Daily Leader* two days before Wales played England at Swansea in January 1907: 'The Coroner's inquiry into the double tragedy at Dewsbury was concluded on Thursday. Mrs Stadden was strangled by her husband William Stadden, a Dewsbury grocer and Welsh ex-international foot-baller, who afterwards committed suicide. It was stated that the pair had generally lived happily together, but the man, who was of an excitable nature, had latterly become jealous of another footballer. A verdict of wilful murder and suicide against Stadden was returned.'

CHAPTER TWO
THE GOULD STANDARD 1891–98

As Arthur Gould is as pre-eminent in football as W.G. Grace is
in cricket, the footballing enthusiasts of Wales might recognise
his services to the game . . . by some national testimonial.

W.J.T. Collins, 1896

I would sooner go to hell than to Wales.

H.H. Asquith, 1905

Arthur Gould stood as captain of Wales at that contentious post-match
banquet in Dewsbury and proclaimed that he 'had never felt as proud
as he did that day. They had accomplished a feat which they had been
trying for many years to perform. They came at the bottom and had
tried every means in their power to get to the top of the tree and it was
truly a proud thing to say that they had conquered the redoubtable
English team.'

The accomplished tree (and rugby posts) climber went on to dominate
the following decade. If Townsend Collins's verdict on him sixty years on
as 'the greatest rugby player who ever took the field' has to be accompanied by the asterisk that he was the devoted chronicler of Gould's club
Newport, no such qualification applies to that monument of Yorkshire
rectitude, Rev. Frank Marshall, who in 1893 proclaimed him 'the central
figure in the football world . . . the greatest centre-threequarter who has
ever played'.

Gould combined unmatched individual skills with cool judgement,
had a lethal outside break and was quick enough to be a highly successful
track sprinter. Gwyn Nicholls, his successor as Wales's midfield kingpin
and an opponent when Cardiff played Newport, wrote: 'He was at top
speed in two strides and away almost before one could realise that he was

in possession of the ball.' Stopping Gould was 'like trying to catch a butterfly with a hat-pin'. His superiority was not effortless. Impressed as a schoolboy by Stokes's kicking for Blackheath against Newport in 1879, he taught himself to kick with both feet. W.H. Gwynn said: 'You simply couldn't stop him getting in his kick.'

By 1896 he had played more first-class matches, scored more tries and dropped more goals than any other player on record. His domination of a decade in which English rugby went to war against itself was sealed by providing the casus belli when that conflict became international. The other enduring name from the 1890s is Bill Bancroft, a cool, impish full-back who developed his skills as a youngster at St Helen's in Swansea, where his grandfather was groundsman. Dai Gent, the Welsh-born England scrum-half who won five caps between 1905 and 1910 and later became a journalist, recalled: 'With no defensive physique to help him, this brilliant player adopted the most daring tactics with absolute confidence', often making 'crowds roar with laughter (though that was never his intention) at the audacity of his tactics'. John Raphael, the England centre who was to die in the First World War, remembered his 'uncanny capacity of inducing forwards to devote their energies to hunting him and to neglect the more respectable pleasures of playing the game'. Bancroft and Indian-born wing Tom Pearson – to Collins 'the greatest wing-threequarter I have known . . . When everything was in his favour he was the greatest wing-threequarter of his day. When everything was against him, he was greater still' – played through the decade and beyond.

Frank Marshall observed in 1894 that 'in no rugby circle is the game pursued with such energy, assiduity and invention as in South Wales', while Wales 'made up for paucity in numbers by their science in play'. Yet far from victory in 1890 presaging a period of Welsh success, England remained dominant, winning six of the next eight meetings. Nor were there many close-run games. One of many reasons for the fame of Wales's win in 1893 was that it was the sole cliffhanger.

Budd, speaking as RFU president at the Dewsbury banquet, trod the boundary between jovial and patronising: 'All Englishmen looked upon the progress of football in Wales with great satisfaction . . . England was the parent of football in Wales, but whether the precocity of the child showed sufficient gratitude to the parent was not a question he was inclined to answer.' Seen in those terms, Wales were severely chastised on their next three visits to England, conceding sixty-six points, including fifteen tries, and scoring only three points. Blackheath as a venue took on the sense of foreboding later associated with Twickenham, although Wales rarely got close enough for any 'jinx' to come into play.

All four nations in turn won the Triple Crown, a notional prize for defeating the other three countries, between 1891 and 1894, with Scotland dominating subsequently. England v Scotland remained, as Budd had described it in 1886, 'beyond doubt the event par excellence of the football year', but the Wales game clearly gained in appeal. While it made a profit of £226 for the RFU in 1892, little more than a third of the following year's England v Scotland match, by the end of the decade figures of £600-£700 were only a little behind the Calcutta Cup in terms of revenue.

Even after England's crushing win in 1894, the *Manchester Guardian* argued that Wales had made more progress over the previous decade. Its clubs were now a match for England's best. Blackheath had the better of early matches against Cardiff in the late 1880s, but the balance was shifting. While Blackheath dominated against other clubs – winning 104 matches and losing only 16 between 1892 and 1898, they lost 16 out of 22 games against Newport and Cardiff in those years. Budd wrote of English club players being 'bewildered by their clever legerdemain passing'. Blackheath had played Swansea but the clubs fell out in 1891 when Blackheath demanded a fixed sum, rather than the half-share offered, for playing at St Helen's. When the match, won by Swansea, attracted a crowd of 15,000, Blackheath tried to renegotiate and were rebuffed.

Rugby's growing popularity did not please everyone. Swansea clergyman Michael Craven denounced it in 1893 as the 'twin sister of the drinking system', while a letter in the *Western Mail* explained that 'scarcely a Sunday comes round that football and theatre are not denounced at nearly all of the Nonconformist chapels in Llanelly'. Adjacent to that letter was just such a denunciation, though from a Cardiff address. It concluded: 'Prize-fights were put down by the strong arm of the law. We cannot hope for the same merciful intervention in the case of football; but the evil, I earnestly hold, should be boldly met by our religious leaders, and not permitted to go on growing . . . The sight presented on Saturday afternoon, when thousands of excited people were coming from the Cardiff Park, was inexpressibly sad.'

Neither Collins nor the cleric Marshall blamed Welsh failures on divine displeasure. Collins argued that other teams had better individual talent, while Marshall pointed to Scotland's and England's 'superior weight, strength and speed'. Much of that weight and power came from Marshall's Yorkshire, who won seven of the first eight County Championships, from 1889, thwarted only in 1891 by neighbouring Lancashire. Each of England's teams in their hat-trick of big home wins had a northern majority of players. The 'Yorkshire forward' – tough, aggressive and physically powerful – such as Jack Toothill, of Bradford, who played in four consecutive meetings from 1891, Harry Bradshaw, of Bramley, or Tom Broadley, of Bingley, became a figure of some menace.

No English player had the historic resonance of Gould or Bancroft in part because of rugby's importance in Wales's collective memory – Gwyn Thomas's 'magnets of remembrance' – but also because Temple Gurdon's sixteen caps remained the English record. Gould and Bancroft both had twenty-seven by the end of the decade. England awarded seventy-nine new caps, averaging slightly over half of each team, in ten meetings from 1890 to 1899. Yet England did have players of class and staying power. Lockwood was living proof that working-class Yorkshiremen offered more than muscle. Collins recalled 'a rather tubby little man who in quiescence did not look a bit like a great footballer, but revealed the mark of "class" as soon as the game started.' Marshall's doubts about his amateurism did not extend to his play, 'combining in one person to the highest degree all the essential qualities of a centre-threequarter . . . of almost infallible judgement, turning up at the right time and invariably being in the right spot, he always does the right thing'. Even the avowedly conservative *Yorkshire Post* thought that choosing W.E. Bromet ahead of him as Yorkshire captain was 'pandering to social position'. Lockwood got the job in 1892 and two years later succeeded Stoddart as England's leader. Historian Tony Collins describes the appointment as 'almost as if a conscript private had taken charge of an elite cavalry regiment'. Lockwood won the last of his fourteen caps, second equal with Charles Gurdon at the turn of the century, aged only twenty-six.

Continuity and drive were supplied to England's pack by the rumbustious Sammy Woods, who also added England cricket caps to earlier Australian ones. It was written that 'he played cricket like a rugger forward and football exactly like a fast bowler . . . he was a demon both in the tight scrums and the loose mauls and when he went down the field, he went with the fury of a charging rhino.' The *Western Mail* saw him as 'angular and bony . . . His forte is dribbling, a sharp following up and vigorous tackling . . . when he does get a chance within measurable distance of the line it is no soft job to stop him'. He played only once at home, in 1890 against Wales, but appeared in the next three away games, the last as captain.

While Wales adopted four threequarters in 1890, England continued to argue that the advantage of an extra forward outweighed another threequarter. International matches became testbeds for the two formations. The *Observer* lamented that a weakened Welsh team in 1892 prevented 'an excellent test of the relative merits of the two systems'.

Looming over everything was English rugby's developing schism, with the rejection at the 1893 RFU AGM of 'broken time' payments to players in lieu of time off work. The RFU's inflexibility led in 1895 to the secession of twenty-two leading Yorkshire, Lancashire and Cheshire clubs to form the Northern Union (later the Rugby League) followed by a steady stream of clubs and individuals. England lost its strongest counties and clubs like Bradford, St Helens and Wakefield Trinity. The number of clubs affiliated to the RFU dropped by nearly half in a few years. Players like Lockwood, and their heirs and successors, were lost. England would not win another championship until 1911. The tensions leading up to the schism extended to Wales. Swansea and Wales half-backs Evan and David James were declared professional in 1892, although a substantial minority of RFU committee men thought the evidence insufficient, and, in spite of repeated Welsh appeals, they were not reinstated until 1896.

The James brothers were powerless against England's forward superiority at Newport in 1891. A year later many critics blamed their absence for Wales losing heavily in spite of copious possession. England's four victories between 1891 and 1895 fell into two groups. In 1891 and 1895, the two matches that Woods played, their pack was dominant. At Newport in 1891, the Welsh Rugby Union had twelve tons of straw spread on top of the ton of salt used as a defence against frost. The *Western Mail* reported: 'The Welshmen hadn't a look-in with their opponents in the matter of weight.' Woods controlled the combined dribble that created

England's third try after the first two were scored by Blackheath wing Percy Christopherson, the first of a series of Englishmen to have their best international days during this sequence. The *Western Mail* blamed Bancroft — 'his collaring was weak and to this I must ascribe in great measure the defeat of the Welshmen'. Poor Welsh defence was also a running theme.

Four years later thirty tons of straw protected St Helen's. The star for a day was another Blackheath player, winger W.B. Thomson who ran three-quarters of the length of the field for England's equalising score, beating Gould, Pearson and Bancroft. The *Cambrian Daily Leader* attributed England's 14-6 victory to their pack: 'Not forwards at all, they were thirteen stone threequarters and every man among them played with splendid spirit.' Woods, England's captain and scorer of the second of its four tries, was seen 'dashing around everywhere. It generally took two of his opponents to bring him down and by the time he had been grounded, he had parted with the ball'. His lieutenants included Charles Thomas, of Barnstaple, England's first Devonian in a decade, whose selection caused such delight that 'the manager of the Exeter Theatre stopped the pantomime and from the front of the stage conveyed the information to the audience, who were most enthusiastic in their expressions of delight'.

In their home victories, 1892 and 1894, England did not dominate up front but won because of Lockwood, individual brilliance from others and Welsh profligacy. At Blackheath in 1892, Budd reckoned England's 17-0 margin 'does not indicate the state of the game'. He, the *Western Mail* and the *Observer* agreed that the absence of the James brothers was crucial. The *Western Mail* described late substitute George Rowles, of Penarth, as 'more of a nuisance than a help' to half-back partner Percy Phillips, while some Welsh tackling was carried out 'rather gingerly'. Lockwood, reported Budd, was 'the shining light among the England players'. England won the Triple Crown without conceding a single point.

In 1894 England, led by Lockwood, finally adopted the four-threequarter formation and slaughtered Wales 24-3, beating them at their own game. The match was played at Birkenhead Park in Cheshire, the last time the fixture was played in the North of England. It took strenuous precautions, costing £100, to counter the brutal weather that kept attendance down to around half the ground's 15,000 capacity. Wales self-destructed even more comprehensively than two years earlier.

Townsend Collins recounted that Gould, with the agreement of pack leader Tom Hannan, a tough, athletic Newport boilermaker, told his forwards to release the ball quickly from the scrum. However, Frank Hill, of Cardiff, 'insisted on trying to wheel and carried some of the other forwards with him'. Collins reckoned Hill might have been tactically right in frozen, treacherous conditions, but his defiance ensured that 'the Welsh pack was a house divided against itself'.

Nor was Wales's defence blameless. Asking why he had not stopped the bulldozer-like Harry Bradshaw from scoring England's second try, Wales wing Norman Biggs replied: 'Tackle him? It was as much as I could do to get out of his way!' Half-back Cyril Wells ran from well inside his own half for England's first score while Lockwood 'covered Gould with merciless persistency' according to the *Yorkshire Post,* which reckoned that he 'has never played with greater judgment or effect'. It was his thirteenth game for England. The *Manchester Guardian* believed him destined to take Gurdon's record, but he won only one more cap. After declining to play in the Calcutta Cup match because he could not afford time off work – exemplifying the case for 'broken time' payments argued by the Northern clubs – he was refused permission to play for Heckmondwike on the same day even though, as Tony Collins has pointed out, the RFU allowed Wells, an Eton housemaster, to play for Harlequins after pulling out of a trial the previous season. Lockwood announced his England retirement – and little over a year later joined the Northern Union. It was not the last time the RFU were accused of double standards.

In between these four English victories came Wales's win in 1893 – a historic cliffhanger and the fixture's first real classic. Yet it was not so very different from the others. It was the first meeting at Cardiff, which since 1884 had staged three internationals against other opponents. In keeping with the spectacular growth of the town, the Arms Park – bordered on two sides by the River Taff and also by a cricket ground – had developed from a simple enclosure into a modern ground with grandstands along both touchlines, although players continued to change in nearby hotels until 1904 and steel fencing erected to 'keep the street urchins from getting into the ground' in 1891 did not succeed in its objective.

The weather, even by late Victorian standards, was horrible. Cardiff was gripped by bitter cold. At midnight on Wednesday there were nine degrees of frost, and thick fog, but Swansea's offer to switch the match to St Helen's was firmly rejected.

England travelled on the Friday, bringing with them one of the first controversies over dual-qualified players. Half-back Robert de Winton had been born on the Welsh side of the border in Hay-on-Wye. It was only on the morning of the match that an RFU committee meeting decided that De Winton could play. A letter in the *Western Mail* implied that there had been earlier Welsh interest in De Winton: 'His reply to the Welsh secretary was that his connection with Welsh football was nil. He had learnt the game at an English school, and had always played with English clubs, and he preferred to throw in his lot with England.'

Cardiff committee man Bill Shepherd worked non-stop from 8 a.m. on Friday to get the game on, devising solutions fitted to Cardiff's reputation as 'Coalopolis'. The *Western Mail* reported on the Saturday that 'some 500 buckets were bought at 8d each; their sides were perforated, they were gradually filled with coal, and fired. A quarter of the area was first treated, and when the necessary softness had been secured the turf was covered over with straw. Each quarter was dealt with in the same fashion, and the process was repeated in succession. It is proposed to keep this up until noon today.'

The *Morning Leader* was reminded of Dante's *Inferno*. 'An acre or more of ground heaped several feet high with live coals from 500 fires blazing far up into the dark night. Dozens of dark, ghoul-like figures were threading their way about the fires, heaping on fresh fuel, while the falling snow rendered the scene one of the most unique and romantic ever seen on a football field. Like Wellington at Waterloo your reporter walked over the field at midnight, and found it in a fairly good condition.' In all 18 tons of coal were burnt.

A well-wrapped crowd of some 20,000 – 'in solid array, a black mass, unrelieved by the slightest vestige of colour' – came to the Arms Park. There was black too on the pitch, where the buckets had stood. For the first half, and longer, England were in control. Their nine forwards, driven by Woods, dominated. Forward Charles Nicholl, an Oxford-educated, Welsh-speaking colossus, admitted that the Welsh eight 'could do nothing with them. They fairly pushed us off the ball every time'. Lockwood outshone the other outside backs. The *Western Mail* thought that Stoddart was 'very weak in defence', while likening Lockwood's efforts to his heroics six years earlier at Llanelli: 'He was safe in defence, ran strongly and was remarkably clever with his kicking.'

There was also the obligatory individual hero. Half-back Howard Marshall, of Blackheath, 'a very fast and strong runner, starting quickly and dodging effectively without turning much from his course or losing speed', scored two tries in the first half of his debut. England took a nine-point lead under scoring values giving two points for a try, three for a penalty or conversion and four for a drop. England, though, could not maintain the pressure. Nicholl broke out of his own twenty-five and found Hannan. He shaped to pass to Gould who, Townsend Collins recalled, twice shouted 'Wait!' before accepting the pass and running in from halfway. Bancroft converted and Wales were within four points. Collins, writing in 1948, reckoned it 'a try with a moral effect as great as any ever scored'. Biggs 'threw back his head and showed his teeth in the grimace of desperate effort' as his try cut the lead to two points. England, implicitly conceding the argument over formations, took Woods from the pack to play as a fourth threequarter. 'Commented upon all over the field', the move worked. Marshall went over to complete the last hat-trick by an Englishman against Wales for 108 years. Gould, with 'a corkscrewing run', went in for his second try, but Bancroft's missed conversion left Wales still a point behind. Then they were awarded a penalty wide out. What happened next is a matter of legend, with contemporary reports offering little assistance. Legend has it that when Gould demanded that the kick be placed, Bancroft insisted on dropping and the Welsh captain stalked off in disgust. Gould, though, recalled that 'the ball was given to Bancroft to drop'. Bancroft much later told J.B.G. Thomas: 'I told him I was going to have a drop at goal, but he was not willing. Then as the crowd grew restive he threw the ball on the ground and walked away. I retrieved the ball, took three strides and drop-kicked. Before the ball had gone 10 yards in flight I shouted "Arthur, it's there", and of course it was.'

Whatever the precise circumstances, it was an extraordinary demonstration of steady nerve and skill, kicked from a wide angle on an icy ground to win a match. The first penalty goal in an international match, it brought about other novelties. The single-point victory in what Rev. Marshall said was 'the finest international match I have ever seen' was the prelude to Wales's first Triple Crown campaign. Had the

Welsh scoring system, three points for a try or penalty and two for a conversion, been used, the match would have been drawn 14-14. Some spectators are supposed to have believed that it had ended as a draw, but a report of Gould being 'lifted shoulder high by a large group of his enthusiastic supporters' suggests that most were fully aware of the victory.

It was Howard Marshall's only international. His career was ended by a knee injury early the following season, when he was captaining Blackheath. His medical career was to earn him an OBE. Nor did De Winton play again, but unused reserve Ernest Taylor became an England regular and was captain by the 1896 match, which was to prove almost as remarkable. It was the first encounter after the Northern Union formation deprived England of its most powerful clubs and counties, yet for a year it was as if nothing had happened. Yorkshire won the County Championship, the North beat the South and there were ten northerners in the team that played Wales at Blackheath in January 1896 (with future Yorkshire cricket captain Frank Mitchell cunningly disguised as representing Blackheath and Cambridge University), including three forward debutants from Castleford.

Gould and Bancroft were there in a Welsh back division that included four Llanelli players. Beforehand, the *Observer* reported that the Welsh backs were 'admitted on all hands' to be superior. Perhaps they were, but they got little chance to show it. The *Western Mail* described it as 'one of the biggest hidings we have ever sustained . . . Two goals and five tries was the score and it really and truly represented the state of play. If Wales made half a dozen incursions into the English half it was as much as they ever did.' Llanelli centre Owen Badger dislocated his shoulder early in the game, but that 'could not excuse the absolute failure of their defence'. England were already ahead, crossed the Welsh line five times by half-time, and twice more before the end. Mitchell, Ernest Fookes, a New Zealander settled in Sowerby Bridge, and half-back Richard Cattell, whom Collins said was 'one of many English players who seems 30 per cent better in an international game', each crossed twice in England's most conclusive victory over Wales between 1881 and 1990. It was possible to believe that nothing had changed. In reality nothing would ever be the same again, the amputation of England's great region of popular passion for rugby – its answer to Wales's industrial south, Scotland's borders and

France's south-west – weakening it in playing terms and making it more socially exclusive.

The Blackheath hammering did nothing to lessen Wales's affection for its captain. Fresh in the public's memory was the national subscription the previous year for cricket idol W.G. Grace. On the following Monday Collins, in his guise as 'Dromio' of the *South Wales Argus*, suggested that rugby follow suit for Gould. The idea was rapidly adopted by the WRU, which subscribed £50. By the end of the month, the RFU had rejected an invitation to subscribe 'on the assumption that the testimonial is a monetary one'. The intention was to present Gould with a house, but the RFU decided in April that this was 'tantamount to giving a monetary testimonial', and therefore professionalised him. The WRU argued that a professional was defined as somebody who received rewards from his club, or a member of it. A national subscription did not directly implicate Newport, while the RFU had recently allowed Richmond to present £50 worth of plate to its captain, W.E. Bromet. Nor had Grace lost his amateur status in spite of receiving what was, by late Victorian standards, a fortune.

By September the Scots were complaining to the International Board about the WRU's 'unsatisfactory treatment' of the case. The WRU retreated to the extent of withdrawing its own contribution to a letter from the RFU, and the Wales v England match, with Gould leading Wales, went ahead in January 1897. Later that month, the International Rugby Board declared the testimonial 'an act of professionalism'. Wales resigned from the Board, protesting that it had fought against professionalism 'under more trying circumstances' than other members and, pointedly, 'with greater success than the English union'. Newport resigned from the RFU.

Gould not only escaped a ban but, with calculated defiance, he was voted on to the WRU committee. He received the title deeds of his house at a dinner on Easter Monday. But Wales did not play Ireland or Scotland in 1897, nor could they play anyone else while outside the IRB. They had no desire to join forces with the Northern Union, but had few alternatives if the hiatus persisted. In England, West Country and Midlands clubs were fearful of losing popular Welsh fixtures while there was sympathy for Wales in the columns of newspapers like the *Sporting Life* and the action of Ernest Taylor, England's captain for the preceding two seasons, in attending the presentation dinner for Gould.

All these considerations exercised the RFU AGM in September 1897 as members debated Rowland Hill's resolution to reinstate Gould. Hill's distaste was evident, describing it as 'an unpleasant duty'. The *Daily Telegraph* reported that Yorkshire delegates were 'almost fierce in their denunciation'. The resolution was, as the *Telegraph* put it, 'not entirely logical . . . but common-sense'. Wales promised to apply IRB rules on amateurism, but retained some local autonomy over what Gareth Williams described as 'blind-side remuneration' and were readmitted in February 1898, in time to play England and Ireland that season, but not the Scots, whose continuing displeasure was clear.

Meanwhile, fall-out from the schism continued. It was not just a matter of the twenty-two clubs who started the first Northern Union season in August 1895. Other clubs wished to regain their most attractive fixtures, and individual players crossed over. The first two post-split Yorkshire champions joined the Northern Union immediately after winning their titles. Swinton, whose centre Jim Valentine had played in all three matches for England that year, and Salford changed codes in 1896. Sam Houghton, full-back at Blackheath in 1896, joined Runcorn in the Northern Union before the Ireland match. Lockwood, declared bankrupt in 1897, was playing for Wakefield Trinity. In the space of a decade the RFU lost almost half of its affiliated clubs.

The implications were clear in the 1897 match at Newport. England lost Castleford forward John Ward to the Northern Union the week before. There was no frost this time, but torrential rain fell. Gould, in his last international, was partnered by a young centre named Gwyn Nicholls. Before the match W.E. Pullin, 'Old Ebor' of the *Yorkshire Post*, a consistent sceptic about Welsh rugby (Welsh writers sometimes put it more forcefully), detected familiar patterns of 'certain enthusiastic Welshmen building up extravagant visions of great victories over England on a foundation of club successes'. He also noted 'a few examples of brawn and muscle from the hills'. Valley clubs had until then played a limited part in Wales teams, but the rise of Penygraig and Llwynypia compelled selectorial attention. Penygraig's Jack Rhapps joined Dai Evans, of Llwynypia, and his Devon-born club-mate Dick Hellings in the Wales pack. The term 'Rhondda forward' would, as Dai Smith has pointed out, become 'a readily employed euphemism for any collier, tinplateman, steelworker or docker', irrespective of provenance. Evans was a policeman. Both he and Rhapps, destined to become rugby league's 'Lion of Salford', joined rugby league within a few months, but the breakthrough had been made. The *Western Mail* observed Welsh fans shouting 'Bravo, colliery!', albeit on a day when conditions rapidly made every player look as though he had completed a shift below ground. Long outmuscled by bigger and more powerful Englishmen and Scots, Wales now had hard men of its own – and at precisely the point when England had lost their most fruitful source.

The Welsh forwards dominated, Nicholls kicked beautifully and Wales were two tries up by half-time. They were scored by Pearson and Arthur Boucher, another of the fine Newport pack of the 1890s and by some way the most versatile, a forward on occasion listed as Wales's reserve back. Wales won 11-0, a margin that the *Western Mail* reckoned should have been closer to twenty points. It also accused England of playing 'a dirty, beastly game. They were kicking the men on the floor and lying on the ball to save themselves without ever attempting to get up to play it in the manner that they are said to be so fond of boasting of.' Old Ebor wrote that it would all have been very different had England picked 'a Yorkshire pack'. Wales's two previous victories had been by a single score or less. This was its first clear-cut win. A precedent was set.

Wales, thanks to the Gould case, did not play another international for fifteen months. The RFU initially hoped to play the 1898 match in Exeter on 26 February, but eventually opted for Blackheath on 2 April. There was, though, no shortage of West Country influence as the Stout brothers of Gloucester – wing Percy and forward Frank, who brought a former footballer's skills to dribbling – scored first-half tries. In 'a wonderfully exciting and well-contested game', according to the *Observer*, Wales hit back to lead 7-6 at the break but were undone – in the words of the unfailingly blunt Bancroft – by their half-backs: 'Our pack got the ball out five times out of six, but Elliott and Biggs never gave a decent pass,' he said. The result was in doubt deep into the second half but was settled by the Yorkshire Kiwi, Fookes. England's best threequarter in the previous season's defeat, he underlined his quality with two tries in the last quarter, the first from 'a brilliant dodgy run' after a cross-kick by Percy Stout. The match deserved to be remembered and England would do so for the next twelve years, but not for a reason they would have wanted.

CHAPTER THREE
THE MOST BEAUTIFUL GAME
1899–1909

Ce petit Chicago.

French visitor to Cardiff, 1905

There is no reason why English players should be less intelligent or less gifted but it is a fact that, relatively, English football is wooden.

Daily Chronicle, 1903

So deeply ingrained are the memories and images of the industrial devastation that followed that it is easy to forget that in 1900 South Wales was a dynamic, fast-expanding society. The population of Wales had all but doubled in the past thirty years, and a further 400,000 was added in the next decade. Growth was concentrated in the industrial south – Glamorgan, Monmouthshire and East Carmarthenshire. Cardiff, with 39,000 inhabitants in 1871, was four times bigger thirty years later, growth fuelled by coal from the Rhondda valleys, whose own population grew in fifty years from less than 1,000 to 113,000. Much of that growth was immigration. The 1911 census found that forty-nine per cent of the inhabitants of the Glamorgan coalfield were English-born. Coal peaked in employment and output before the First World War.

Wales's rugby team was cast in the image of that society, with players like the duo who secured a draw against England in 1904 – Swansea steelworker and Sunday School superintendent Will Joseph and Gwyn Nicholls's Nottingham-born business partner Bert Winfield – representing a convergence of the forces that made it. T.H. Thomas, who as Herald Bard, a senior official of the Gorsedd of Bards who organise the

National Eisteddfod, showed that the older, more traditional Wales was not immune to the national pleasure taken in rugby success, argued in 1909 that it belied conventional assumptions: 'Wales is a very small country. The success which has attended her efforts in athletics is therefore a sort of miracle. It has been attained by the exercise of those qualities in which the critics of the Welsh declare us to be deficient – hard work, self-control, discipline. The game has been intellectualised by our players . . . our teams "play with brains".'

Those brains generated a distinct style. Dai Gent, the Llandovery-born half-back who bucked contemporary trends by moving to and playing for England after finding his progression in Wales blocked, remembered in 1932 the rugby played in Wales between 1898 and 1903 as 'a beautiful game to watch . . . still the most beautiful game I have ever seen'. It worked on a strict division of labour between pack and backs. 'Forwards . . . were expected to be forwards, and practically never entered into competition with the backs or interfered with them.' Their task was to win the ball in scrum or line-out, to tackle and dribble. Handling was left to the backs. 'The seven backs on each side have ample room to manoeuvre, and it was really delightful to watch these manoeuvres carried out without the interference of forwards straying about as they do in these days.'

The shift in back play was personified by the transition from Gould to Nicholls. Gould was, in Nicholls's words, 'greater in individualism than in combination'. Nicholls had ample star quality. His regular Wales partner Rhys Gabe remembered his possessing 'some indefinable glamour'. He was, though, an enabler of others. 'His abiding ambition was to create openings for his wing or centre to carry on,' said Gabe. 'He was never selfish and if anything, he might occasionally have been selfless to a fault.'

Nicholls told Gabe that a misplaced pass was invariably the fault of the passer. Passing, observed John Raphael, an English opponent in two severe beatings and a narrow defeat who took acutely perceptive note of his persecutors, was not merely a matter of superior handling. 'The best Welsh players have a wonderful appreciation of the minimum amount of action necessary to put a defender temporarily out of service,' he said, 'with their precision, that the weight of an opponent was merely on the wrong foot would often be sufficient.'

Nicholls expounded his philosophy in the coaching book he wrote after his retirement. 'In an ideal Welsh game you really see fifteen great chess masters working in partnership and without consultation,' he said, 'each man knowing instinctively not only the best thing to be done, but that all the other fellows know it also and are falling, or have fallen, into their places accordingly.'

Some of these chess players attained grand master level. John Daniell, who played against the best and was later regarded as an exceptional judge of players, recalled 'an era of very great players in Wales, forwards as well as backs, although the latter stole the thunder'. Nicholls's memory, perpetuated by commemorative gates outside the Cardiff ground and a biography by David Parry-Jones, has endured best. His effectiveness was encapsulated by E.H.D. Sewell. 'He never betrayed his intentions,' Sewell said. There was always doubt as to what he would do 'until the thing was done . . . then what was done seemed the only thing to do'.

Continuity through the era was provided by the Swansea duo of Dicky Owen and Billy Trew, with Owen beating club-mate Bill Bancroft's record of thirty-three caps by two. Each was slight and fragile-looking, although in Owen's case this was an illusion. A.A. Thomson called him 'unobliteratable' and he relished the 'hip-tackle' that brought down much bigger men. Dai Smith and Gareth Williams argue that this made them particularly appealing for Welsh fans, many of whom were also on the small side. 'Huge forwards . . . singled out for awesome wonder by their sheer unusual size . . . could be objects of pride only. The Swansea pair could have come off the terraces which their admirers packed.'

Trew was versatile, capped as a wing against England in 1900 and 1901, then later returning as a centre or outside-half. That he could occupy a position called 'outside-half' was down to Owen, who did not so much play scrum-half as invent it. Half-back play, and the distinction between the positions, was still evolving. Gent was asked which side of the field he would like to play by his partner Walter Butcher when first picked for Gloucestershire in 1904. There were no such questions with Swansea or Wales and, as the *South Wales Daily Post* said in 1907, 'every inside player of note has modelled his play on Owen'. He was small, listed at between 5ft 1½in and 5ft 5in, and relished a London paper's description of him as 'a wizened little man'. A lightning-quick passer, he cultivated the reverse pass and a dazzling range of feints and deceptions. Gent described him and Trew as 'revelling in talks of the theory of the game'. His was the probing mind that devised the move that tore open the previously invincible All Blacks for the only score in Wales's historic win in 1905. He did not fit seamlessly with every partner, famously failing to gel with Cardiff's brilliant Percy Bush, but his club and country partnership with Dick Jones went into Swansea folklore as the 'Dancing Dicks' for moves that Raphael, for one, found 'utterly baffling and bewildering'.

Trew's genius was not in question. Gent, after thirty years as player and journalist, rated him 'easily the finest rugby player I have ever seen'. But Trew's talents were hard to describe, an elusiveness that led Dai Smith to call him 'the Ghost in the Machine'. Collins talked of Trew as the Nicholls ideal made flesh, and credited him with 'unassuming effectiveness' and 'unexcelled judgment' – the highest praise in his personal lexicon – that 'enabled him often to double-value the powers of the men who played beside him'.

From 1902 to 1906, Wales fielded at least three of a threequarter line of Teddy Morgan and Willie Llewellyn on the wings, with Gabe and Nicholls between them, that the cultured Raphael reckoned 'to football what Greek culture is to literature'. Among the forwards, George 'Twyber' Travers did for hooker what Owen was doing for scrum-half. Quickness around the field had something to do with landing him in the front row of scrums still packing down in much the order in which players arrived but long legs, speed of thought and movement and understanding with Owen also fitted him for the role.

Wales lost five matches out of thirty against the other home nations between 1900 and 1909. It took a very good team to beat them – the Scottish sides that triumphed at Inverleith in 1901, 1903 and 1907 all went on to take the Triple Crown. If Wales's most famous win was against New Zealand in 1905, and the most disappointing defeat was a year later against South Africa, more local dominance was underpinned by their mastery of England. It was England's misfortune that this juggernaut was on their doorstep just as they were most vulnerable. After losing all three matches in a season before 1899, they repeated the experience in 1901, 1903, 1905 and 1907 – the last season relieved by victory over newcomers France. The 1905 All Blacks went through England like Viking invaders, scoring 721 points to 15 in recording 23 wins, including a 15-0 dismissal of England, before losing to Wales and barely escaping with victories over Swansea and Cardiff.

*

Welsh losses to the Northern Union, while resented enough to make the professional scout a popular folk devil, scarcely compared to England's amputation of its two strongest counties. The English game's limited social range was shown when Leicester wing Jack Miles attracted interest in 1903 not only as the first of many 'Tigers' to play for England, but because he was 'the first man to arrive at national honours who has begun his career in the rugby fifteen of an Elementary school'. The writer hoped to see rugby played in elementary schools 'as it is in Leicester, Bristol and Coventry'. Among England's few gains from this decade of wrath was that these three cities' clubs, along with Bedford and Northampton, produced their first England players between 1900 and 1908. Yorkshire and Lancashire may have gone, but the towns and cities of middle England were beginning to compensate.

England selections also reflected the County Championship performances of Devon, who had four players in the 1906 team, Cornwall and Durham. The growth in rugby in the Royal Navy underpinned Devon's progress, but the availability of talented servicemen could be a mixed blessing. Percy Royds, later Rear Admiral, RFU president, Conservative MP and historian of the rules of rugby, was a hard-tackling centre for England in 1898 and 1899, but was unavailable the following year when he was winning a medal for rescuing diplomats in Peking from the Boxer Rising.

Nicholls sympathised with England's predicament. 'An English XV is more or less a scratch side,' he wrote. 'The men are drawn from a great variety of clubs playing various styles of game, and almost totally unfamiliar with each other.' While this was undoubtedly so, England did not always help themselves. A further seventy-one new caps were awarded in matches against Wales between 1900 and 1909, starting with thirteen, including the whole pack, in 1900. Thirty-one players had been used the season before. Nicholls was much less sympathetic to English half-back selection, arguing that they consistently picked individuals rather than the best combination. When Richard Livesay and Arthur Rotherham played at half-back at Swansea in 1899 it was the last time England fielded the same pairing in consecutive years until 1951. Sixteen men played at half-back for England against Wales between 1900 and 1909, not far short of the maximum of twenty. In all twenty-five different combinations were tried in thirty-seven matches throughout the decade.

England's rugby players could have fielded a fine cricket team at this time. Reg Schwarz (1901) went into history as one of an extraordinary clutch of South African googly bowlers, Bob Spooner (1903) was the supreme batting stylist in an age of elegance. Neither Edward Dillon (1904 & 05) nor Raphael (1902, 05 & 06) fell far short of Test class. However, forging an effective rugby combination was beyond them.

Gurdon's caps record of sixteen remained unscathed, although John Birkett, whose father Reg played in the first international in 1871 and scored England's first try, was by 1909 on his way to erasing it. There were still, though, players of substance. Birkett, who eventually collected twenty-one caps and ten tries, struck A.A. Thomson as 'a threequarter with the build of a forward . . . to any full-back faced with the agonising problem of tackling him, he must have seemed like a running mountain'. Gent – diminutive, quick and hard to contain – would not have disgraced Wales, and played for their Probables team at the Welsh trial in 1905 before opting for England. Half-back James Peters, a Devonport dockyard worker, was England's first black player and an early victim of South African sporting racism when the 1906 Springboks objected to his playing. Race may also have played its part at Swansea in 1907 when Peters, an England reserve, was prevented from taking his seat until a spectator 'explained matters to the constable'.

England's packs were respectable, conforming to Collins's description of the archetypal English forward: 'An honest and skilled scrummager; in the open he was useful with his feet, either as a scientific dribbler or in the kick-and-rush game. He was a sound tackler, had safe hands for a pass and for a catch at the line-out or on the field; and he was a runner with varying degrees of cleverness, but invariably resolute, with confidence in his own powers.' Some were much better. Losing John Daniell, who practised dribbling round cricket stumps, was 'undoubtedly a great blow' to England in 1902. Sewell reckoned that Noel Slocock was 'a terror for work in the tight, a fine man at the line-out, grand at following up and never let go of anything once he had a hand to'. Indeed, he rated him as the best current all-round forward before a knee injury ended his career in 1908. They were well served at full-back. Leicester's Cornishman Edward Jackett provided extreme competence in succession to Herbert

Gamlin. A protégé of Woods, Gamlin had been chosen to play cricket for Somerset as a seventeen-year-old in 1895, and had taken the wicket of England batsman Archie MacLaren – but only after he had scored a world record first-class score of 424.

Gamlin played, and in particular tackled, with his mentor's ferocious vigour, becoming known as 'The Octopus'. Gent admitted being 'scared to death' of being tackled by him and described him vividly as being 'six feet odd in height, with exceptionally long arms and legs, his face always grimly set and slightly bow-legged . . . Gamlin's genius lay in arranging – yes, arranging – when the man in possession should be tackled . . . [he] would watch the movement coming up . . . then, by perfect positioning, force the movement to go in a certain way, induce a player or two to pass, and then crash into the man on the spot where he [Gamlin] had decided the movement should stop.'

It was a skill for which he had plenty of use. If it said something of Wales's dominance that this fearsome defender conceded eighteen tries in five matches against them, it says still more that Gamlin emerged from those games with his reputation enhanced.

England's problem, Raphael argued, was that 'she had no distinctive style of her own. She copied various features that she saw Welsh teams bringing out successfully, without understanding their real object. There was no cohesion in her play and the result was that much individual excellence was wasted . . . it was the English system of defence that was so hopeless; perhaps one ought to say that there was no system.'

England's best hope was that some external factors might hamper Wales. None did. The nine international players who went north were the fewest of any peacetime decade until the 1950s. When traditional Welsh religiosity had its last flaring with Evan Roberts's revival in 1904-5, a few junior clubs closed and the 100,000 converts included Jenkin Thomas, who said: 'I used to play full-back for the devil, but now I am forward for God.' The *Western Mail* reported 'a peculiar something in the air which conveyed the impression that the match would suffer from the influence of the Revival' and 'Great Enthusiasm and Spontaneity' at meetings in Birchgrove and Morriston when Wales played England in 1905. Yet that was possibly Wales's best year, beginning with a record beating of England and ending with the overthrow of the All Blacks. David Lloyd George, the first Welshman in centuries to attain Cabinet rank, had even more than the usual politician's sensitivity to the shifting zeitgeist. In 1895, he complained that the valleys had 'sunk into a morbid footballism'. In 1908, he kicked off Cardiff v Blackheath at the Arms Park and declared it 'a most extraordinary game . . . much more exciting than politics'.

Injuries did not halt Wales. Dick Hellings scored with an injured collarbone in 1900. Losing Pearson in 1903 let Jehoida Hodges – who had crossed in the 13–0 win at Cardiff two years ealier – out of the pack to score a hat-trick. Nor did illness hamper their progress. When Dai 'Tarw' Jones, as a Treherbert collier the archetypal Rhondda forward, contracted typhoid in 1904 he recovered to play two more years of international rugby, be suspended *sine die* for involvement in 'blind-side remuneration' too blatant to be disregarded and play in the first rugby league Tests. England wing Reg Forrest, similarly afflicted in Dublin in February 1903, played against Scotland before typhoid was diagnosed, then died in April. A new twist in foul weather at Bristol in 1908 merely led the exuberant Percy Bush to offer to 'play with the fog' before using it to cloak an outrageously effective deception, passing one way and running, whooping, the other. Perhaps a referee got closest to thwarting Wales. Crawford Findlay's officiating of the 14-14 draw at Leicester and Wales's defeat in Dublin in 1904 did nothing to dispel Welsh conviction that he carried social prejudice, shown in his suggestion that Welsh working men join the Northern Union, on to the field.

The draw at Leicester was England's sole championship point from eleven meetings between 1899 and 1909. The pattern mirrored England's dominance in the early 1890s. England were usually competitive at home, and could feel that the odd result might have been different. Matches in Wales were almost unrelieved massacres. While England remained nomadic, using two London grounds and three in the provinces, Wales alternated between Cardiff and Swansea. The latter venue inspired English foreboding as once Blackheath had done for the Welsh. Wales exceeded twenty points at St Helen's in 1899, 1903 and 1907, perhaps contributing to the *Yorkshire Post*'s jibe in 1907 that 'Swansea is not an inspiring place at the best of times, but today it must be described as one of the dirtiest and most dreary to be found in the Principality'.

The lasting claim to rugby fame of Denys Dobson, from Newton Abbot, was that he died in 1916 in Nyasaland (now Malawi) under the feet of a charging rhino. Though no stranger than Wales wing Norman

Biggs's death by poison dart in Nigeria, its renown rests on a former teacher's reaction that 'he always had a poor hand-off'. Dobson had been known for his late consolation try at Swansea in 1903, converted in a Devon-Durham combination typical of the era by John Taylor of West Hartlepool. It was England's only score on Welsh soil between 1899 and 1911. The 1899 try – by prolific Percy Park wing Tot Robinson – was also a late consolation, concluding a contest that laid the template for the next decade. The central figures, though, spoke more to the past than the future. Evan and David James were 'my Greek Gods' to their Jewish mother, and scarcely less esteemed by the rest of Swansea. As labourers at White Rock copper works, site of the modern Liberty Stadium, these diminutive deceptionists – one Irish captain told team-mates to 'go for the one that hasn't got the ball, because he'll be the one that has' – personified a town that celebrated their reinstatement in 1896 with a torchlight procession.

Their Wales recall attracted a record crowd of 25,000, the *Cambria Daily Leader* observing 'one solid mass of humanity flowing towards the St Helen's ground'. A policeman stolidly guarded the pavilion enclosure gate, 'blissfully unconscious . . . that the enclosure was rapidly being filled by the people who did not think it above their dignity to vault the railings'. The fencing around the pitch gave way three times, although less frequently than England's defence. Bancroft, captaining Wales, had shown frank pre-match confidence of a sort that disappeared once rugby discovered media training, saying that he would be disappointed if Wales did not win by at least two tries.

He was not disappointed. The final tally was six tries to one, twenty-six points to three. After a tentative start, the James brothers would 'distinguish themselves as they had never done before' even though Evan dislocated his shoulder after fifteen minutes, playing on in 'a lot of pain'. No less troubled, in the mental sense, were England's half-backs Rotherham and Livesay, stars of victory over Wales twelve months earlier, who were 'completely fogged and nonplussed'. Rotherham, getting a taste of his future eminence as Master in Lunacy, 'wasted a good deal of energy in empty protest when he found the brothers James too good for him'. The *Daily Graphic* reported 'what our American friends would call a landslide' while the *Morning Leader* disapproved of 'a heavy Englishman unnecessarily flinging down little David James'.

Wales had practised at Cardiff Arms Park under the supervision of the former Newport and Wales captain Tom Graham. Four tries, two in each half, were scored by debutant wing Willie Llewellyn, a trainee pharmacist from Llwynypia who had been seen as a potential weak link. A regular for the next six years, Llewellyn's hero status was confirmed in 1910 when his chemist shop was untouched amid the looting and wrecking of the Tonypandy riots. But for Gamlin, England might have suffered more. The *Cambrian Daily Leader* thought 'his coolness was "North Polian" and some of his saves were really marvellous'. Daniell, another Somerset man, led England's forwards well, particularly in a lively opening, before showing Bancroftian directness in a post-match interview. When a Welsh reporter remarked that 'you were badly let down', Daniell responded: 'My word, you are right, but your fellows played magnificently. Personally, I would have preferred seeing my own pack [Cambridge University] playing. Our men were all sixes and sevens and they scrummaged very badly. The Welshmen pushed us about as they liked.' Six weeks later, the James brothers joined Broughton Rangers, the rugby league club, for the second time. This time, in rugby terms at least, there was no coming back.

Nor was there for England over the next eleven years. That period brought Wales five Triple Crowns and two Grand Slams, albeit when France were still not playing all the other nations and nearly half a century before the term Grand Slam was coined. Matches in Wales followed the pattern of 1899. Rugby's steady growth in appeal was recognised not only by railway companies, who ran twenty-two excursions into Swansea in 1903, but also by less welcome followers. Four pickpockets from London were arrested at Gloucester station early that morning after 'several watches appeared to have been stolen' on an excursion. Two years later, numerous forged tickets were circulating at 1s apiece.

Welsh captains remained uncowed by fear of motivating England with over-confident predictions. Llewellyn's pre-match view in 1905 was: 'Of course one can never say definitely, but my opinion is that with a fair amount of luck Wales will win. I believe the Welsh halves will be a good deal better than the English pair if they have the chance to get the ball.' Such confidence was justified. Matches in Wales became predictable, although still distinguished by outstanding performances. In 1903 Jehoida Hodges, a forward, was sent to the wing after Pearson – recalled after five years and made captain – was injured by a Gamlin tackle. Gabe, playing inside Hodges, recounted what happened next. 'My instructions to Hodges were, whenever the ball came out to the Welsh backs and was moving towards the left-wing, he should run like hell, as I was quicker and would catch him up,' Gabe said. 'I told him I would run straight towards Gamlin and then give him the ball with every chance of scoring.' This worked so well that Hodges scored a hat-trick in seventeen first-half minutes. Wales led 21-0 at half-time. Gabe recalled becoming 'as sore and bruised as if I had been mauled by a bear, as a result of delaying my passes as late as possible so as to give Hodges a clear run in!' Hodges expressed his appreciation for Gabe's selflessness, but added that 'on the whole I think I would rather play in the pack'.

Two years later, in a 25-0, seven-try hammering at Cardiff, described as 'one of the greatest lessons in the history of rugby football in the marvellous effectiveness of combination', it was Dick Jones and Swansea full-back George Davies whose 'brilliancy was exhilarating', while the fearsomely quick Teddy Morgan crossed twice. In 1907, it was six tries and 22-0. Wales were still experimenting with the seven-man scrum and the 'rover' formation learnt from – and used to devastating effect against – the 1905 All Blacks. Cardiff's Reggie Gibbs 'roved' to devastating effect, Owen was simply himself and Trew 'the master mind . . . that created most of the movements that ended in tries'.

England's performance in 1907 was described as 'woefully weak' by the *Cambria Daily Leader*, while the *Morning Leader* condemned their pack as 'a helpless rabble'. Jackett showed himself to be Gamlin's true successor at full-back, his solidity preventing a bad beating becoming even worse. John Daniell's disconcerting frankness also had an imitator, albeit by attribution rather than direct quotation, when England's 1903 skipper Bernard Oughtred reportedly said that his team had been 'beaten to blazes'.

In 1909, at Cardiff, England at least held Wales to single figures, 8-0. The selectors reflected the 1908 County Championship by picking four Cornishmen – Jackett, the severely criticised half-backs Tom Wedge and 'Maffer' Davey, and the splendidly named Penzance winger Barzillai Beckerleg Bennetts, 'Barrie' to his friends. Cardiff wing Johnny Williams, who had 'a characteristic hunched-up way of running', and captained Wales in Paris in 1911 because he spoke French, scored the second of two first-half tries and was close to claiming two more.

Predictability has its downside, though, even for winners. The *Western Mail* is not an infallible guide to the Welsh psyche – its quest to persuade Wales to vote Conservative may be the least successful marketing campaign in national history – but it possibly had a point in stating in 1905 that 'Welshmen are ready to confess to a desire to see a variation in the way of a win for England'. Winning loses much of its appeal without fear of defeat. Even in 1899, substantial numbers were streaming away before the end. By 1907 a a *Cambrian Daily Leader* report said: 'No one parading the main streets of Swansea today would imagine that it was an International Football day. The excursions have arrived as usual – but without the excursionists. "The Docks" declines resolutely to interest itself in the subject of the match, the employees at the great manufactories stick solidly to their work, and the town consequently presents its normal appearance.' That only 12,000 spectators saw Trew's masterclass was partly a reflection of the disappointment felt at Wales's 11-0 loss to South Africa at St Helen's a few weeks earlier, but easy wins were nevertheless becoming dull.

Matches played in England were closer contests. Wales won comfortably twice. At Gloucester, in 1900, England's selectors surpassed themselves by choosing thirteen new caps, including all eight forwards. Two of those newcomers, Blackheath full-back Sydney Coopper and Birkenhead Park forward James 'Bim' Baxter, eventually became the most powerful men in English rugby: Coopper as RFU secretary and Baxter, after winning an Olympic sailing medal and refereeing two of the rowdiest rugby internationals in history, at Paris in 1913 and Swansea in 1921, as selector, International Board delegate and gunboat-diplomat manager of the 1930 British and Irish Lions. This experience, with England beaten 13-3 by tries from the maimed Hellings and debutant Billy Trew, still a winger, may account for Baxter later presiding as a selector over one of England's more stable periods. England captain Richard Cattell also appears to have lacked diplomatic skills, as 'Welsh forwards nodded agreement as one of their number described England's captain as a pig'.

In 1906, thirteen of the Welsh XV who had beaten New Zealand before Christmas won 16-3 at Richmond. Nicholls, 'the Nicholls of old' according to the *Observer*, thought the margin unfair to England. The *Observer*, though, praised the solidity of Wales's seven-man scrum and the 'leisurely excellence' of their backs. Hodge scored from a charge-down and Morgan, recalled by Sewell as 'exceptionally quick over thirty yards' with a 'characteristic waggle at full speed' and in the midst of a thirteen-match spell that produced fourteen tries for Wales, bamboozled his high-quality marker George Hudson for another of Wales's four tries.

England got rather closer in the other matches. In 1902, at Blackheath, Wales scored first through Gabe, who landed unconscious after Gamlin's tackle to the solar plexus, but England led 8-3 by the break with tries from the ill-fated Dobson and forward John Robinson, a Yorkshireman winning his second cap nine years after his first. 'The tradition of failure at the ground which had previously haunted Welsh teams seemed to be in the air again.' England still led 8-6 five minutes from time, and were denied only by a tackle on Coopper by Llewellyn that Nicholls reckoned among the two best he ever saw. Debutant Owen, looking to Sewell like 'a schoolboy who had come to the wrong game', put into a scrum, then dummied a pass. His opposite number Oughtred, who had earlier lost his shorts, now mislaid his judgement and strayed offside. Irish referee Robert Jeffares was jeered by the crowd for the penalty award, and full-back John Strand-Jones – who would go on to take up a chaplaincy in Karachi – drop-kicked the goal. While the market in books such as Arthur Tysilio Johnson's *The Perfidious Welshman* (1910) and T.W.H. Crosland's *Taffy was a Welshman* (1912) owed most to Lloyd George, who was denounced with magisterial incomprehension by John Maynard Keynes as 'this goat-footed bard, rooted in nothing', Owen and the James brothers also marked the English psyche.

Two years later it took another late kick, this time a drop-goal from the mark, worth four points, to salvage a 14-14 draw for Wales at Leicester. Both teams felt they should have won. The sun shone 'with fervent brilliancy' as Leicester played host to between two and three thousand Welshmen and 'excursionists from all parts of England'. The *Leicester Mercury* described post-match chaos at the Post Office: 'Scores upon scores of people squeezed themselves into the office, and dozens of hands could be seen upraised frantically waving telegrams'. Around thirty telegraph clerks filed 100,000 words of newspaper copy plus 'many hundreds' of private wires.

There was plenty to write about. Crawford Findlay gave so many penalties against Owen for 'feeding the scrum' – seven before half-time – that the Welsh player gave the ball to his English counterpart to put in, but England wing Elliott Vivyan missed several kickable opportunities. England led 6-0 at the break thanks to the dominance of a pack that included South African-born Bedford Grammar School pupil John Milton, the first player to follow his father – Sir William Milton, Cecil Rhodes's secretary and a key figure in popularising the game in the Cape – into an England team. In the second half Morgan crossed for Wales, then England wing Edgar Elliot dribbled over for his second try. Elliot was judged by the *Daily Telegraph* 'not to have sufficient pace for a winger' and so followed his uncle Charles, who had been derided for making a mark when he had a clear run to the line in 1886, as a butt for critics. Elliot's second try was converted by Gamlin, who was 'playing a really fine game for his side' in his final season. Llewellyn scored for Wales and Winfield's touchline conversion put his side 10-9 ahead, but a try by centre Arthur Brettargh, converted by veteran skipper Frank Stout, his only goal in fourteen internationals, restored England's four-point advantage.

'The excitement had scarcely subsided' when Will Joseph made a mark near halfway and handed the ball to Winfield. Joseph was a steelworker, Owen's cousin, and a quoits international denied recent honours because the England v Wales match had been suspended following a row over shares of gate receipts. The archetypal 'safe pair of hands', a kicker credited by Sewell as possessing 'machine-like certainty', Winfield could have been playing for England. He had had an England trial, playing well below his usual standards and missing out on selection, only after losing by six votes to five to Strand-Jones for the Wales full-back vacancy in 1902. He had then told journalists: 'Wales is where I now earn my living. It is Wales that I will represent on the rugby field.' He now, like Strand-Jones two years earlier, found himself with Wales's fate at his feet. The kick went over and there was still time for Mr Findlay to disallow a Morgan try for a forward pass. Gabe said that he could 'forgive and forget everything the referee did that day, but not that final decision'. England centre Edward Dillon was not impressed, saying: 'The Welsh always blame the referee. They do not understand the rules properly. They are not educated like we are. In Wales you don't find the same kind of people as in England.' This may explain the relish with which the *Western Mail* branded Dillon 'a complete failure' when England were demolished at Cardiff the following year.

The 1908 match should have been remembered as a nine-try classic of attacking rugby. Instead it went down in history because of the weather. It was played at Ashton Gate, the football ground belonging to Bristol City, much to the applause of the *Western Daily Press*. The paper argued that: 'Bristol is the natural home of the English and Wales match, but it is only now that this fact has been realised by the English Rugby Union.' The game was wrecked as a spectacle, however, by thick fog. Even so there were numerous visitors from across the border, the *Press* reporting: 'There was no mistaking they were Welsh, if the brogue did not give them away, the leek did. There it was in thousands of button holes . . . fog or no fog, they were out for the day and wanted Bristol to know it.' The paper also detected a distinctive Welsh phenomenon. 'It was a curious fact,' it noted, 'that hundreds of Welshmen were to be seen in the city while the match was in progress at Ashton Gate.'

Those who were actually in the ground saw little more than those outside, the *Press* report describing 'dim outlines of white flitting here and there'. By half-time visibility was twenty to thirty yards. Wales had started well and were twelve points up in twenty minutes before, 'from a distant corner of the field came cheers of an unmistakable Saxon quality, for Williamson had scored. Further cheers indicated that Roberts had kicked the goal.' Wales were always ahead, Bush creating one score by passing to Gabe and drawing the cover by running – whooping, but empty-handed – in the opposite direction. England, though, kept hitting back, the fog giving one score a peculiarly dramatic quality. 'Expectantly the crowd waited, and when a figure in white emerged from the fog with the ball grasped firmly under his arm, Englishmen let their enthusiasm go without restraint. It was Birkett. He had got the ball somewhere in the centre of the field, and apparently forced an opening. When he came into view there was only Winfield to stop him and with a splendidly judged swerve he went round the Welsh full-back and completed the last few yards to the line.' It ended 28-18 to Wales, but was still one of the best England performances of the decade. England kicker Geoffrey Roberts, later Recorder of Bristol and a prosecutor at the Nuremburg trials, detected a miscarriage of justice when dropped from the team for the next match. *The Times* said that 'both fifteens frequently disappeared from sight. So did the goalposts when I was vainly trying to put the ball between them . . . I had not played so badly and in any event the selection committee could not have seen whether I did or not.' Debutant half-back Rupert Williamson, much-praised scorer of two tries, might also have registered a grievance. He was to win five caps for England, and had a different half-back partner each time.

The *Western Daily Press* had predicted that, when they saw the attendance in Bristol, the RFU would lament income lost by not playing there before. They had a point: in spite of the fog, it was more profitable than any previous England match, pulling in nearly £1,200 to break the record set against the All Blacks in 1906. The RFU, though, was already committed to a course of action that would mean England never again playing Wales in Bristol, or at any other English ground that had hosted the fixture up until then.

CHAPTER FOUR
THE TWICKENHAM EFFECT 1910–22

There is an indefinable something in the atmosphere and surroundings of Twickenham which is not congenial to the Celtic temperament.

Welsh writer, 1912

For Welsh rugby the years between 1906 and 1914 constituted not so much a landscape of declining standards as a plateau where the consistency of earlier success was maintained, but where innovation was now the victim of intense club rivalry and constant familiarity, and where unpredictability was somehow lost sight of in the wheels and cogs of smooth-running machinery.

Gareth Williams, 1991

On a grey, damp afternoon in the middle of January 1910, a Bridgend stonemason named Ben Gronow kicked off the first international match played at Twickenham. The ball was caught near the twenty-five-yard line by England's captain and outside-half, Adrian Stoop. The standard tactic was to kick back into touch but, instead of this, Stoop's half-back partner Dai Gent recalled half a century later: 'He started to run at once, at top speed, up the field and diagonally towards the left. Though surprised we all quickly tumbled to what he was doing and moved up on his inside. Outside him he had Solomon, Birkett and Poulton and the ball was passed along the line at top speed. When it reached Poulton on the left wing, he was hemmed in and wisely put in a cross kick which dropped in front of the posts.' England retained possession and Gent launched another movement. 'This time along the line towards Chapman on our right wing, and in a flash Chapman was over in the north-east or right-hand corner.'

The RFU had begun seeking a ground of their own in March 1907, encouraged by the example of Scotland, who had built the first dedicated national ground, Inverleith, in 1899. The finance committee of England's governing body argued that no current ground was good enough. Blackheath and Richmond had adequate playing surfaces, but both needed temporary stands to accommodate 15,000 spectators and neither could offer a secure tenancy. Though £1,100 was spent on improving capacious Crystal Palace to host the All Blacks in 1905, 'nobody would say it was totally fit'. The committee advised the RFU 'to purchase land in the neighbourhood of London and lay the site out as a permanent football ground'.

By October, they had settled upon a former market garden in Twickenham, a dozen miles south-west of Central London, just beyond the traditional stronghold of Richmond. It came to be known ever after as 'Billy Williams's cabbage patch', in honour of an RFU committee man, and was purchased for £5,573. A further £20,000 was spent before the first match, Harlequins v Richmond, was played in September 1909. The venture was a declaration of confidence that, while results remained discouraging, with no championship success since 1893, English rugby was regaining the ground lost since 1895. An England team with the regulation eight new caps was evidence of progress. Though traditional London clubs were represented – two Blackheathans, a Richmond man and three from rising power Harlequins – Gloucester, with three men, Bristol and Bedford represented the developing West Country and Midlands clubs, while Redruth centre Bert Solomon came from the far south west and Fred Chapman from Westoe in the north east.

Stoop, an Old Rugbeian of Dutch extraction, won his first cap in 1905 but dropped off the England half-back carousel after the Swansea debacle of 1907, in which he had fulfilled the down-side of a pre-match assessment of him – 'on one day positively brilliant and on another not worth playing'. He captained England only twice, but left a lasting imprint with that opening attack at Twickenham, epitomising an innovative tactical philosophy based on refining Nicholls's ideas, analysing angles of running and passing, standardising half-back play and, above all, attacking at any opportunity rather than awaiting a favourable field position.

Owen was reportedly 'flabbergasted'. For the *Sportsman* – stereotyping fearlessly despite Wales's comebacks of 1902 and 1904 and England's serial collapses of recent years – the score 'contributed more to the undoing of the Welshmen than anything else. The emotional Welsh nature responds very readily to early success, but is just as easily depressed when its opponent gets on and up early.' Certainly England dominated before half-time, when they led 11-3. Chapman kicked a penalty then converted a brilliant try by Solomon, who from thirty yards out 'ran towards Chapman and feinted to pass. Having thoroughly drawn the defence on to the wing, he doubled inside and then gained a great try.' The supposedly deflated Welsh revived after half-time, Gibbs scoring a try, and 'once at least were within an ace of getting in'. England, though, held on for an 11-6 win, their first in the fixture since 1898 and Wales's first defeat against any country since 1907.

The new stadium showed limitations: kick-off was delayed for fifteen minutes by traffic congestion and, Gent recalled, 'in the confusion there was no team photograph taken'. The approaches to the groud were unprepossessing: 'The narrow winding Oak Lane with the dangerous deep ditch on one side connecting Mogden Lane with the East Stand.' Nor were initial crowds spectacular: 18,000 in 1910, 20,000 two years later. Neither matched the attendance at Bristol in 1908. It was, though, vastly more lucrative. The profit at Bristol was just under £1,200. The first Twickenham match generated more than £2,000, a sum that had nearly doubled by 1914. The stadium paid for itself in three years.

One reason was that the spectacular opening, in rugby terms at least, was no false dawn. England went on to become champions in 1910, and add Grand Slams in 1913 and 1914. Whether this would have happened anyway, or represented a genuine Twickenham effect, is a 'chicken and egg' question. England certainly had some exceptional players. If Stoop was the brain at Twickenham in 1910 and his fellow Harlequin and Old Rugbeian Poulton the romantic hero, the original was Blackheath back-rower Charles 'Cherry' Pillman, who had turned twenty only the week before. The *Observer* thought him 'the player who won the hearts of the crowd', while the *Sportsman* reckoned he 'probably contributed more to winning the match than any other single individual. It was Pillman who especially checked the Owen and Jones manoeuvres.'

Looking back in 1958, the Welsh captain John Gwilliam argued that the previous half-century was defined by the progress of intelligent forward play. Pillman represented a significant evolutionary step. For a bemused

South African, 'he played a game apparently invented by himself'. He was quick – Collins thought 'he made a nonsense of the dictum that you can pass the ball faster than a man can run' – acutely aware, Gent describing him as the first forward to 'make intelligent anticipation an art', a lethal disrupter of opposing backs and a regular try-scorer. Solomon, an Olympic medallist having played in Cornwall's defeat by Australia in the 1908 Games in London, did not play for England again. Allegedly uncomfortable with upper-class team-mates, he returned to Redruth saying: 'That's it, I've finished.' Much more was seen of another debutant. Irish-born Bill Johnson became, Gent would recall, 'a great full-back (with) a good sense of position, a beautiful fielder of the ball, a wonderful tackler and always revelling in stopping rushes', and initiated a great Bristol tradition. Of England's seven Grand Slams before 1980, only those of 1921 and 1923 were won without a Bristolian full-back. Still to come before the war were combative 5ft 5in Headingley forward John King, Cyril Lowe, as a military pilot the first authentic flying wing, and goal-kicking Cambridge forward John 'Jenny' Greenwood, who shocked team-mates by reading books relevant to his studies, allegedly unprecedented for a student player.

If England were newly prosperous, Wales had yet to decline. Trew and Owen were as accomplished and confident as ever. In 1911 Owen told the *Daily Post*: 'That we shall win, I have not much doubt,' and he fulfilled his prophecy, the *Observer* hailing 'the genius of Dicky Owen', who played with 'all of his old subtlety' in a 15-11 win over an England team who the *Daily Post* reckoned were stronger than the year before. Wales's own exceptionally quick back-rower Ivor Morgan scored on his home ground. The *Post's* bracketing of him with Trew and Owen as the architects of victory might appear to be local bias, but their praise was echoed by English papers. Essayist A.A. Thomson remembered Morgan as 'a wing-forward who performed prodigies of valour as a raider, but worked like an honest man in the scrum as well'.

The 1914 pack, led by Rev. Alban Davies and immortalised as 'The Terrible Eight' after an epic battle with the like-minded Irish, was as good as any Welsh forward combination. Former England captain Vincent Cartwright, showing that the old player who believes that decadence began with his own retirement is not an exclusively modern phenomenon, proffered the faint praise that the Welsh 'bore more resemblance to a real good pack of forwards than any other I have seen in the past five or six seasons' and credited them with the only acceptable wheel seen all season at Twickenham.

Welsh results against Ireland and Scotland between 1910 and 1922 were marginally better than in the previous eight seasons. The difference was that England were vastly improved, the outcome being a rare period of mutual strength. Welsh ascendancy was transferred towards England, with Wales cast in the role that France would play in the 1970s and 1990s: that of consistent challenger to a hegemonic power. England won four championships, each a Grand Slam, and shared two in those eight seasons. Wales won two and shared one. Scotland and Ireland had one shared championship apiece. France won four matches.

Home advantage became all-important. England did not lose a championship match at Twickenham until 1926. Wales remained strong at home, the only exception being England's victory at Cardiff in 1913. England had also come close at Swansea two years earlier. The match was not the only seafront attraction at the time. Two days before the game, local engineer Ernest Sutton, twenty-eight, became 'the first man to fly in a heavier than air machine' in Wales when he took off at Oxwich Bay. A crowd estimated at forty to fifty thousand suggested that England's win at Twickenham in 1910 had genuinely revived interest in the fixture, and brought the usual unwelcome outriders. A rumour, not long after the siege of Sydney Street, that anarchist Peter the Painter was abroad in Swansea proved merely to be South Walian humour. The *Daily Post* could, though, carry an enthusiastic account of the rounding up of 'a gang of notorious pickpockets', concluding in the pursuit and capture of three who had been at the match. There were reckoned, said Detective Inspector Roberts, 'to be at least fifty, and they all came from the East End of London'. Their victims may have included the man on the Paddington excursion who was robbed of £20, borrowed a sovereign from the stationmaster and had that taken before he was back on the train. The pickpockets were not the only miscreants. An acrobat was arrested after an impromptu pitch-side show with a bicycle and two chairs that amused the crowd but not austere Welsh Rugby Union secretary Walter Rees, who called the police when his order to desist was ignored. The entertainer was dragged away 'by the combined forces of seven constables . . . amidst the vigorous booing of the crowd'.

Others were equally keen to press charges of theft after Wales's 15-11 win. The *Referee* thought Wales 'certainly very lucky', while the *Daily Post* reckoned Leicester stalwart Alf Kewney 'quite 15 yards offside' in scoring to launch a revival that hauled England, who had been 12-3 down, back to within a point. Owen remembered weeks before his suicide in 1932 that 'England were the cleverer side'. That interview did not mention his dribble to set up the final score for Cardiff forward Joe Pugsley, but Owen still recalled Morgan's try. 'Trew and I had handled in a triangular movement,' he said, 'which drew the defence to one side to allow Ivor Morgan to score.' The *Observer* thought that the heroes of the day were Morgan and 'the English Williams, the full-back'. Few questioned that valuation. Williams 'fielded the ball safely and kicked with a fine length' according to the *Sunday Times* and laid out Trew with a tackle as the Welsh captain was giving Morgan his scoring pass. It was the 'English' part of the description that was disputed.

Stanley Williams was born near Newport, was educated there and had played for its club since 1904. A Wales reserve for the past two seasons, he had failed to dislodge incumbent Jack Bancroft, brother of the more famous Bill. When the WRU protested against Williams's defection, the RFU cited 'the absence of any international disqualification'. Williams played very well in every England match that season. The WRU's concern was the precedent set. Were the RFU claiming Newport as an English club, and Monmouthshire as an English county? The RFU responded that they were not, but that 'in view of what he told us we considered he was English and not Welsh by parentage, and as he was ready to play for us if selected, we decided we were justified in selecting him. Players may be born and live in Wales, but if his parentage is English we consider we have a right to play him if he is ready to play for us.' The WRU was not convinced, but declined an offer of arbitration. After that season Williams retired from international rugby. He was as colourful off the field as he was safe and undemonstrative on it. He was mentioned twice in dispatches, was awarded a wartime DSO and then, in 1936, was 'lost overboard at sea during a return journey from South America'.

If Williams was outstanding in a losing cause in 1911, so was Jack Bancroft the following year. Getting to Twickenham remained an adventure. The *Observer* described 'extraordinary scenes at Waterloo . . . Men had literally to fight for places and all carriages were filled to overflowing'. Scenes at Twickenham testified to rugby's well-heeled clientele: 'Motors were unable to get along the road at anything beyond a crawl, and the large waste pieces of ground outside the Rugby Union enclosure were crowded with waiting cars.'

Inside the stadium, Wales were besieged. Their survival for nearly seventy minutes of incessant pressure was largely down, on the day that Owen overtook Bill Bancroft's caps record, to the younger Bancroft. Thomson recalled: 'At full-back for Wales he seemed frequently to be playing the whole of the English team by himself . . . Frequently, looking like a lone defender, he performed the task of half-a-dozen men, tackling and kicking as if he had as many arms and legs as a Hindu deity.' Telling a Welsh friend that he had seen 'The Great Bancroft', and being told 'that was merely the great Bancroft's little brother', he suggested that Bill 'must have had wings as well'.

Welsh resistance finally broke half an hour into the second half. The *Observer* reported that a pass went behind wing Henry Brougham, 'but Pillman, who had just come across, secured it, he made a few yards, boring still further to the left and when hopelessly shut in himself he gave an in-pass to Brougham, who slipped in behind two Welshmen and was over . . . the scene in the stands was extraordinary. Everyone stood up. Hats, sticks, anything handy, were waved in the air.' The end, after a second score from half-back John Pym, further belied theories about the undemonstrative English: 'Thousands burst through the barriers, despite many large notices ordering people not to cross the enclosure, and surrounded the players and carried several of them shoulder high into the dressing room. Such enthusiasm has seldom been seen in an English rugby enclosure.'

Both England scorers were debutants, although Brougham had earlier experience of international sport as a rackets medallist at the 1908 Olympics. Two more rookies, the forwards Alfred MacIlwaine, of United Services, 'who can never have played better', and John Eddison, of Headingley, lived another seventy years, surviving into their nineties. All four played every game in 1912, but only MacIlwaine, picked once more in 1920, appeared after that. A fifth debutant was listed alongside MacIlwaine and Eddison on all four teamsheets. Dick Stafford, of Bedford, was a rugby prodigy, 6ft and 13st, renowned as a 'devastating tackle' and for 'tremendous dashes for the line'. He played for Bedford at the age of fifteen and had an England trial at seventeen. He was only eighteen when he played against Wales, but he was already Bedford's captain and had led it to 'an unprecedented run of success, particularly against Metropolitan clubs'. He played the entire championship season and was re-elected Bedford captain. On 24 October he played for East Midlands, but was taken ill three days later. On 8 November, a specialist diagnosed spinal cancer. He died aged nineteen on 1 December. His funeral was the biggest in Bedford for twenty years.

Premature deaths became the norm rather than the tragic exception when war broke out two years later. None was mourned more widely than Ronnie Poulton's. He was seen as a sporting analogue to another Old Rugbeian, the poet Rupert Brooke, also killed in 1915. His finest hour against Wales was in 1913 – 'Poulton's match' according to E.W. Ballantine of the *Observer* – England's first win in Wales since 1895. Poulton was heir to a vast biscuit fortune – adding 'Palmer' to his name in 1914 – had a matinee idol's air of effortless ease and an individual style. Travelling overnight from the ski slopes of Switzerland, to be 'met on the platform and hurried off to practice on the evening before the match' against Wales in 1912 accentuated the devil-may-care impression he gave, but in reality he was serious-minded and, by rugby standards, radical. His closest friend, William Temple, became Archbishop of Canterbury, his bequests included the Workers Education Association and, as captain of England, he was publicly critical of the RFU. He warned the governing body that it risked confining the game to a single class when it banned ten West Country players and officials for breaching rules on amateurism.

England arrived at Cardiff in 1913 hoping for dry weather – and were predictably disappointed. W.J.A. Davies, England's outside-half, recalled 'the strong confidence of Wodehouse, our captain, in his belief that we were going to give Wales a good hiding, and his keen disappointment at breakfast on the morning of the match, when it was raining'. Davies was a dual-qualified player, but clear-cut in provenance and allegiance. Born and educated in Pembroke Dock, where his grandfather was a well-known dockyard officer, he went to England on a naval dockyard apprenticeship. In 1921, he told the *Western Mail*: 'All my rugby was played in England . . . until I left Wales I knew nothing of rugby. It was said I was going to be selected for both the English and the Welsh trials. I made it clear at once that if I was going to be selected at all I would play for England.' England would be intensely grateful for his decision, although this was his only international in Wales.

Poulton remembered: 'The morning was spent in animated discussion of numerous devices for winning the match, none of which by any chance came off . . . except the off-repeated injunction from our captain "Remember your feet and use them, and don't forget the watchword" – but that, I fear, is unprintable'. The match echoed that of 1912. Led by Norman Wodehouse, another naval man and cousin of humorist P.G. Wodehouse, England's forwards held their own into the wind and rain of a scoreless first half. After half-time one English device did 'come off' – Poulton. Publicity posters had said simply: 'Come and see R.B. Poulton.' Wales would happily have seen less of him. His running on ground that was 'like a water-meadow after a herd of cows had been forced to pass through it against their will' had a bemused Welsh threequarter asking: 'How can one stop him when his head goes one way, his arms another and his legs keep straight on?' Poulton located 'a small green patch in a sea of mud' from which to drop a goal, then led a dribble that created havoc in the Welsh defence and was seized upon by the alert Pillman for the try that completed a 12-0 win.

After failing to score against England for two seasons, Wales managed it at Twickenham in 1914 when Newport wing George Hirst dropped a goal. Willie Watts, a Llanelli centre who was making his debut – and not to be confused with fellow debutant Davie Watts, a collier from Maesteg – charged down a Poulton clearance to score and give Wales a 9-5 lead deep in the second half. Their Welsh forwards were well on top, although Raphael in the *Observer* complained that 'some of their methods were over-vigorous'. That England escaped – 'luckily' according to the *Daily Telegraph* – owed much to the men who had sustained them over the previous five seasons. Johnson, wrote Raphael, was 'always to be depended on in an emergency'. Poulton was 'zig-zagging through the Welsh defence as only he can'. A.A. Thomson noted that his swerve was so subtle that 'you had the optical illusion of seeing him go, not past the full-back, but right through him', while spectators behind the goal-line 'declared that it was the defenders trying to tackle him who appeared to swerve'. Poulton created England's first try for the Australian loose forward Bruno Brown. Eight minutes from time, Willie Watts fumbled the ball. In the ensuing chaos Pillman, true to form, won the chase to the line then 'rejoined his comrades amid a hurricane of cheers' before Chapman landed the conversion for a 10-9 victory that launched England towards a second consecutive Grand Slam.

The rivalry was scheduled to continue on 2 January 1915. By then James Watson, a debutant on the wing at Twickenham, was dead, the first of twenty-seven English internationals to fall after following Blackheath's resolution that 'it is the duty of every able-bodied man of enlistable age to offer his services to king and country'. Sewell noted that thirty-nine of the fifty-eight men commemorated in his tribute to rugby's war dead joined up within two months; 'they did not wait for conscription'. Trench warfare took disproportionately savage toll among junior officers – the likeliest ranks for privately educated young men. Others lost from those involved in the 1914 match included Poulton, Raphael, Alfred Maynard, the 'gloriously strong fellow' who had charged down a Welsh drop-goal in the desperate final minutes to preserve England's win, and Davie Watts, the Maesteg collier. Willie Watts was wounded. Pillman survived and won the Military Cross but lost his younger brother Robert, who was capped against France in 1914. Pillman did not play again and had two sons killed in the Second World War. Other English losses included John King, initially rejected as too small to serve, Noel Slocock and wing Edgar Mobbs, who famously kicked a ball ahead of him towards the German trenches. The thirteen Welsh dead included French-speaking wing Johnnie Williams and two of its pioneers – the drop-kicking former footballer Charles Taylor and Richard Garnons Williams, one of the 1881 team, who rejoined his regiment at the age of fifty-eight and died a year later.

Resumption of competition after six years generated an extraordinary sequence of matches. England's defeats at Swansea in 1920 and Cardiff in 1922 were noteworthy as their only championship defeats between 1912 and 1925, and were staggering by virtue of their severity. They lost 19-5 at Swansea and 28-6 at Cardiff, conceding eight tries, still a Welsh record against England. Weather contributed to both defeats, re-establishing the English belief that Wales, like London taxis, were unstoppable in the rain.

There were also significant differences. The 1920 match was an individual triumph on a scale not repeated for nearly half a century. Even in a team of some versatility — scrum-half Ben Beynon had scored the winner for Swansea Town in a famous FA Cup victory over Blackburn Rovers — Newport centre Jerry Shea stood out. He pursued parallel careers as a track sprinter and welterweight boxer. A month after the match against England he shared a ring with world champion Ted 'Kid' Lewis, one of the greatest of all British boxers. Though outclassed in one round by Lewis, he was good enough to beat champions like Johnny Basham and Frank Moody.

If his gifts were singular, so was a playing style that completely inverted the Nicholls ideal. Shea was an individualist 'who never knew when he had done enough', and as a result could be criticised even on his greatest day. Sewell wrote that 'he regarded his wing . . . as if he were not on the earth at all'. Llanelli fans poured into Swansea on 'train after train, packed like sardines in a box' to see their idol Albert Jenkins make his debut alongside Shea. It seemed, complained the writer 'Scarlet' in the *Daily Post*, 'as if Jenkins was deliberately ignored by halves and centre'. Jenkins said afterwards: 'I am glad Wales won. I was starved.' Shea dropped two goals, landed a penalty (also dropped) and scored a try which he then converted to become the first player to score in every possible way in an international match. He also created a try for Cardiff wing Wickham Powell with a break and perfectly timed pass — Collins exclaimed: 'Would that it had ever been thus!'

England did not help themselves. W.J.A. Davies was left out, prompting captain Jenny Greenwood to remark that 'the selection committee were not very bright'. Greenwood was also 'staggered' when he found that a change had been made after the team photograph was taken, the selectors deciding that conditions suited Leicester wing Harold Day better than the original choice, Wilfrid Lowry, of Birkenhead Park. Day recalled how he had been 'fetched out of my seat in the stand to play for England against Wales. It poured with rain the whole match and the ground was churned into a dreadful mess.' His recollection suggested limited gratitude, even though he scored England's try. Lowry's thoughts were not recorded, possibly on grounds of taste.

Wavell Wakefield, one of England's twelve debutants that day, was destined for much happier days and a career that would mark him as one of his country's greatest players. He remembered that his team was 'all at sixes and sevens, for the players were strangers to each other'. His memories were 'disjointed' but dominated by 'the curious bird-like cry which Jack Wetter, the Wales half, continually uttered all over the field. I remember also my great annoyance at having my jersey held on to when I was dribbling.'

England could plead ill-luck in hitting a flawed genius at his best when they were effectively starting from scratch after a six-year break. Wakefield wrote that 'the selectors could not be expected to be certain of their material'. Two years later, though, most of their team at Cardiff – including a pack described by one critic twenty-five years later as their best ever – were fresh from a resounding Grand Slam in 1921. There were points in common. Davies, injured rather than dropped, was again absent. Day was present, recalled for his second cap. Players wore numbers for the first time in a championship fixture but were 'an indistinguishable mass' after only fifteen minutes. England probably welcomed their anonymity since 'while they signally failed to adapt themselves to the conditions, the Welshmen revelled in them'. Similar weather at Cardiff in 1920 led an Irish player to lament 'the lack of foresight of the Welsh Union in not providing lifebelts'. Wales scored five tries before half-time. Wing-forward Dai Hiddlestone, a thirty-one-year-old from Neath, was 'ubiquitous and tireless, following the ball with speed and dogged persistency, tackling like a tiger and always to the fore in the rushes and dashes for the line'. He claimed the fourth try. The sixth went to Swansea wing Frank Palmer, who had broken a rib in the first ten minutes. England switched Davies's locum, Victor Davies, 'a notable failure', with centre Edward Myers, who created a last-minute try for Day.

They showed rather more resource in explaining the defeat. Wakefield recalled: 'It was most difficult to stand up at all, a difficulty which the Welshmen overcame by having phenomenally long studs in their boots, longer studs indeed than I have ever seen, and I imagine they had considerably outgrown the regulation size.' England's captain, Bruno Brown, told the *Western Mail*: 'Your two winging forwards were very effective . . . but at the same time I must say that the mud was our biggest enemy. We are not as used to it as the Welshmen are. Given a good dry day we should have done vastly different. Still, the win will do Wales good.' It did, to the extent of taking the title and only missing the Grand Slam and Triple Crown through a draw with Scotland at Inverleith. Tough forwards like Cross Keys collier Steve Morris and Tom Parker, of Swansea – remembered by Rowe Harding as 'a great personality, with the countenance and figure of a knight of the Crusades', and who was unbeaten in seven matches as captain – made Wales a force to match any in British rugby. A far better pointer to the future, though, was provided a year earlier at Twickenham.

If England loathed Cardiff's primeval swamp, Wales were exercised about English selection policy. Eight of England's 1921 team had been born in other countries. A ninth had played two sports for another country. None, admittedly, was quite as conspicuous as medical student Jannie Krige – who had played his only international opposite Shea at Swansea in 1920 – or half-backs Bekker and Van Schalkwijk, who had been overwhelmed in England's final trial by the combined forces of Leicester snow and incumbents Davies and Kershaw.

This year's South African was less obvious, going by the name of Frank Mellish. Bruno Brown had been around for so long it was almost forgotten that he originated from Brisbane, where in fairness rugby union was in abeyance. Nor would anyone have suggested that centre Edward Myers was disqualified by being born in New York, and any dispute over wing Alastair Smallwood, born in Alloa but raised in Newcastle, was a matter for the Scots. The problem was with the others, who were each by some definition Welsh. Three – Davies and the forwards Tom Woods and Ernest Gardner – were in the Navy. The others were from Newport, resurrecting the Stanley Williams row. Big Reg Edwards had been playing in Welsh trials since 1908. Centre Ernest Hammett was Somerset-born but before the war played amateur football and tennis for Wales. In 1920, he was selected for both England and Wales, and had a novel reason for choosing England. His preference, he explained, was for Wales but England asked first and he had accepted. His integrity had mixed outcomes. The football skills were evident at St Helen's when he dribbled, then crossed soccer-fashion to the unmarked Day, who scored the try that gave England the lead. Later, Hammett was as helpless as his team-mates against Shea.

The WRU asked the RFU for clarification on qualification rules, not least a ruling that a player who accepted an invitation to a trial was committed to that country. None was forthcoming. Sewell credited Baxter with halting the recycling of visiting students, but England continued to push limits in other ways. Roderick MacLennan, a Glasgow-born Gaelic-speaking Old Merchant Taylors prop who was capped three times in 1925, had, Sewell wrote in 1944, 'as much prior right to play for England as Goebbels has to bat for Yorkshire'.

England's inclusiveness was perhaps best seen in the context of the recent war and the fellow-feeling that had been rooted in a common cause. If South Africans and Australians had fought for England – which was rarely, in those days, differentiated from Great Britain or the United Kingdom – why should they not also play for it? At the same time Welsh puzzlement at England's policy was equally understandable – why should a nation that already had more players than any other insist on chasing players whose Englishness was debatable? Mellish played for South Africa against New Zealand later in 1921 while Woods played rugby league Tests for Wales a year later.

It was also natural that Wales, lacking a successor to Trew and Jones, looked wistfully towards Davies, hailed by Baxter as 'the greatest match-winner who ever put on a football boot', and who had never been on a losing England side since his debut against South Africa in 1913. He was credited with 'the hands and agility of a first-class cover point', and had 'the eye of a hawk for a gap in the opposing defence' and a lethal swerve, kicked brilliantly and was an effective England captain from 1921 'if only because everyone liked him'.

He also now had a partner who complemented those skills. Cecil Kershaw – 'hawk-faced and as militant as an old-time Corinthian' according to Leo Munro – was another hereditary naval man, albeit a son of the wardroom rather than the dockyard and, by happy coincidence, was also stationed at Portsmouth. Davies and Kershaw met at the final Navy trial in 1918, played for the Grand Fleet against the Rest of the Navy in 1919 and formed England's first great half-back pairing. Kershaw recalled: 'It didn't just happen. It was bloody hard work. We practised first, often four nights a week, at the Portsmouth United Services ground. We worked up an instinctive co-operation. If I got the ball in a game no matter where I went, I knew that if I tossed it in the air, Dave would be there.' A gifted sportsman with the quick feet of an Olympic fencer – he competed in the 1920 Games – he was, in Sewell's memorably vivid description, 'a powerfully built young man whose force of character showed itself in his every movement, by his almost contemptuous hand-off, his cannon-ball service and the guile that deceived everybody except his partner'.

There was quality outside them. Wing Cyril Lowe said after his retirement that he wished he had played in a position with more involvement. P.G. Wodehouse penned humorous verse on the infrequency that Lowe received the ball, but twenty-five caps and eighteen tries – both England records – suggest that he was not entirely starved while his defensive qualities, in spite of being 5ft 6in and 8st, reminded the *Morning Post* writer Ernest Ward of Lockwood. Myers was 'a man for the big occasion', his solid build and tackling complemented by a burst of speed and, recalled fellow Yorkshireman Jim Kilburn, with 'thighs that thrust aside tacklers in the manner of a snow-plough'.

Greater than any, however, was the pack leader, Wavell Wakefield, a force of nature at 6ft and 14st, faster than most wingers and recalled by journalist Howard Marshall as 'a complete footballer . . . who could run and handle the ball as well as any threequarter or control in a dribble like Stanley Matthews'. He was not merely physically gifted, but saw rugby as 'a game for the tactician, for the man who is mentally alert'. Applying his own wit and intellect, he did for forwards what Owen and Stoop had done for half-backs with his advocacy – and practice – of the specialisation by position that New Zealanders had long taken for granted. This involved the introduction of cover defence, back row 'corner-flagging' and drawing opponents into contact before attacking quickly from 'second phase' possession. A formidable pack gathered around this dominant, charismatic figure – 'England's greatest ever forward', according to John Daniell, who was frequently cited as its best judge of them.

While still comparative newcomers in international rugby – only Davies and Lowe had played for England before the war – they were mature men, shaped by wartime service. Full-back Barry Cumberlege won a military OBE, Lowe was an air ace credited with nine 'kills' (and claimed more). Davies served on the staff of the commander-in-chief of the Grand Fleet. They were also allowed to mature as players. England introduced two debutants in each Wales match from 1921 to 1923, easily the most stable period in more than ninety years when the fixture usually opened the season. Though Leonard Tosswill complained in 1925 that few new English players had emerged since the war, forcing them to 'depend for some years now on pretty much the same set of men', this was almost certainly to their advantage. The urge to fiddle had to be suppressed.

The fruits to come were evident at Twickenham in 1921. The *Sunday Express* perceived an omen when a leek tied to the top of a post by a Welsh fan, who evaded police tacklers to place it there, fell to the ground. In the first minute debutant wing John Ring, scorer of seventy-six tries for Aberavon that season, swerved past Cumberlege but was collared just short of the line by Myers. Less than fifteen minutes later, in what Sewell reckoned was the fastest of more than ninety international matches he had seen until then, England were twelve points up. Kershaw, 'a host in himself', crossed for a try, Davies dropped a goal, Myers intercepted and Kershaw sent Lowe over. Wales 'played like men dazed and hypnotised'. For F.J. Sellicks in the *Daily Mail*, Shea had the air 'of a man utterly bored with life in general and this game in particular', outside-half Jack Wetter 'shattered a great reputation' and Wales's forwards were 'heavier, but deplorably slow'. Ring claimed a second-half try for Wales, but Smallwood crossed twice to complete an 18-3 win, England's largest over Wales between 1896 and 1990. Only full-back Joe Rees, who described it as the toughest game he had played in, escaped criticism. Jack Jenkins, capped once by Wales in 1906, displayed the charity characteristic of the marginal former international when he wrote that he had never seen 'a more brainless XV'. There were extenuating circumstances. Three Welsh players – Wetter, wing Tom Johnson and centre Jack Jones, the youngest of three Pontypool brothers who played for Wales – were badly hurt. England were a truly exceptional team who went on to beat Ireland and Scotland with similar ease and were extended only by France in winning a conclusive Grand Slam.

What did appear brainless was the reaction of the Welsh selectors. Eight changes were made for the next match, in which Scotland claimed a first win on Welsh soil since 1892. Victories over France and Ireland, which was fast descending into civil war and fielded its weakest team in decades, rescued something from the season but by its end Wales had capped thirty-three players, including eight half-backs. This, not the rain-affected victories over England on either side, was the harbinger of the 1920s. Later in 1921, American writer Lincoln Steffens declared, after visiting the Soviet Union, that 'I have seen the future, and it works'. Welsh fans at Twickenham had seen it as well, and it worked very badly.

CHAPTER FIVE
REVENGE OF THE FORSYTES
1923–32

The experience of South Wales and its people between 1923 and
1939 bears all the hallmarks of a major tragedy.

Kenneth Morgan, 1982

The English; Are They Human?

A book by G.J. Renier, 1931

That the Welsh plateau became an abyss, with no further victory over
England until 1932, reflected the state of its economy and society. It was
not alone in its suffering, but depended more than anywhere else in Britain
upon heavy industry, and suffered accordingly as it collapsed. In 1907, the
economist W.J. Perkins had written: 'While coal remains the most effective
and economical source of power . . . the position of Wales is assured.' Now it
found out what happened when that assurance was removed amid a general
depression. Employment in the coal industry dropped from 265,000 in 1920 to
138,000 in 1933. Those still in jobs suffered savage pay cuts – the wage bill fell
from £65m to £14m, implying a 60 per cent reduction in pay. By 1933, nearly
one third of the working population of Wales was jobless. In the Rhondda
Valley it was close to double that. More than 430,000 people, more than half
between the ages of fifteen and twenty-nine, left Wales between the wars, 'a
Black Death on wheels' according to Gwyn Thomas.

Just as pre-war Welsh rugby was played with the confidence of a
prospering society, so it now reflected economic and psychological
devastation. As Gareth Williams put it: 'Tactical bankruptcy on the field
reflected the financial insolvency off it.' Wakefield observed the
symptoms displayed by Welsh players. 'So few have been consistently

good,' he said, 'and though there have been many individuals who, for a season, have seemed full of promise, they have dropped back into obscurity afterwards.'

From where Wakefield was standing – a middle-class, London-based Englishman who would spend twenty-five years as a Conservative MP – 'obscurity' encompassed rugby league. Tony Collins calculated that twenty-five Welsh players a year 'went north' between 1919 and 1926. Thirty-seven internationals, the most in any decade, were lost in the 1920s. Shea and Ring, who became league's most consistent try-scorer, went to Wigan. Joe Thompson played against England in 1923 when only just 20 and joined Huddersfield two weeks later, so soon that he had not yet received his Wales cap. As rugby union's attitude to league recruits precisely echoed the Act of Succession's view of Catholics – it is 'as if they are legally dead' – he waited until 1975 to receive it. Among Wales's brightest moments in a decade of frustration at Twickenham were tries by Newport wings – George Andrews in 1927 and Jack Morley in 1929. Both ended up in rugby league. The greatest losses of all had no time to become Welsh internationals. Jim Sullivan was already close to a Welsh cap at seventeen when he joined Wigan in 1921. Eight years later Gus Risman went to Salford as an eighteen-year-old. Between them they dominated rugby league for thirty years. There is every chance they would have done the same in union.

These losses confused already panicky and capricious selectors. This was the only decade in the near-century in which the England v Wales fixture opened the season that Wales fielded more new caps, sixty-five, than England. Ben Beynon, alphabetically the first among the debutants in 1920, was the 300th man to play for Wales. Number 400, Dai Jenkins, won his first cap against Australia in 1927, twenty-five matches later (both also ended up playing league). The previous one hundred took forty-three matches to accumulate. The next hundred took thirty-nine, the one after that forty-five. In 1924, thirty-five players, including fourteen different threequarters, appeared in four matches. This lunacy at last prompted the WRU to replace its thirteen-man, district-based match committee with a more compact body that came to be known as the 'Big Five'. This did not noticeably improve matters. A year later Townsend Collins, writing in the short-lived *Wisden Rugby Almanack* of 'the blackest period in the history of Welsh Rugby Football', enumerated with gloomy precision the thirty-four men who played in that season's five matches – two full-backs, four wingers, seven centres, five half-backs and 16 forwards. There were also five different captains. The writer who complained later in the 1920s that Wales lacked an outstanding personality was almost certainly right. Good captains take time to develop authority. Wales's were given none. Only once in twenty-six matches between 1923 and 1929 was the Wales captain the same as in the previous game. Losing captains were routinely dropped from the team.

There were some points of continuity. An unstated truth about Welsh rugby is that the scrum-half factory has consistently outperformed its more publicised fly-half operation. Wales were well served by two scrum-halves of differing style: the impish Bobby Delahay, an early traveller on the well-trodden path from Bridgend to Cardiff, played against England in four of the five matches from 1922 and was followed by powerful London Welsh Guardsman Wick Powell, who played four of the next six. There were, though, limits to what continuity at scrum-half could accomplish when Wales fielded a different outside-half every year from 1920 to 1934. Albert Jenkins, of Llanelli, was a centre of formidable gifts, one of the few Welshmen mentioned specifically by Wakefield. He played fourteen internationals spread over nine seasons. Another Scarlet, loose forward Ivor Jones, played sixteen matches over seven seasons. In New Zealand with the 1930 Lions, his hosts – connoisseurs of his position above all others – thought him perhaps the greatest they had seen. He was twenty-nine and played another eight seasons for Llanelli, but did not win another cap.

Forward selections were particularly perverse, ignoring not only Wakefield's innovations but the Welsh tradition of specialisation formerly represented by George Travers. Idris Jones, of Llanelli, whose little brother Elwyn was Lord Chancellor in the 1970s, was regarded as the best hooker in Wales in the mid 1920s, but never chosen in that position in five appearances. It did not take international opponents to expose Welsh weaknesses. Winger Rowe Harding recalled seeing Wales's chosen eight outscrummaged in training by six Cardiff policemen. Little consideration was given to combinations. As the caustic Sewell noted, Wales played England in 1924 with forwards from eight different clubs 'and the only real Welsh combination seen was the way in which the pack lost its temper as one man'. Since spectators at this match also adapted the popular hit of the day to sing 'yes we have no threequarters', it was hardly surprising that Wales lost.

Losing was what they did – and not only against England. They won seven matches in six seasons between 1923 and 1928. But for the 'annual consolation' against still uncompetitive France, Wales would have won only two. It was little wonder that Harding, who played against England four times, twice as captain, found international rugby 'on the whole, a gloomy experience'.

The contrast with England was stark. England's depressed areas were not those in which rugby was strongest. The game expanded at club level – the formation of more than 200 clubs in the 1920s took RFU affiliations back above 1895 levels – and many private and state schools switched from football to rugby as an indication of both social aspiration and distaste for football having continued for a season at the start of the war. This created a market for coaching manuals and led to a renewed flow of grammar school boys into the England team in the 1930s. Whether or not Harding was right that coherent selection made England successful 'more than once . . . with individually the worst team in the four countries', something worked. England won Grand Slams in 1923, 1924 and 1928 and were desperately close to the title in 1925, losing to possibly Scotland's best ever team 14-11 in the first ever match at Murrayfield. There was, whatever Jenny Greenwood's doubts about the committee's mental acuity, a cohesion and continuity in selection rarely seen before or since. Men from this era dominated England's 'most-capped' list for the next forty years. Only Birkett had won twenty caps in nearly fifty years of international rugby before 1920. Seven players – Lowe, Davies, Wakefield, Ronald Cove-Smith, Tom Voyce, Sam Tucker and Henry Periton – reached that mark in the following decade.

This created a demand for tickets that both necessitated and funded the expansion of Twickenham in 1923 to hold 53,000 – larger and, with more than one third of the ground seated, more profitable than either of the Welsh venues. If Ivor Brown saw it as 'the last fortress of the Forsytes', these were good years for them and the southern middle classes, with Conservative-dominated government throughout the inter-war years apart from two brief and unthreatening Labour interregnums.

Yet Twickenham was not universally loved. Gent disliked the size of the crowds – 'terrible things; an unlikeable mass of delightful people' –

while Sewell found it 'a most uncomfortable, poorly nourished and gloomy place to sit at'. He would still find takers in 2009 for his description of 'a tiresome place to get to and a penance to escape from'.

It was is in this period that Twickenham truly entered the Welsh psyche. Watcyn Thomas, who first played there in 1927, recalled 'vagaries that often lead to the defeat of visiting international XVs. Bounded on three sides by stands it is a ground of atmospheric eddies and whirlpools, which make kicking and passing go fortuitously astray. But above all, it is the electric atmosphere that unnerves the man playing his first international there. Raucous shouts, jeers and cheers rebound from the roofs of the stadium, so there is a constant roar in the ears of the player down below, enough to daunt and unsettle the most experienced of club players . . . the initiate is inclined to charge around like a tormented bull, instead of conserving his energies.' Harding disagreed about the sound, but agreed that it was disconcerting. 'To my ears the noise seemed an incessant high-pitched wailing, weird and eerie, as though the sound came from a congregation of lost souls hovering about the high stands,' he said.

The sounds associated with international rugby were no longer heard only by those at the match or its immediate vicinity. The 1920s saw the birth of broadcasting in Britain – formed in 1922, the BBC was selling 2.5 million annual radio licenses within six years. The 1927 match was not only Thomas's debut, but radio's as well, with former Harlequins player Teddy Wakelam providing the BBC's first running sports commentary from 'a somewhat rickety-looking hut mounted on a scaffold platform at the end of the then single-decker West Stand'. Wakelam was accompanied, just outside the box, by a blind man who had formerly been a keen rugby watcher 'so that I could talk as if explaining the game directly to him'. Alongside was Charles Lapworth, whose colourful earlier career included spells in Hollywood and as a radical socialist, editor of the *Daily Herald* in its most uninhibited period, but evidently not much exposure to rugby. His on-air questions – 'Do they always play with an oval ball?' and, following an injury, 'Who will they send on now?' – served to remind Wakelam that not all his audience were rugby aficionados and would need aspects of the game explaining. A surviving recording conveys Wakelam's urgent but clipped tones – an England attack concludes with Wales captain Lou Turnbull making a mark, earning a 'Well played, Sir!' from Wakelam, while a voice in the background intones the numbers from a map of the pitch, divided into numbered squares, which had been printed in the *Radio Times*. Afterwards, Wakelam received a letter from the wife of a former Welsh international, who complained that 'her husband had got so excited listening-in that he had started playing himself and had smashed up most of her sitting-room furniture'. Wakelam treasured it for years as a tribute to the vividness of his account.

It is a fair bet that these were not the only Welsh domestic breakages of this era, attributable as much to frustration as passion as Wales regularly threatened, but never quite managed, to beat the old enemy. These are the years of the 'jinx'. While England won consistently, it was not in the manner of Wales's victories twenty years earlier. There were no hammerings and that record 18-3 win in 1921 remained an English high-point. England won seven and drew two between 1923 and 1931. Their aggregate winning margin was thirty-five points, equivalent to a converted try per victory, but the gap never reached double figures. Wales's average margin between 1899 and 1909 was fourteen points, and three of their wins were by more than twenty. With the points system unchanged, scoring was a little higher. Just over 18.6 points per game were scored in matches between the four home nations between 1923 and 1932, compared with 16.6 between 1900 and 1909. Wales v England, easily the highest scoring match in the earlier period, was only fifth out of six in the later one.

England's dominance was neither quite as sustained nor as complete as the Welsh golden age, and came from a different source. Wales had good forwards, but their greatness lay in having the best back division seen before the 1970s. When on top, they scored heavily. England had good backs, but more significantly a pack not matched for sustained excellence until the 1990s. So they routinely won, particularly against primitive Welsh methods and selections, but did not slaughter opponents. Wales's worst hammerings in the 1920s were by Scotland.

So the fixture did not lose appeal as it had done in the late 1900s. The typical Welsh fan of the period was described, none too flatteringly, by his Cambridge-educated compatriot Harding as being 'usually a small, sallow man, emotional, talkative and, if need be, abusive. He probably has a scarf of outrageously clashing colours, a cloth cap which accentuates the dead whiteness of a face which perhaps does not see daylight for forty-eight hours in the week, and if it is an international match he wears a leek of gigantic proportions and smells of leeks and beer in about equal strength.' The fan continued, in spite of defeat and depression on and off the field, to travel hopefully – funded by accumulated pennies rather than the 'weekly shillings' cited by Max Boyce half a century later – and to induce wonder in his temporary hosts.

In 1927, the *Observer* chronicled the 'Celtic invasion of London' from its arrival at Paddington to Waterloo, where they 'greatly outnumbered the English enthusiasts. The arrival at the ground of the first big contingent of Welshmen, wearing huge red rosettes, daffodils and leeks, was signalised by an outburst of harmony from under the clock. Starting with hymn tunes, the visitors proceeded to music-hall ditties. Later "The Red Flag" was sung. It was a purely mischievous rendering, apparently without any political significance, and after the last bars there were roars of laughter.' It was only a few months after the General Strike, and the miners were still out. The *Observer* was still a Conservative paper, made anxious by any hint of subversion. It was probably right in seeing none. Martin Johnes is certainly correct when he dismisses the equally Conservative *Western Mail's* belief that sport was a solvent for class tensions. Nor does Welsh support seem to have taken on an overtly political tone. The *Western Mail's* attribution of a pitch invasion during the Scotland match at Swansea in 1921 to 'followers of Lenin and Trotsky' owed more to a fevered political atmosphere than reality. The real culprit was overcrowding.

Nor, except in the basic sense of wanting to beat England, were Welsh rugby fans anti-English. Gent reported that in 1924 the Swansea crowd 'cheered for minutes in admiration' of an admittedly remarkable English try, an epic length-of-the-field team effort concluded by wing Hal Jacob. Two years later at Cardiff, Leo Munro recalled that the crowd 'cheered for about a minute when W.W. Wakefield bored through for "a man's try" against Wales. And this on a day when tempers were frayed, and the play was inclined to pugilism, and one man, making his first appearance for England, said "if this is international football, I don't like it".'

Fans who had, as Harding pointed out, once 'been in the habit of seeing the best rugby in the world' found much to admire in the play of English teams, particularly at Swansea in 1924. The *Rugby Football Annual* and the writer 'Freelance' in the *Daily Post* both saw a margin of 17-9 as seriously understating English superiority. 'Freelance' saw clear echoes of Welsh teams past, noting England's 'knack of introducing all the subtlety and trickiness which in the good old days made Wales stand out ahead of all competitors in the Rugby world'.

It rained heavily, creating 'conditions as bleak as rain and hailstones could make them'. Earlier England teams might have been demoralised. This one made one late change, bringing in Ronald Cove-Smith, a bad omen for Wales. Cove-Smith was the common thread through England's greatest successes in the 1920s, winner of more caps, twenty-nine, than anyone except Wakefield and the only player to appear in all four Grand Slam-winning teams. England won on each of the six times he played against Wales. Tall and powerful, with a moustache and chiselled features that cried out for a military shako or sola topee, he was 'dogged, tough and solid' to appreciative team-mate Wakefield and appealed strongly to Townsend Collins as 'a great forward and a great leader – a ruthless scrummager who knew how to limit the opportunities of opposing backs by skilful wheeling to the touchline'.

Those qualities were essential in 1924 to a triumph of tactical organisation and precise execution. Davies, Kershaw and Lowe had all retired in 1923, so new captain Wakefield led five new caps who included Arthur Young, an unpredictably brilliant scrum-half partnered by the well-established and utterly dependable Myers, and that infallible harbinger of success, a Bristol full-back. In his single international season Bevan Stanislaw Chantrill, who was twenty-seven and had not played in any of the trials, surprised 'those who thought him only an ordinary good club man', before emigrating to become a gold prospector in South Africa.

Mindful of inevitable nerves, Wakefield demanded 'that we kept it tight and dribbled it for the first quarter of an hour', giving his newcomers time to settle. A Welsh score after 20 minutes might have undermined their confidence, but instead provoked an explosion of three tries in six minutes. The second, following Myers's equalising score, was the masterpiece. Left-wing Jacob, near his own line, sliced a kick badly across the field. Carson Catcheside, on England's other wing, would have done well simply to find touch. Instead he beat a pursuer and ran up the touchline. Then, Gent recalled, 'away went the English forwards after him in support, Voyce and Wakefield leading. On reaching the halfway line, Catcheside was forced to pass and gave a beautiful inside pass to Wakefield. Then it looked for all the world as if every member of the England side was up in support, and in the right position too, and the Welshmen were completely bewildered by the nature of the passing and the number of the men concerned in it. Eventually the ball reached Jacob, who also had gone up in support, close to the left touch-line, and he scored in the left-hand corner!'

Wales hit back in a ferocious period after half-time that saw England depleted, Voyce finishing with a fractured rib. It may be this period of play that supplied the anecdote of England captain Wakefield remonstrating with a Welsh forward who had administered a severe 'shoeing' to a prone Englishman receiving a heartfelt apology from the miscreant, who explained that he had thought it was Wakefield he was assaulting. However, a total of five tries, including two for debutant Catcheside, gave England a 17-9 victory, and the first of another Grand Slam. This year, no other opponents got to within eight points of them, as Wales had done.

Wales got even nearer in every subsequent match in this period. In 1926, at Cardiff, the crowd had to be persuaded to retreat from the touchline by the Chief Constable, whose order to shut the gates produced 'an ugly scene' with many still outside brandishing tickets. The match was similarly heated, producing leader-column harrumphing from the *Western Mail* about 'fisticuffs and deliberate roughness'. One Englishman was laid out by an uppercut, another had stitches, and 'white sleeves' were seen doing unconscionable things in the scrummage. Wakefield's try was cancelled out by one from Andrews and Wales pressed hard at the end of a 3-3 draw. The players, the Welsh touch judge and the *Western Mail* were convinced that Delahay, 'playing the game of his life', had contrived 'a perfectly fair score' in the final minutes but the referee did not agree.

Two years later, an extraordinary defensive effort from England's full-back, naval man Kenneth 'Monkey' Sellar, was the difference in a 10-8 win on another sodden day at Swansea. The fire brigade pumped water off the pitch, one bank of supporters 'appeared to be on fire' as smoke from hundreds of cigarettes hung above it and thousands more expected from

Llanelli to watch a team including five Scarlets failed to appear. Fans were quoted later that day as asking 'Where are the excursions to Bath?', which was where the Scarlets were playing that day. Wales dominated the scrums, taking thirty-two heels to twelve, but England were rapidly 10-0 up. Outside-half Colin Laird, England's youngest ever player when capped against Wales the previous year at 18 years and 134 days, helped set up the first try for Blackheath wing William Taylor, then scored himself under the posts after a break by Taylor. Laird, described by Wakelam as 'a player of many parts, very quick off the mark, with a fine eye for an opening and an exceptionally good passer', might have played until the Second World War, which broke out on his thirty-first birthday, but illness cut his career short at twenty. Wales spent most of the second half on England's line in a feverish assault recorded as 'great human drama' by the *Daily Post*. 'The human maelstrom that writhed and surged within a few yards of the line, the tense anxiety of the crowd, which again agonised between hope and disappointment, the furious attack and dogged defence, the inches that again and again separated Wales from an outstanding victory, the waves of sound from the human orchestra, which expressed its exultations, its expectations, its swift changes of high hope incessantly renewed, chequered with mortification.'

Defying the maelstrom was Sellar, echoing Jack Bancroft's heroics of 1912. *Express* writer Leo Munro remembered: 'The line could not be crossed. "Monkey" Sellar held it. There were moments when he seemed to be holding it single-handed, fielding the slippery ball, kicking it to earn the respite of a matter of seconds, and again diving in the churned mass at the boots which drove the ball towards his goal. He was "smothered" sometimes beneath the mounds of red-jerseyed giants, but when they sorted themselves out, there was Sellar, last man up, still smiling cheerfully and ready for more "fun".'

Many critics thought that while Wales's threequarter line were well-educated – all four went to Cambridge – they were too slow and unimaginative, linking poorly with two Llanelli half-backs both christened David John. The scrum-half, who answered to Arthur, was dead in little over a year while partner Dai John's limited international opportunities occasioned Llanelli fans – not hard to aggrieve – almost as much frustration as the treatment of Arthur Jenkins, whom the *Daily Post's* writer 'Wing-Three' reckoned would have 'dropped at least a couple of goals and got a try as well' given the same opportunities. From London, the High Tory *Morning Post* pronounced, with evident satisfaction, that 'Cambridge and Llanelly don't make a good cocktail'.

If Wales could blame the referee in 1926 and Sellar two years later, 1930 had a strong element of deus ex machina as veteran hooker Sam Tucker descended from the sky minutes before kick-off. The Bristolian was thirty-four and the last survivor of England's great packs. Munro portrayed him as '"Sam" to everyone at Bristol from "the best people" in the stand to the small boys sneaking inside the barriers of the Memorial Ground . . . the expert hooker whose great strength of neck, shoulders and arms bound the front row of the scrummage like a wall.' His warmth and experience were exactly what a young and experimental England side, which had nine new caps – old habits were resurfacing – and were widely expected to lose, needed. The rookies included Peter Howard, whose colourful career would incorporate the England captaincy at twenty-two, youth secretaryship of Sir Oswald Mosley's New Party, journalism for the *Daily Express*, co-writing the famous polemic *Guilty Men* with Michael Foot and years as head of the Moral Re-Armament movement, before dying in Lima at fifty-eight. He remembered walking 'as a man like a God' in the streets of Oxford after being chosen for England. Other debutants included Brian Black, a South African at Oxford, and front-rower Douglas Kendrew, from the Woodford club in Essex. Army front-rower Henry Rew, already capped three times, was the man whose late illness caused England problems.

Tucker would always go the extra mile for England. Nine months earlier he travelled overnight by train to Paris to play against France after Ron Sparks, of Bath, was ruled out. This call-up, though, demanded a really remarkable effort. He was called two hours and twenty minutes before the 2.45 p.m. kick-off, too late to catch a train from Bristol to Cardiff and told firmly by Daniell that 'you've got to come along, even if you have to come by aeroplane' – although neither Bristol nor Cardiff had an airport. Tucker found a pilot at Filton aerodrome who said that he could take him, but 'could not guarantee a landing place because he knew the racecourse was flooded'. The story was recounted in Tucker's words by his fellow Bristolian John Mason, rugby correspondent of the *Daily Telegraph*, recalling a party piece that 'could command total silence in the old Bristol bar'.

Tucker got to Filton at 1.45 p.m. 'There was the pilot with a small biplane two-seater already revved up. He stuck a helmet on my head, helped me into the front seat, strapped me in and with a roar we started off. Now I'd never been in a plane before so my feelings could be imagined. I was in an open cockpit with what looked to me like a bit of fuselage and a few pieces of wire between me and eternity. We arrived over Cardiff Arms Park at roughly 2.00p.m. The pilot told me through the intercom that the rugby ground was below us, but he could not see a landing place anywhere. I told him to try to land somewhere as it seemed a pity to turn back now.

'After circling three or four times he said he thought he could land in a field he had spotted. He said: "Hang on, it might be a bit bumpy on landing". I remember being shaken rigid and gripped the front of the cockpit as I felt certain we were going through into the next field. He helped me out and in that order gave me my bowler hat and kit which had been stowed in the back of the plane. I asked him where we were. He said he had no idea but there was a road a couple of fields away. I thanked him, raced over the field and then through a ploughed field to the road. Not a soul to be seen. Then a small lorry came along loaded with what I think was coal. That driver was a real pal and did the journey of three miles to the Arms Park in under ten minutes, having picked me up at 2.25p.m. I forced £1 on him. But I was still in a quandary. At that time it was not an all-ticket match but first come, first served.

'There were thousands of people outside the gates and I could not get through. Then I spotted an inspector of police whom I knew as Trevor, who had played for both Cardiff and Wales. He would not believe my story at first, but finally I convinced him and he shouldered his way through and I got to the gates with five minutes to spare. I still had to run all the way round the stand to reach the old changing room and I made it five minutes before kick-off. I was in a bath of perspiration, but I hurriedly changed and ran on to the field with the rest of the England side.'

The congestion outside the ground was repeated inside it. Once more the crowd broke through the railings around the pitch, encroaching close to the posts. Bryn Thomas, who under his byline of 'J.B.G.' was the most famous and influential of Welsh rugby journalists, recalled that, as a schoolboy spectator, 'I only saw parts of it by jumping up at intervals'.

Wales expected to dominate the scrums, but Tucker won three-quarters of them before half-time. Long-striding Harlequins wing Jim Reeve, who was killed in a car crash in 1936, scored two tries – one a solo effort when he came off his wing, took a pass directly from a scrum and sliced through a flat-footed defence – and England won 11-3 in what the *Rugby Football Annual* termed 'a most disturbing defeat' for Wales. Tucker had promised to attend a function at his old school so returned immediately after the game to Bristol – by train. Rew was fit to play against Ireland, but Tucker retained his place and was England's captain by the third match of the season, leading them to an extremely close-fought championship. His one regret was that his descent into Cardiff meant that Bath's Norman Matthews, a rival from many local derbies who was changed and ready to play that day against Wales, never did win an England cap.

Home defeats should hurt more but it was Wales's failures at Twickenham that entered folklore, in part because victory was so tantalisingly close. Wales were never out of it, but something always happened to preserve England's unbeaten run. Most remarkable were the kicks that ensured an England win in 1923 and saved a draw in 1931. The 1923 match is probably when Welshmen became convinced that Twickenham was cursed. It was played 'in a storm that blew the ball around like a piece of confetti'. England's first try was the quickest – and one of the strangest – in international history. Wakefield kicked off into the wind and wing forward Leo Price, a speedy, gifted ball player who a year earlier was picked to play for England against Scotland at both rugby and hockey on the same day, gave chase. He gathered it, dropped for goal and missed but chased as the ball was blown back towards him. He regathered and a few seconds from the start registered a distinctly wind-assisted try. With the scores level at 3-3 Len Corbett – the intelligent Bristol centre of whom H.J. Henley recalled that nothing 'affected his air of icy detachment' or disturbed his sleekly ordered brown hair which suggested 'a ballroom rather than a football field' – found himself isolated and with few options, save one. He passed through his legs to Smallwood – an unorthodox move that had earned his captain, W.J.A. Davies, a stern rebuke when he had used it against France a decade earlier.

As Corbett passed, he shouted: 'Drop!' Smallwood, close to the touchline and near to halfway, had only dropped one goal in his life but, as *Wisden* reported: 'Drop Smallwood did, and to such purpose that, carried along by a strong wind, the ball sailed just over the cross-bar — to the amazement of everybody present.' Vivian Jenkins told of the Welsh fan who exclaimed 'that's ****** it', then, realising that he had shocked a nearby female spectator, turned to her and said: 'I'm so sorry, but it has, hasn't it?'

Similar scenes, and no doubt similar language, occurred in 1931. Wales were both helped and hindered by the erratic Powell, who took advantage of English inattention to drop a goal from the mark but then, mistaking a signal, threw a line-out long into midfield no man's land, where debutant Bristol centre Don Burland picked up and ran to the line. Wales led 11-8 after a fine Morley try, converted by full-back Jack Bassett. England were almost immediately awarded a penalty on halfway, a colossal distance for a kick at goal, with leather balls and boots. Munro recalled a Welsh fan looking at kicker Brian Black and saying: 'What does he think he's doing?' and laughing. Black 'placed the ball carefully, swiped the mud from his boots and let fly. The ball flew on and on, the touch-judges standing behind the posts waved their flags. Goal! Black's wonderful kick had saved England. The match was drawn.'

Munro again looked down at a small group of Welsh fans: 'They were white-faced and silent, while Englishmen all around them roared with relief . . . the crowd slowly dispersed, but the lads lingered on. And presently "Damn bad luck to Wales, Dai", said one. "Yes, damn bad," Dai agreed, but then that was a great kick of Black's . . . damn him.' Tucker, England's captain in his last international, felt Wales had deserved to win.

Bristol centres and drop-kicks combined to decisive effect in 1927: 'Corbett's match' according to Rowe Harding. Captaining England, the Bristolian landed an early drop then scored a spectacular solo try from halfway, 'going off with terrific pace, darting through his opponents, dodging one here, handing off another there until, with a final burst, he was over the line'. Wales played for an hour with fourteen men after Newport forward Dai Jones fractured his shoulder helping set up a try for Harding, and lost only 11-9.

In 1925 Cambridge wing Henry Hamilton-Wickes 'as good as won the game himself' — scoring one try, setting up another for the Oxford outside-half Harold Kittermaster and then helping in the final score, a solo effort by another of Wakefield's musketeers, the rumbustious Gloucester loose forward Tom Voyce. Gassed at Passchendaele and wounded several times, Voyce played with the hectic urgency of a man who believed that every second should be cherished. That Twickenham score was a characteristic effort, as recounted by Wakefield: 'I passed to him some thirty yards from the line, hoping he would heave the ball out at once. But Tom was going to score himself if the whole Welsh team tried to stop him, and score he did, just beating a Welshman who was coming across to tackle him before he fell safely across the line.'

In 1929 debutant forward Harry Wilkinson, of Halifax, scored both England tries in an 8-3 win, the second after 'Laird cut through in irresistible style'. The *Observer* also reported that Wilkinson 'was equally brilliant in his tackling and covered up weaknesses of some of his colleagues'. With the talismanic Cove-Smith captaining the side, England could hardly lose. Wales probably were unlucky not to beat England at any time between 1922 and 1932. But if losing one rugby international can be put down to misfortune, to lose seven looks like incompetence.

Rugby is played in the mind as well as on grass. A jinx becomes real when players start to believe in it and it affects their confidence and behaviour. Something always did happen at Twickenham. Occasionally it was genuinely bad luck, such as Dai Jones's injury in 1927. More often, though, it was because England had players of skill, experience and resource. In modern vernacular, they knew how to win. If there is a degree of luck in a huge place-kick or a spectacular drop-goal by a player who does not usually attempt them, they are also achievements of nerve and technical skill. The *Daily Post's* verdict on England's tries in the particularly close-run thing of 1928, that they came from 'quick thinking, by the fullest and most effective use of speed, and splendid determination . . . by surprise, that incalculable factor', sums up the era.

England were better. Whether they had to be is another matter. Much Welsh suffering was self-inflicted. There was a complete failure to appreciate that Wakefield's innovations affected not only the pack – where Wales were beguiled by their successes of 1920 and 1922 into fielding huge, slow-moving eights – but backs as well. Threequarters, who would once have run into space, were now encountering marauding back-row forwards. Incoherence and inconsistency in the selection not only of teams but of captains reflected a failure to show the courage of any convictions. If the right players were picked, it was in strange positions or in the wrong combinations. Fragile but authentic talents like outside-half Windsor Lewis, who played against England in 1927, were lost in the chaos. Perhaps Wales had players who could have beaten England but, as Dai Smith and Gareth Williams wrote, 'to expect the Welsh Match Committee to find the appropriate blend between them was like asking them to contemplate the mysteries of Einstein's physics'.

There was improvement around the turn of the decade. In 1931, they at last gave a captain, the reliable Penarth full-back Jack Bassett, a proper run. Whether that led to Wales winning the title for the first time since 1922, and missing out on a Grand Slam and Triple Crown only because of Black's last-minute monster at Twickenham, is a matter for conjecture. Among the gilded youth that was emerging from secondary schools and universities, players with staying power as well as talent were coming through.

That Bassett was not only still in the team but still captain against England at Swansea in 1932, in spite of an earlier defeat by the South African tourists, was encouragement in itself. That there was only one new England cap gives a misleading impression of stability. The Rest beat England in their final trial and nine new caps were named against South Africa, including seven forwards. One of them, Les Saxby, of Gloucester, had declined a trial two years earlier because he thought that he was too old.

The game at St Helen's was attended by the Prince of Wales. He saw England 'beaten more decisively than the score of a goal, a drop-goal and a penalty to a goal suggested' according to the *Rugby Football Annual* editorialist O.L. Owen. Gent recorded Welsh 'superiority fore and aft that enabled them to do nine-tenths of the attacking'. The pattern echoed England's victories just before the war, a scoreless first half followed by the dominant team turning its ascendancy into points. Ronnie Boon, a confident sprint-champion wing, scored the try 'turning inwards and had all the England players running the other way' then darting through 'a narrow, rapidly closing line of opponents'. Later, 'after sidestepping and wriggling past two or three opponents', he dropped a goal. England's late try was no threat to Wales's triumph, but had an extremely strong suspicion of a knock-on. The crowd 'set up a mighty roar of disapproval that lasted until the whistle went for no side'.

The *Daily Post* reaffirmed rugby's standing as the national game. 'No Welsh town successes in Association yield quite the same thrill as a Welsh national side's success in Rugby,' it argued pointedly, given that, while Wales were beating England at St Helen's, Swansea Town had been defeating Manchester United a few hundred yards along the seafront.

It also asserted that the rugby team's victory 'will pass into history as the breaking after ten years of the spell of Welsh defeat at rugby by England'. Ten years remains the longest Wales have gone between victories over England. Their victory in 1932 should be a famous match. It is not. That it gets only a passing mention in *Fields of Praise*, the monumental centenary history of the Welsh Rugby Union by Dai Smith and Gareth Williams, shows the importance of the Twickenham effect in Welsh eyes. England were beaten, but the bigger beast remained to be slain.

CHAPTER SIX

POETRY AND PARITY 1933–39

Wales pressed, and pressed again
And yet, why, why
Could we not break
Her long chain of misfortune at Twickenham
> Cynan (Albert Jenkins-Jones), *Y Dyrfa* (The Crowd), 1931
> (translation: Gareth Williams)

I have never witnessed anything comparable in emotional excitement to the scene before an international match in Cardiff.

> Bernard Darwin, 1940

Cynan's poem, a winner at the 1931 National Eisteddfod, told of a former Welsh international named John, who was on his way to begin missionary work in China, remembering how he had scored a winning try at Twickenham. John was not entirely a product of poetic imagination. Cardiff centre John Roberts, one of the Cambridge quartet of 1928 and capped thirteen times in all, was known to be planning to go to China – he spent six years in Amoy, starting in 1932. His younger brother Bill also played for Wales, once, at Twickenham in 1929. He was destined to become a journalist and pig-breeder (readers may insert their own joke here). Oxford's outside-half from 1928 to 1931, he won a late call-up for Wales's final trial, played himself into the team against England, was called 'the most fortunate player of his generation' by veteran journalist W.J. Hoare, and just as rapidly played himself out of it by making nothing of copious amounts of possession. If the fabulous destiny of John Roberts appealed to poets, Bill offers a better explanation of Welsh failure, a nineteen-year-old elevated suddenly on limited evidence then quickly discarded – never to figure again

– after one match. He also epitomised selectorial fondness for Oxbridge Blues.

Welsh teams in the late 1920s and early 1930s possibly suffered from a degree of class tension. Watcyn Thomas wrote with direct reference to the 1929 team: 'What a fetish the Welsh selectors had for Oxford and Cambridge in those days'. He remembered how the austere Walter Rees, secretary of the WRU for the barely credible span of 1896 to 1948, had asked one home-based player who was claiming for travel from West Wales: 'Good Lord, man. Have you come from Moscow?' But Rees's attitude gave way to smiling indulgence for claims for journeys from Oxford or Cambridge.

Thomas was the man to defuse any tensions. His personality was as big as his 6ft 3in, 15st frame. He was a graduate, but of Swansea rather than Oxford or Cambridge. Born and raised in Llanelli – the Welsh answer to childhood Catholicism, leaving marks just as indelible – he was fluent in Welsh, English and the distinctive vernacular of the rugby union forward. He reflected his times by playing outside Wales. The 'Black Death on wheels' meant that sixteen of the thirty players in the final trial of 1934 were doing so. After playing club rugby at the Welsh St Helen's, he now taught in the Lancashire town of the same name, at Cowley School, and played for Waterloo. This distanced him from Wales's internecine struggles, with the bonus that the selectors never learnt that he trained, and mixed freely, with players at the rugby league club St Helen's Recreation. Outside-half Harry Bowcott, a Cambridge Blue, British Lion and himself a former captain of Wales, recalled nearly seventy years later: 'We all respected Watcyn.'

Jack Bassett, captain and full-back in 1931 and 1932, was discarded after the only poor game of his fifteen for Wales and Thomas was appointed to lead the team at Twickenham in 1933. The Possibles won the final trial. This was not always a recipe for success, but this time it had the valuable effect of propelling Wilfred Wooller into the team, apparently from nowhere. Wooller was still a schoolboy, albeit a highly unusual one because he was twenty and still at Rydal, but only to seek the academic upgrades necessary for a place at Cambridge. The *Rugby Football Annual* would lament that, as a North Walian of English parentage, he was 'inspired by Welsh instead of English blood', but seems not to have had the same qualms over back-rower Arthur Vaughan-Jones, a Welsh-speaker from Pontardulais and one of four servicemen selected for England. Bassett's place went to Vivian Jenkins, of Bridgend and Oxford, who was previously regarded as a prime prospect at centre and was 'extremely annoyed' when Bridgend tried him at full-back at the request of the Wales selectors. Alongside Wooller was Claude Davey, a bulldozing, hard-tackling centre in the later mould of Jack Matthews and Scott Gibbs. Davey's experience (he had nine caps already) and defensive ferocity – Vivian Jenkins recalled that 'when he tackled, he took off' – were an essential balance to Wooller's callowness. He had played with Wooller at Sale, and recommended that Wales act to secure an exceptional talent. With forward Raymond Bark-Jones playing at Waterloo, four of the Welsh team had club affiliations in north-west England. Bark-Jones was also a North Walian, so after waiting for ages, Wales had two at once. All three front-rowers came from Llanelli. While policeman and former miner Archie Skym had joined Cardiff when he changed forces, tin-worker Bryn Evans and steelworker Edgar Jones were still Scarlets. Almost half a century later Dai Smith and Gareth Williams described the Twickenham team of 1933 as 'geographically, socially, occupationally, linguistically . . . the most truly representative *national* side ever to pull on the scarlet jersey'. It also boasted considerable all-round sporting talent. Ronnie Boon, Jenkins, Wooller and scrum-half Maurice Turnbull played cricket for Glamorgan. Turnbull, the first Welshman to play Test cricket, also represented Wales at hockey and squash. Skym was later a bowls international.

Talented they may have been, but they could not escape the Twickenham factor. Jenkins contracted flu and played only because team-mates warned him he might not get another chance. Powerful England centre Don Burland rapidly exposed Wooller, who, Gent thought, 'looked and played like the youth he is for fifteen minutes'. Wooller remembered that Burland 'came crashing into me and through me three times. I had never played against anybody so physically strong and my orthodox sideways tackle was simply brushed aside.' England, he reckoned, should have scored each time but a loose pass and a superb tackle by Jenkins meant that they crossed only once. Even then most observers thought that Royal Navy outside-half Walter Elliot, who would serve alongside Wakefield as a Conservative MP, knocked on in touching down, but the try was given. Evans had a broken nose, which Thomas recalled 'bleeding like a tap' in the scrums.

Illness, injury, a Bristol centre running amok (plus a Bristol full-back, Tom Brown, later banned for the Orwellian offence of 'discussing the advantages of rugby league'), an England team loaded with servicemen, one of whom was qualified for Wales, and a questionable try. Had Brian Black attempted the conversion from halfway, every ghost of Twickenham past would have been present in 1933. Instead, Black missed from much closer range. Who advised Wooller how to cope with Burland is unclear. Thomas recalls 'having a quiet fatherly word' and suggesting going low. Wooller remembered waiting behind the posts for Black's kick 'visibly perturbed. I didn't quite understand how to solve my problems in defence. Claude Davey patted me on the shoulder in a reassuring way . . . "Don't worry," he said. "Take him straight. Aim for his stomach. You are much faster than him and that will stop him".' Perhaps both happened.

England, reckoned the *Rugby Football Annual*, had had enough chances to 'take a commanding and perhaps crushing lead'. The opportunity did not recur. *The Times* said of the forward battle: 'For once the Welsh backrow activists were more intelligent than the English.' Jenkins showed no sign of illness in his 'remarkably safe all-round play' and next time Wooller was faced with Burland on the burst: 'I sank my shoulder about two feet deep into his stomach when he was fortuitously reaching high for an ill-directed pass. He went backwards with a grunt. Suddenly I felt at ease on an international field.'

England still led 3-0 at half-time but, within a minute of the restart, Boon gave Wales a 4-3 advantage. He gathered a miscued clearance and, as Wooller pointed out, cheerfully ignored a double overlap outside him to drop a goal. Now England suffered an injury. Ten minutes after half-time, centre Ronnie Gerrard tackled Davey then 'fell to the ground like a stone, with blood pouring from his eye. He was led off and not allowed to return.' The injury was not as bad as it looked – Gerrard played against Ireland three weeks later and his biographer discounts the suggestion 'freely said amongst the English spectators' that the injury was deliberate – but it was seriously disruptive. Skipper Carl Aarvold moved from wing to centre and Wakefield flanker Reg Bolton spent the last half-hour of his first international marking the predatory Boon.

England still nearly scored next. Wooller recalled: 'Elliot intercepted and made a break for the right hand side of the field towards the corner of the open stand. Instinctively I had turned in the centre and was covering across towards the wing. Then came the long chase. It must have been close on sixty yards. I was catching him as he approached the line unopposed. I had to make a decision on the timing of the tackle because he was so close to it. Later I woke up on occasions at night wondering in panic what would have happened had I left my leap one stride longer. Fortunately the timing was exact and I felled Elliot six feet from the Welsh line.'

Five minutes from time, Davey drew England full-back Brown and sent Boon looping round Bolton to the line. Jenkins took the conversion and the scoreboard clicked around to 9-3. Game over, or so it seemed. In fact Jenkins had missed and England were still within striking distance. Had they done much more than merely hang on and stop Wales scoring again, there might have been serious controversy. Along with a similar incident in the 1931 match, when a Black conversion went over the top of a post and confusion reigned until the referee confirmed the goal at half-time, it led to the International Rugby Board's ruling in 1934 that in future, to avoid such confusion, matches should restart with a drop-kick after a missed conversion.

Welsh celebrations were in keeping with the achievement. Thomas recalled 'one of our reserves telling me next morning that I was up rather early, when I fact I had just returned to our hotel at 6.45a.m.', and told with relish the story of the inebriated Welshman, unimpressed by the circus at Olympia, exclaiming: 'Lions? Watcyn Thomas would eat the bloody lot, mun!'

Although the only game anyone remembers, this was Wales's third consecutive year unbeaten by England. They had the right captain and had players with time on their side – Jenkins and Wooller were still playing in 1939. They would be joined from 1934 by a brilliant outside-half in Cliff Jones, then in 1936 by Haydn Tanner, the link between Owen and Gareth Edwards in Wales's holy trinity of scrum-halves. Conditions at home were improving, insofar as hitting rock bottom after inexorable decline – Welsh unemployment peaked in 1933 – constitutes improvement. The South Wales Miners' Federation showed renewed vigour. Steve Winmill, one of the better forwards at Twickenham in 1921, participated in a 1935 'stay-down strike' at the pit that nine years later claimed his life.

In spite of showing stability in 1931 and 1932, and then making inspired changes in 1933, the Welsh selectors had not lost their gift for the inexplicable. Thomas was dumped as captain after rearranging a particularly baffling forward selection in Wales's next match in Dublin. Walter Rees's partner in the longest-running double act in rugby history, Horace Lyne, the WRU president from 1906 to 1947, was to forward play what Rees was to class cohesion. Lyne, who had played for Wales in the 1880s, was no Identikit reactionary. He had argued in 1886 for a liberal attitude to broken-time payments and in 1918 proposed extending the wartime amnesty for rugby league players. He was still, though, as late as 1935, railing against forward specialisation. The 1934 selection panel exceeded even the greatest efforts of the 1920s by fielding thirteen new caps against England. Only Davey survived from the match at Twickenham.

Organisation remained often shambolic. On the morning of the 1936 match, Davey, appointed captain, failed a fitness test. Although his problem was known in advance, Rees could find only three of the five selectors. Then 'they endeavoured to trace G.R. Rees-Jones, the reserve. No-one knew whether he had travelled to Swansea and by 1.40 their anxiety could be imagined.' Fortunately Rees-Jones arrived 'to a great cheer from the members of the team. He did not know what it was about.' The captaincy went to schoolmaster Idwal Rees, who would be lost to rugby two years later when he became head of Cowbridge Grammar School at twenty-nine.

Wales's most gifted players did not always adhere to the Nicholls ideal of team-play. Wooller's greatness as a player who seemed '10ft tall and [took] steps 10 yards long' was universally recognised. He could, however, as the *Rugby Football Annual* noted in 1936, vary from 'the great to the grotesquely uncertain'. Collins questioned his judgement, arguing that 'he knew the "how" but not the "why" and the "when"', while he reckoned Jones 'noteworthy for what he did himself, and not for what he enabled others to do'. This was not merely the prejudice of the veteran – Collins was born in 1865 – since he was fully appreciative of Tanner.

Judged purely on results, Wales's great match-winner was Jenkins. Wales lost five of the six matches he missed in seven years, but won a clear majority of those in which he played.

This was the tightest period, in more senses than one, in the championship's history. France were expelled in 1931, in response to professionalism and violent play in the French championship, and the remaining eight pre-war seasons saw scores drop to their lowest since the very early days, the average points-per-game falling below ten in 1936 and 1939. England scored only nineteen points in winning the Triple Crown in 1937. Scotland won two Triple Crowns but only nine matches in eight seasons, while Ireland and Wales won more matches but fewer prizes.

Wales's triumph over England in 1933 was followed by two wins apiece and two draws in the run-up to the war. Scoring was so low as to make Wales's 14-8 win at Cardiff in 1938 look positively bacchanalian. England's 9-0 victory in 1934 was followed by scores of 3-3, 0-0 and 4-3, and the decade rounded off by a 3-0 at Twickenham in 1939. Wales scored three points in their first three matches when Jones, acknowledged as a superb attacker, was at outside-half and managed only two tries, both by Wooller, between Boon's score at Twickenham in 1933 and Alan McCarley's opener at Cardiff five years later. Peter Candler's riposte to McCarley was England's first try since 1934.

The International Rugby Board, selectors, referees and players wrestled with the vagaries of the scrummage. Teams were issued with unhelpful commands. Arthur Rees, with namesake Idwal the most enduring of the class of 1934 and a future Chief Constable of Staffordshire, recalled being told to leave a tunnel in the scrummage 'which the entire England pack promptly came through'. When two exceptional hookers, England's Bert Toft and 'Bunner' Travers, scion of the Newport dynasty, emerged late in the decade, their confrontations were often decided by what referees and selectors deemed permissible.

Tension sometimes spilled into violence. England captain Douglas Kendrew, appearing at the dinner after the 'desperate battle' of 1935 with a black eye, explained: 'I cast my bread on the waters early in the game and it came back to haunt me. I have no grouse, it is ended.' His successor in 1936, Bernard Gadney, was possibly less philosophical about being punched, to the warm appreciation of the St Helen's crowd, by rugged Swansea debutant Eddie Long. England selector John Daniell, scribbling in a notebook which survives in the Twickenham library, recorded: 'Referee dreadful. Lost all control of the game.' Wooller recalled matches against England as 'a grim and necessary duty'. 'Too much by tradition . . . was at stake and with the balance of power distributed as it was between the two countries, match after match produced a dour tough struggle which left each side quite exhausted.'

As well as becoming more socially inclusive – rugby's expansion in state schools in the Twenties was reflected by eleven per cent of England's players in the Thirties being grammar school educated – England continued to pick overseas students, with a particular predilection for South African full-backs. Their justification was voiced by the most exotic of the breed, St Petersburg-born wing Alexander Obolensky, when his qualification was questioned by the Prince of Wales immediately before his debut against New Zealand in 1936. Scion of an ancient Russian family and probably the only man at Twickenham who considered himself the Prince's social equal, he said with icy hauteur: 'I attend Oxford University, *Sir*.' He then passed into rugby's Valhalla by virtue of an extraordinary two-try debut, his improbably romantic life and a desperately premature death. Yet England's – and the fixture's – most effective wing of this period was his team-mate that day, Hal Sever, of Sale, a match-winner in 1937. Gadney, another headmaster-to-be, was a strong and aggressive scrum-half. England, though, forsook potentially their most dangerous attacking weapon in the Waterloo and Lancashire pairing of Ray Leyland and Jack Heaton, who according to Ian Hamilton-Fazey, 'had the misfortune to be an attacking general in an age when the England selectors were more interested in stolid, safe defence'. England did pick them in Lancashire's County Championship-winning year, 1935, but exiled Leyland to the wing and paired Heaton with the solid and dependable Peter Cranmer. Hamilton-Fazey wrote that Heaton's style 'required backs to combine in support of each other in running play and he never got the chance to show this off'. England were never let down by Cranmer. Wooller remembered that his 'attack presented little difficulty (but) he was the most difficult defender to outwit whom I ever played against'.

Continuity among Welsh forwards was represented by the future senior policeman Arthur Rees, of London Welsh, a loose forward of pace, intelligence and low cunning who led Daniell in 1935 to bemoan referee Hazlitt's inability to deal with 'all the scrummage and line-out practices of the Welsh'. For England, continuity took the formidable form of Northampton prop Ray Longland, who played in every match from 1933 to 1938, then in wartime internationals was called 'the pick of England's forwards' as late as April 1945.

Low-scoring matches do have an inherent excitement. Every twist is potentially decisive. Certainly, the lack of points had not robbed the England-Wales fixture of any of its appeal. The misery of the Welsh Valleys was reflected in the *Swansea Daily Post's* reflection in 1936 on 'the practical disappearance of Shoni Rhondda. The cap and muffler man has gone'. There were, though, more than 70,000 at Twickenham in 1935, with 'thousands of latecomers from Wales being admitted inside the boards of the ring-seats. They watched the remainder of the match sitting on the grass at the edge', helping make so much noise that play went on for more than a minute after the final whistle, which was inaudible amid the din. More than five thousand people were locked out of St Helen's in 1936, with the 50,000 crowd inside including several hundred who burst – or were swept – in when one of the gates was stormed. Two of them came from the Swansea district of St Thomas. 'One lost his gloves and had a mackintosh torn off his back and lost irretrievably. The other wore a 4s 11d hat, but retrieved and wore a 15s hat. Both got in free, but are many shillings out in the transaction.' They were still luckier than the unemployed miners who had walked down from the Swansea Valley and staked out a nearby bridge as their vantage point, only to find that the police had orders to keep it clear. The gates were closed again at Twickenham in 1939 when *The Times* observed 'an avalanche of motor omnibuses and private cars. These so exceeded the resources of the spacious car parks that they nearly blocked the approaches on the North side. Even the sidewalks were covered.'

The succession of tight games led to a series of players enjoying 80 minutes of fame, or infamy. In 1934, at Cardiff, Waterloo wing Graham Meikle showed himself, in Gent's words, 'quick and resourceful', scoring twice on his debut and missing a third try only when the ball ran dead as he touched down. Meikle scored against Scotland and Ireland as England won their first Triple Crown in six years, yet by the end of the season Gent was unconvinced that he was international class, misgivings shared by the selectors, who discarded him. It was a shared family fate. His elder brother Steve scored on his debut against Scotland in 1929, but never played again. John Daniell, not easy to please, wrote that the 'forwards excelled'.

Wales's forwards did not. *The Times* reckoned them weaker than the average Welsh club pack, perhaps because most were locks or wing-forwards. Most grievously miscast was John Evans, of Newport, captain of Wales on his debut and a lock who was forced to play hooker. Unsurprisingly he was, as the *Daily Post* declared with the usual charity of a Welsh paper commenting on players from another town, 'a complete failure', and was dropped. He was one of three Welsh internationals – Cecil Davies, of Bedford, also subsequently dropped, was another – killed in the Second World War. Full-back Bryn Howells, of Bridgend, by contrast, played superbly. His misfortune was replacing the indispensable Jenkins, who promptly returned to end Howells' international career.

Full-backs also figured prominently in the draws of 1935 and 1936. England were saved in the first by Harold Boughton, of Gloucester, described as a veteran because he had had a trial in 1929, but in truth was still only twenty-four. England tried six other full-backs during the trials before summoning him to play at Twickenham. Wooller appreciated 'the skills of a great full-back, the temper of a prop forward and the right hook of a boxer', suggesting recognition of a kindred spirit. Those full-back skills included falling on the ball in front of dribbling forwards, then somehow hanging on. Journalist Rupert Cherry recalled: 'Afterwards he showed me his back, all black and blue, where the Welsh had kicked him. But he never flinched – never missed a tackle.' Boughton's late penalty, after a Welsh forward strayed offside, equalised an earlier try by Wooller that former international Victor Davies did not believe 'anyone in the world could have stopped'.

Wooller was stopped, along with everybody else, in the scoreless draw at Swansea in 1936. Both teams, uniquely, were fresh from victory over New Zealand. Wales had two enforced changes, England none. Howard Marshall wrote that he 'never saw a more lively or excited crowd before a match'. Attention inevitably focused on Obolensky, and one fan was quoted as joking that 'you'll need somebody on a motorcycle to catch him' as supporters exchanged banter before the match. Instead Wales had

Jenkins, who had spent four hours in an early version of the modern video analysis session, sitting in a cinema repeatedly watching a cycle of cartoons and newsreels to catch the few seconds of film of Obolensky's tries at Twickenham against New Zealand two weeks earlier. It was time well spent, as Jenkins confirmed. 'Just as I thought, he tried to emulate his first try against New Zealand, veered in and went out again. I ran right into him and hit him into the straw bales in the front of the stand.'

This was the first appearance against England by scrum-half Haydn Tanner, who was still at school but was clearly one of those rare phenomena who arrives as a ready-made international player. To Gent, who knew his half-backs, he was 'surely the best scrum-half Wales has had for years and years . . . beautiful passes and varied this with some good breaks from the scrum'. Tanner had already beaten New Zealand with club and country, but was unable to add England to the list because their full-back 'Tuppy' Owen-Smith – in spite of a name straight out of Wodehouse, the latest thing in imported South African talent – ankle-tapped the rampaging Wooller in the last few minutes. Owen-Smith played full-back with the casual assurance of the absurdly gifted. He was a Test cricketer, scored a spectacular century for South Africa against England at Headingley in 1929, was one of *Wisden's* Cricketers of the Year, and won a boxing Blue at Oxford. J.B.G. Thomas recorded that 'he just ambled quietly to and fro across the field until the situation demanded his intervention'. Then he might 'tackle a right-wing dashing upfield, and then deal with a cross-kick near the left touchline and almost immediately make a splendid mark beneath his posts, without apparently having ever covered the distance between the three points'.

While Obolensky's opportunities were limited at Swansea, as they were for the rest of his brief international career, Sever struck *The Times* as an 'always menacing, challenging figure'. That threat was fulfilled in 1937, although not in the manner expected. Sever, interviewed by Miles Harrison late in a very long life, recorded that his father said before that year's game: 'I just hope one side doesn't win by a drop-goal to a try.' Wales, to a man, would have agreed. Jenkins, unusually, missed touch. Sever, standing next to England prop Robin Prescott, remembered: 'It bounced off his right shoulder and I was standing behind him and caught it . . . I was not an Obolensky who could run right across the field, so I just took the opportunity and dropped a goal. Nobody was more surprised than I was when it went over.' With a drop still worth four points to three for a try it was enough to beat the single Welsh score by Wooller, who was 'at his poorest', according to Gent. He also argued that rugby was being ruined by negative tactics, in particular loose forwards like Eddie Long standing 'well out in the open away from loose scrums . . . at least one more for the opposition to beat, even though he doesn't tackle them himself.'

Sever scored again in 1938, although it brought England little benefit as they went down 14-8 in a wind so violent that E.W. Swanton, of the *Evening Standard*, reckoned every Welsh player was blown from his place while standing for the anthems. Both Wales tries showed astute adaptation to the conditions – McCarley dribbling from halfway for the first and Idwal Rees claiming the second after a perfectly judged up-and-under from Cliff Jones had confounded England full-back Hubert Freakes, yet another South African.

Howard Marshall commended the excellence of Welsh forwards, who had been reshuffled into a South Africa-style 3-4-1 scrummage formation during the game by pack leader Arthur Rees, but also blamed the RFU, which issued an official pre-match statement saying that the prop forward 'on the side on which the ball is put in must observe the spirit of the scrummage law, and abstain from attempting to hook the ball'. While 'admiring the altruistic intentions of the Rugby Union', Marshall thought an international in Cardiff the wrong place for gestures. England hooker Bert Toft 'was to be observed performing fearful and inevitably belated gyrations', while his opposite number 'Bunner' Travers, hailed in 1939's *Rugby Football Annual* as the best forward in the British Isles, enjoyed a productive afternoon.

No such scruples, though, restricted Toft or England in 1939 at Twickenham, in playing conditions more usually associated with Cardiff. Captaining England and described by the *Illustrated London News* as 'more than a mere hooker of brilliance . . . an inspired leader who knew how to get the last ounce out of his men', he led a forward effort that won twelve scrums to five before half-time and had the writer called 'Forward', who supplied the Welsh perspective in *The Times,* complaining bitterly 'at the manner in which England's outside forwards were permitted to hook in the scrummages'. England closed the 1930s with a scoreline appropriate to the era, 3-0. Toft also had a foot in the try, scored by debutant Richmond prop Derek Teden 'perilously close to touch in goal'. New Welsh wing Sid Williams was hailed as 'a player in the best Welsh traditions, able to swerve, dodge, kick and maintain speed', but inevitably most of the praise focused on the Englishmen. Teden was 'the best front row in the four nations next to Travers', Oxford back-rower Robert Marshall was 'head and shoulders above' the other forwards and scrum-half Paul Cooke 'got the ball away with unexpected power and gave evidence of wonderful stamina'. All three seemingly had great futures.

CHAPTER SEVEN
WAR AND PEACE 1940–51

Wales was the tough match, Scotland for fun and Ireland for food.

Micky Steele-Bodger, 2008

Called him an Englishman. Insulting language to an official, that'll be it.

A Run For Your Money, 1949

Instead, like their fathers' generation, Teden, Marshall and Cooke went off to the war against Hitler's Germany declared on 3 September 1939. None of that trio of great English promise survived to see peace in 1945. Cooke and Teden were dead by the end of 1940 and Marshall, decorated for ramming a U-boat, died in action in the final months of the war. The Second World War was not as savage for active combatants as its predecessor, but the English toll was fourteen. Obolensky was the first to fall, in 1940, followed by others including Gerrard, Brian Black and the first Grand Slam-winning captain, Noel Wodehouse. Wales lost three players, the two hapless front-rowers of 1934 and the multi-talented Maurice Turnbull.

Twickenham was requisitioned, the East car park resuming its former vocation of growing vegetables. Cardiff Arms Park was bombed in 1941, damage to the newish North Stand, built in 1934, inspiring the popular cartoon of an American serviceman saying 'that must have been a helluva game' when told that the last international there was Wales against England.

Careers were truncated, if not ended, by an eight-year hiatus between championship seasons. Toft went into the RAF and is still warmly remembered by Ruth Melly, a WAAF who served under his command, as 'a perfect gentleman'. Wooller suffered the peculiar horrors of a Japanese prisoner-of-war camp.

In keeping, though, with the less febrile mood during the Second World War, there was also some international rugby. The England v Wales series continued in 1940, with two matches played in aid of the Red Cross. The *Illustrated London News* report of England's fourth try in their 18-9 victory in the first of them, at Cardiff in March 1940, is inescapably poignant: 'Obolensky, making ground all the way, went clean over to the right before passing to Teden, who ran with measured power close to touch. His inward pass was followed by a scramble after which Kemp dived on the ball for his second try.' Obolensky was dead by the end of the month, Teden before the end of the year. Tommy Kemp, England's captain, survived to resume playing international rugby after the war. Others would play their only internationals in wartime. Wales's outside-half, Willie Jones, of Neath, 'a little fellow with a screw-kick and a capacity for getting out of tight corners', was compensated for never winning a full cap by playing in Glamorgan's County Championship-winning cricket team of 1948, captained by Wooller. If there was an air of 'phoney war' at the time of the first Red Cross match, those attending the second one at Gloucester can have been in no doubt about its reality after the minute's silence for Obolensky, killed in a flying accident the day before. England won 17-3 in Wooller's last international, in which he was partnered at centre by debutant Jack Matthews.

The war being anything but phoney by the start of 1941, with the Battle of Britain raging and invasion fears gripping the nation, there were no internationals that season, but a form of Test rugby returned the following year with the introduction of armed forces internationals organised by an inter-services committee. After two matches in March 1942, the games settled from the 1942-43 season into a consistent rhythm of two per season: at Swansea in November, and Gloucester in the spring. The secretary of the Swansea organising committee that raised around £15,000 for war charities was Reg Bancroft, son of Bill. While by definition not fully representative, the services matches developed the feel of internationals – 'something of peacetime glamour pervaded the famous St Helen's ground' when 30,000 watched in March 1942. Gent noted in 1944 that the area outside the pavilion at Gloucester was 'getting like the space at the back of the West stand at Twickenham, which has been a parade ground for years and years'. Wales's victory at Swansea in March 1942, erasing a twelve-point half-time deficit to win 17-12 as England 'cracked up completely', created a pattern. Wales won seven of the eight forces internationals – England winning only at Gloucester in 1944 with three final-quarter tries, the last by Bob Weighill, later RFU secretary.

As in the First World War, rugby league players in the services were granted an amnesty, and Wales benefited much more than England from the decision. Welsh league players all had union backgrounds. For many the service internationals fulfilled a dream reluctantly forsaken when they went north. Bev Risman remembers that for his father Gus: 'It was hugely important to him, one of the big things in his life. He enjoyed union internationals very much and when I started playing he told me not to go to league too soon, but to make the most of my opportunities in union first.' Gus also learnt about the oddities of amateurism when he claimed £4 in travel expenses and received £8. Back-rower Trevor Foster, a Welsh triallist in 1938, nearly turned down Bradford Northern because he wanted his Welsh cap before going to rugby league. Now he got his chance. Others, such as Sid Williams and outside-half Willie Davies, both of whom went north in 1939, played again with former colleagues – in Davies's case, his half-back partner and cousin Haydn Tanner. Bleddyn Williams, who played for Wales as a teenager, remembers: 'They were fantastic players. Risman was a superb back who could play anywhere, a great distributor who made a lot of openings. Trevor Foster was one of the great back-row forwards. I learnt a lot from all of them.' His one disappointment was not having the chance of playing alongside another league star, his eldest brother Gwyn. 'We were picked for the same match, but before it was played he was posted to North Africa, where he was wounded in the knee and did not play again.'

Even in this exceptional period for Welsh league talent – twenty-seven internationals went north in the 1930s and more than half of the players in the 1939 Challenge Cup final between Halifax and Salford were Welsh – England still had far more league players. Unlike their Welsh counterparts, few had a union grounding and the selectors knew little about them. Micky Steele-Bodger remembers: 'Selection was pretty haphazard. If somebody knew about you and you were playing reasonably well, you'd probably stay in the team.' League stars played for England – the victory at Gloucester owed much to the attacking flair of

Johnny Lawrenson and the goal-kicking of Ernest Ward – but were rarely as potent as their Welsh equivalents.

England made extensive use of Commonwealth servicemen. Knight, a New Zealander, scored in the first service international at St Helen's. His compatriot Rankin was hailed by the *Observer* as 'a wonderful full-back, undoubtedly the best in Britain'. The recruitment policy peaked in November 1944 with a threequarter line featuring two Australians, a Frenchman and Ward, with a South African at full-back. Longland and Toft renewed a front-row partnership dating back to 1936 while Seaman J.D. Robins, one of eleven Coventry players capped for England during the war, played in the second row. Robins would reappear in peacetime fixtures, but not in the same shirt.

That team, though, was no match for an exceptional Welsh performance, and were dismantled 28-11. Risman, man of the match according to the Swansea *Evening Post*, scored thirteen points, Trevor Foster showed 'skill in the breakaways' and Bleddyn Williams scored three tries, emulating the debut hat-trick in the 34-7 win at Gloucester in 1943 that had earned a rebuke from his wing, league player Alan Edwards. 'Centres are supposed to make tries for their wings, not score themselves,' said Edwards. It was, Williams recalls, 'said as a joke, but made a serious point about team-work and thinking what you could do for other players'.

John Gwilliam, an exact contemporary of Williams, said: 'I've never seen anything quite like Bleddyn at eighteen or nineteen. Later he had more experience, but not the zip he had then. He'd got it all – speed off the mark and perfect passing, kicking and sidestepping. He was quite alarming really.' Williams offered speed and youthful exuberance alongside the established gifts of the league stars. He played for Wales until 1955 and was a Lion in 1950, but still regards the services teams as the best he played in. England had players of quality and resolve – Longland and Toft packed down with Robin Prescott, who was greeted like an old friend by the Swansea *Evening Post* when in November 1943 he was initially omitted, then recalled as captain – but nothing in Williams's class.

Political journalist and rugby columnist Alan Watkins, who saw the Swansea matches as a schoolboy, remembered them in 1989 as 'the best rugby I ever saw . . . it was the presence of the rugby league players that made these matches memorable'. There was also an underlying philosophy that helped. As Williams recalls: 'The games were very fair and the objective was to entertain. The idea was that you'd throw the ball about rather than keeping it tight.' As the war ended, so did the amnesty. Cliff Jones, echoing Horace Lyne in 1918, would have liked it to have been extended 'with suitable modifications and safeguards'. With war extending into the 1945-46 season, it was another year before ordinary peacetime rivalries resumed. Instead there was a warmly remembered tour by New Zealand Services and, in the spring of 1946, home and away 'Victory' internationals.

International rugby returned to Cardiff, which the youthful West Walian Alan Watkins, more used to St Helen's, thought 'squalid . . . constructed – and not very well constructed – of rusting corrugated iron and rotting wood. The prevailing smell was of urine.' His Cardiff contemporary David Parry-Jones has different but still distinct memories, particularly of the North Stand: 'The seats had been reduced to matchwood; and . . . the damaged area was still no more than casually roped-off. Any careless schoolboy who lost his footing could easily have plunged to his death on the concrete terracing below.'

True to the spirit of renewal – and minus the league stars of their 24-9 services win at Gloucester in 1945 – Wales fielded teenage cousins from Pontypridd Grammar School, Wynford and Glyn Davies, at half-back against England at Cardiff in January 1946 and conceded twenty-one points in the first half before recovering to a 25-13 defeat by the end. Outside-half Nim Hall offered a foretaste of the future by dropping two goals for England. Hall was part of a remarkable St Mary's Hospital side favoured in wartime by the partiality of Lord Moran, its dean, for talented rugby players and the status of medical students as a reserved occupation, while other teams were disrupted by the demands of war. Hall had kicked two drop-goals in one of the most memorable wartime club matches, the 8-3 win by St Mary's in January 1945 that ended Coventry's four-year, 72-match winning run. Steele-Bodger, a veterinary student commended by *The Times* for his positioning in England's combined rushes, scored one of their tries and also left Glyn Davies knowing what actor Richard Burton meant when, in a memorable essay about his rugby experiences, he recalled 'a more onomatopoeic name for its owner would be hard to find . . . he was, I promise you, steel, and he did, I give you my word, bodger.'

According to Steele-Bodger, 'Glyn Davies was a lovely little man and an excellent player and I felt quite sorry for him. I was a couple of years older than him and we gave him a very hard time. I'd go low on him and Tommy Kemp would go high and he told me afterwards that he did not enjoy the game very much.' He would still make more of an impact than Wynford, who had to compete for a place with the implacable Tanner. A more seasoned Welsh team levelled the series by winning 3-0 at Twickenham. Steele-Bodger has vivid memories of Tanner: 'A terrific player with a very good break . . . bigger than most scrum-halves and very, very strong.' His try, reported by R.C. 'Crusoe' Robertson-Glasgow in the *Observer*, typified those strengths. From a scrum thirty-five yards out, 'Tanner did not pass, but went straight for the line, then gave the ball to T.R. Evans. Evans, faced by Uren, passed inside again to Tanner who scored a try which, rightly enough, brought the immediate and personal reward of congratulations from two invading spectators.'

No caps were awarded. Watkins has recalled the bitterness of Hugh Lloyd-Davies, full-back for Wales at Cardiff, who 'kept claiming what was morally true, but factually incorrect, that he was a Welsh international'. Davies led a picaresque life that, Watkins recalled in a tribute, included a schoolboy affair with, and later marriage to, his French teacher, wartime service as a pilot, a decisive contribution to the 1947 Varsity match followed immediately by expulsion for addressing a Welsh-speaking university official over-familiarly in that language, becoming the first Blue to play rugby league, and a nine-month prison sentence for pawning stolen jewellery. In all, fifty-four Englishmen and forty-seven Welshmen wore national shirts between 1940 and 1946 but were never recognised as international players. England's total included Owen Chadwick, later Regius Professor of Modern History at Cambridge and member of the Order of Merit, churchman Gerry Hollis – who played twelve times – and Micky Walford, Olympic hockey medallist. Cardiff stalwart Stan Bowes and Swansea's D. John Davies, whose son Mervyn would make up for any disappointment, were among the Welshmen.

The official resumption of England v Wales fixtures came at Cardiff on 15 January 1947. It was not, as in 1920, the restart of the entire championship.

That came on New Year's Day as France celebrated their return after a sixteen-year absence by beating Scotland 8-3. England fielded fourteen new caps, wing Dickie Guest being the only exception, and were led by Sale second row Joe Mycock. Wales had two pre-war caps – Tanner, captain for the first three post-war seasons, and Llanelli full-back Howard Davies. Many nominal debutants had, though, played in service and Victory internationals. Bleddyn Williams says: 'It really felt like a continuation,' but Steele-Bodger recalls it feeling different for him: 'You'd see somebody like Dickie Guest and think "I've read about him, this is fantastic!"'

Many were experienced in more than just rugby. In 1948, England included two players – Headingley lock Humphrey Luya and Oxford full-back Syd Newman – who had been prisoners-of-war. Newman, a South African, represented another England tendency, to call up overseas students once more. That this happened particularly after the two wars was no surprise. The common wartime cause conferred a shared identity even though Indian independence in 1947 presaged the end of empire. The New Zealand, Australian or South African – even an Afrikaner like Clive van Ryneveld in 1949 – was in the *Playfair Rugby Annual's* words 'one of us'. So England gave caps to fine cricketers such as Van Ryneveld and New Zealander Martin Donnelly. Four South Africans played in the trials in 1950 and the selection of New Zealander Ian Botting, only a few months after he had played for the All Blacks in South Africa, occasioned what *Playfair* termed 'worldwide controversy'. Belief that this had gone too far was reflected not only in J.B.G. Thomas's description of Botting's selection as 'farcical' and ironic shouts of 'Come on the Home and Colonials', but in the Pathe newsreel's description of the 1950 match as 'Wales's 15 against England's foreign legion'.

England's recruiting did not stop at the dominions. Barry Holmes, an Argentinian studying at Cambridge, played full-back for the whole of the 1949 season. They also looked at Gwyn Rowlands, a goal-kicking medical student of Welsh parentage, who did not make the final trial, but was then picked for the Welsh one. Rowlands felt that he could not immediately switch sides and turned Wales down. Upset by the accompanying controversy, he wrote to the RFU asking not to be considered in future, but there were lasting effects for his immediate family. His mother, who had shown little previous interest in rugby, was furious that he had turned down Wales and, when his father disagreed with her, 'cast my father out of the bedroom and never took him back'.

There was no repetition of the Anglo-Welsh duopoly of the previous post-war period. The two countries shared the championship in 1947, but the dominant force was Ireland, who won the only Grand Slam in their history in 1948 and took three championships in four seasons. The Irish resented suggestions that this was attributable to the Republic's wartime neutrality – as comedian Dave Allen put it: 'They knock the crap out of the German army and couldn't out of 15 Irishmen'. A tough, combative pack allied to the genius of outside-half Jack Kyle would have been formidable at any time. In 1948, Wales and England occupied the bottom two places in the championship for the first time since 1899, which was also the date of Ireland's last Triple Crown. England finished bottom again in 1950 and 1951.

None of this dented the appeal of the matches. The immediate post-war period produced unprecedented crowds for spectator sport. Cardiff v Newport matches attracted crowds of more than 40,000, while important county games in England could pull in 15,000. So it was hardly surprising that astonishing numbers travelled from Wales to London for the match against England. A 1949 Ealing comedy, *A Run For Your Money*, was based on two Welsh miners going to Twickenham. While the match was simply a plot device to enable a series of misadventures, and some of the accents in the pit scenes were more RADA than Rhondda, the film evoked the great biennial trek – overnight trains arriving in London packed with informal male voice choirs, sporting leeks and red berets – although a real Paddington Station announcer would have known not to precipitate bedlam by summoning 'Mr David and Mr Thomas Jones from Wales' to the stationmaster's office. That Wales won 16-5 in the film was also incidental, but popular with Welsh audiences.

In 1948, it was reported that Twickenham 'can never have been fuller'. It was fuller still in 1950, with a record crowd of more than 75,000, although Pathe's estimate that half the crowd was Welsh was possibly over-excitement brought on by singing which led *The Times* to muse that 'unless the RFU are careful, Twickenham will end up as one of the more famous Welsh grounds'. It was entirely possible that one third of the crowd was Welsh – with many more outside. *The Times* reported that 'the roads outside all became blocked by vehicles and disappointed people, mostly Welsh'.

The atmosphere engendered by the Welsh fans made a deep impression on essayist A.A.Thomson, a Yorkshireman of Scottish descent. 'An hour before the kick-off the ground is packed,' he wrote, 'the usual military band makes a fairy ring in the middle, but the musical programme is taken over by ten thousand Welshmen and, by the Lord Harry of Monmouth, how they sing.' The singing, he suggested, was the cover for 'commando units', whose mission was to get past the police and fix a leek to the crossbars. 'Suddenly a frantic cheer goes up . . . over the crossbar goes one leek . . . All the raiders depart. The police smile. The choir sings "Guide us, oh, thou Great Jehovah" with grandeur if some irrelevance. Honour is satisfied. Let battle begin.'

The crowd took on a life of its own: 'Turbulent, lyrical, Rabelaisian, swaying like barley in a strong wind as the ball goes backwards and forwards along the Welsh threequarter line. Standing in the middle of the south bank, I was swept off my feet and passed along the line as my red bereted companions swayed, like one man, with the ebb and flow of the game, and if Ken Jones had not made a clever reverse pass to his inside man, I should no doubt have found myself deposited in the East Stand.' Wondering why this happened only at Wales games, Thomson concluded: 'I was the victim of a superbly concentrated national will to win. Englishmen, Scotsmen and Irishmen go to cheer on their heroes to victory; they are with the players in spirit. Welshmen go to victory themselves, wholly in spirit and half in body too. When Bleddyn Williams goes for the line, the entire Welsh contingent at Twickenham goes with him.'

If Welsh fans retained their essential character, so did England's selectors. There was not much they could have done about naming fourteen new caps in 1947, still less about the knee injury that ended Steele-Bodger's career at the age of twenty-four or Holmes dying of typhoid in Argentina. Even so, thirty-one new caps over the next four years seemed excessive and helped explain England's declining rugby fortunes. Only Luya remained from the 1948 team to play Wales the following year. Four of the 1949 team played in 1950, and only two from that year did so in 1951. Not until 1953 had England's captain played the previous year's fixture. They capped fifty-six different players in five matches between 1947 and 1951. Only Gordon Rimmer, the rugged Waterloo scrum-half, played even three of them. His was a distinctive England career; he was picked five times against Wales, but always dropped before the end of the season. England fielded five full-backs, twelve front-rowers and at least three different players in every position during these five matches.

Yet Wales felt a healthy respect for several England players. They had good reason to be wary of Nim Hall, 'a good all-round player and a drop-goal expert' in Williams's memory, who impressed the venerable Collins as having 'brains as well as individual skills', but whose gaunt appearance led Alan Watkins to think that 'he looked at death's door, even as a young man'. Hall's most dangerous adversaries were the examiners at St Mary's Hospital, and he eventually fell foul of new regulations that demanded 'passing all examinations in a reasonable time'. Most leading Welsh clubs played Northampton and so their players were bemused, although certainly not disappointed, that rumbustious flanker Don White, a formidable England debutant at Cardiff in 1947, did not reappear against Wales until 1952. His club-mate Dick Jeeps suspects that 'he was rather too rough for some selectors' taste'.

Wales too had their period of flux, fielding twenty forwards in the first three years after the war, the only continuity provided by the big bald policeman Gwyn Evans on the flank. But by 1951, they were fielding twelve of the previous season's XV. The Welsh core came from the exceptional Cardiff team that provided an unprecedented ten of the XV that played England in 1948 – Cardiff's best ever year, though Wales's worst of this period. The fixed point amid this turmoil was provided by wing-threequarter Ken Jones, who in the 1949 match in Cardiff confronted Jack Gregory, a colleague from the Great Britain relay quartet that won a silver medal at the previous year's Olympics. That was Gregory's solitary England cap. Jones was much more than a sprinter in boots and was rated by the astute All Blacks full-back Bob Scott as 'the complete wing-threequarter'. Jones played for Newport but Wales's other ever-present, Jack Matthews, and five of the eight Welshmen who played three of those five games –Williams, Tanner, Evans, Billy Cleaver and Cliff Davies – were Cardiff players. Williams would have played all five but for a highly personal Twickenham jinx. In spite of being an automatic choice almost until his retirement in 1955, he did not play there after 1948. If the lethal pace he once had had gone, his maturity was characterised by his famously mesmeric sidestep. Steele-Bodger recalls: 'When he started he always went off the same foot, but then he learnt to do it off either, jolly galling when you thought you might get him taped.'

Williams's permanent move to centre after playing outside-half against England in 1947 opened hostilities in a classic Welsh controversy. The debate then raged over whether Billy Cleaver or Glyn Davies should play at outside-half; Alun Richards' characterisation of it as 'like comparing a poet to an accountant' did no more justice to Cardiff's Cleaver than did his West Wales nickname of 'Billy Kick', but caught the flavour of debate over the choice between him and Davies, who had become a classic running outside-half. Forward instability was eased by newcomers like the tough Newbridge lock Don Hayward, who formed an effective partnership of contrasts with Neath's line-out magician Roy John, whom New Zealand journalist Terry McLean reckoned 'could do the Indian rope trick without the rope', and a front row including reformed Englishman John Robins and Rhondda collier turned Somerset policeman Dai Davies.

Nevertheless, England started the post-war era the better. For a crowd limited to 40,000, it was, said *The Times*, 'a portmanteau of disappointment, packaged in dismay and disillusionment'. Wales scored two tries to one, but still lost 9-6 when Hall, 'no great maker of opportunities for other players but . . . among (the) master drop-kickers', landed one of the last four-pointers to follow a converted try by the rampaging White. Wales had little cause for complaint. England centre Eric Scott was badly injured after only fifteen minutes, so Steele-Bodger moved out of the pack to reinforce the threequarters. 'I found myself marking Ken Jones, the Olympic sprinter,' he remembers, 'and thought, "My God, now I'm in trouble",' but the efforts of the remaining seven forwards ensured that Jones had few opportunities. Scott had formed an all St Mary's midfield with Hall and fellow centre Billy Bennett. Wales, too, opted for a club unit and much criticism focused on the 'Cardiff triangle' of Williams at outside-half and Cleaver and Matthews at centre. It was an odd alignment to modern eyes, accustomed to Williams and Matthews as a centre pairing for the ages and lifelong friends who still meet every day at the Cardiff Athletic Club, yet they were paired against England only once. Williams remembers of the 1947 match: 'I pulled a thigh muscle in the first ten minutes, but with no replacements in those days I couldn't go off. I could hardly run and I didn't play for a long time afterwards.'

Nor did he enjoy the opening stages at Twickenham in 1948, when he conceded a penalty for playing the ball with his hand after a tackle – an offence he remains adamant he did not commit – that England full-back Newman converted from near halfway. This 3-3 draw had echoes of the previous year, with a serious injury – Newman broke his arm fifteen minutes from the end after playing brilliantly – and a terrific English rearguard action. Steele-Bodger says: 'I don't think we got out of our half. Wales had the ball all the time. They attacked and we defended.' A report that 'Wales must find a set of backs capable of utilising the innumerable chances given them by their magnificent forwards' sounds odd considering that they had a threequarter line containing two immortals, Jones and Williams, and Matthews, who was a great by most other standards. But even immortals have off-days and this one was rooted in the selectors' desire to get all three, plus Cleaver and Davies, into the same team. Cleaver, described as having 'few ideas in attack', played centre while Matthews' past as a sprint champion doomed him to the wing. He took years to live down a dropped pass from Cleaver in the final minutes. He says: 'Billy just heaved it out and it hit my shoulder. He wasn't a great passer, just used to flick the ball from his wrists.' It wasn't Matthews' day. Williams recalls how 'earlier he'd scored a perfectly good try, taking a quick throw-in to Tanner who passed it back, which was disallowed'.

Matthews left a happier impression in 1949, when he and Williams played together at centre. Nearly half a century later English journalist Terry Cooper could recall 'one Matthews tackle which caught his South African-born rival Clive van Ryneveld in the midriff. The Oxford man made little impact afterwards.' A still more vivid memory was provided by one of Glyn Davies's best performances. 'The incisive running and side-stepping skills of Davies created two of his side's three tries. Davies had all the qualities associated with a Welsh number 10 – quick, decisive and with an instinct to find gaps.' Williams recalls that he was given space because Tanner, still incomparable in his final season, kept England's back row fully occupied. The chief beneficiary in Wales's 9-3 win was Cardiff wing Les Williams, who scored two tries, greatly increasing his market value for his departure to rugby league. His move to Hunslet was

Forerunners *(Above)* Wales's first ever winners at Dewsbury in 1890: WRU secretary Richard Mullock is a shadowy presence at the back, try-scorer Buller Stadden absent. The rest are (back): A. Duncan (umpire), S. Thomas, A. Bland, W. Williams, W. Bowen, J. Meredith, W. Treatt (WRU) (middle), H. Hannen, A. Gould (captain), W. Thomas, W. Evans (front) C. Thomas, D. Gwynn, W. Bancroft, R. Garrett. *Alamy*

(Below) England cross for one of their five tries in their 17-0 victory at Rectory Field, Blackheath in 1892.

Wales at the end of their first Golden Age

Swansea in 1911: (back) J. Pugsley, A. Webb, W. Perry, A. Coldrick, H. Jarman, T. Evans, D. Thomas (middle) I. Morgan, W. Spiller, R. Gibbs, W. Trew (captain), F. Birt, J. Williams. (Front) J. Bancroft, R. Owen.

Giants and innovators

(Left) Cherry Pillman of England, who 'played a game apparently invented by himself', anticipating before 1914 much in modern back-row play with its dual responsibilities in defence and attack. *PA Photos*

(Right) Dickie Owen of Wales, the ur-scrum-half, diminutive master of deception, rugby intellectual and enabler of others. The constant factor in Wales's first Golden Age. *PA Photos*

Top Row:- E.R.Gardner, T.Woods, E.Myers, A.T.Voyce, A.F.Blakiston, A.M.Smallwood. F.W.Mellish, B.S.Cumberlege. Middle Row:- E.D.G.Hammett, R.Edwards, L.G.Brown, W.J.A.Davies, (Capt.), C.N.Lowe, W.W.Wakefield. On Ground:- C.A.Kershaw.

English inclusiveness

The XV of 1921 that included four men born in Wales, an Australia, a South African, others with birth qualifications for Scotland and USA and Ernest Hammett, who would rather have played for Wales. They won 18-3.

World Rugby Museum, Twickenham.

Fields of Praise
Swansea, 1907.
Pioneering hooker
George Travers
(centre, dark shirt)
looks on as a Welsh
colleague tackles
an Englishman.
Getty Images

Twickenham 1915.
'HQ' in its First
World War repose,
the original
grandstand standing
alongside the
touchline.
*World Rugby Museum,
Twickenham.*

Cardiff 1922. A reprise
of wartime conditions
for those with memories
of the trenches. England
are sponged down at
half-time, pensive
expressions reflecting
five Welsh first-half
tries. *Getty Images*

On the Road *A Run For Your Money*. Reporter Alec Guinness (right) waits while miner Donald Houston telephones in a scene from the 1949 film about Welsh fans on a trip to Twickenham. **Rex Features**

The Celtic Invasion: Welsh fans on their way to Twickenham in 1937, leeks and berets on display just in case anyone doubts where they are from. **Getty Images**

Travelling hopefully: Invariably unlucky on his visits to Twickenham, Wales's post-war hero Bleddyn Williams is seen here in 1950 dressed for what proved a more fortunate trip to New Zealand with the Lions. **PA Photos**

Giants of their Time A Man for All Surfaces. England's debutant scrum-half Dick Jeeps kicks at Twickenham in 1956. Jeeps was a loser on this day, but returned to win on many others. *PA Photos*

A Welsh Sergeant Bilko. Clive Rowlands in 1963, silent for once, perhaps contemplating a future as Triple Crown captain, coach, manager, broadcaster and union president. *Mirrorpix*

England's recurring nightmare of the 1970s: a JPR Williams try. This is the first of them, launching Wales's remarkable comeback at Twickenham in 1970. *PA Photos*

A rare moment at Twickenham in 1978 when Gareth Edwards (peering over ruck, left) wasn't at the centre of things. Opposite number Malcolm Young clears, Derek Quinnell (centre) surveys the scene, Bill Beaumont peers from the depths. *PA Photos*

Turning Points Referee David Burnett (centre) orders Paul Ringer (no. 6, back to camera) off at Twickenham in 1980. Victim John Horton (no. 10, left) is helped to his feet. Wales took longer to recover. *PA Photos*

End of the line. England's Rob Andrew is held firmly by Jonathan Davies (left) and Ieuan Evans in the first World Cup at Brisbane at 1987, a 16-3 Wales win that provoked an English revolution. *Getty Images*

Triumph of the Wills
England captain Will Carling, about to shake off Welsh defender Mark Titley and launch the 34-6 massacre, first of many modern Welsh nightmares at Twickenham, in 1990.
Getty Images

Will Greenwood, scorer of more tries than anyone else in the history of this fixture, slices past Wales's Gavin Thomas for his record-equaling sixth at Cardiff in 2003. *PA Photos*

Welsh revenge
James Hook, latest in the line of players who particularly excel in this fixture, fires over a drop-goal in Wales's victory at Cardiff in 2007.
Getty Images

The pride and the passion More colourful, though perhaps less tuneful than their predecessors of the past. Just as partisan, but still trusted to sit unsegregated. The point of it all, the element of continuity. Fans of both teams proudly showing their colours at the World Cup quarter-final at Brisbane in 2003, a contest from which both sides took some satisfaction. *Getty Images & PA Photos*

sealed in Bleddyn Williams's front room, later in the year. England's points came from a Hall drop, worth one point less than his 1947 effort, while the ill-fated Holmes hit a post with a long-range penalty. Tanner retired after playing seven consecutive full championship seasons, and losing seven to the war. Without the interrupton, he could have been the first player from any country to win fifty caps. Departing with him was Travers, who had returned for a final international season at thirty-five. The normally tight-fisted WRU, evidently not believing that he was the same Travers who played in 1939, gave him an unprecedented second Wales cap.

It was, though, the 1950 match that left indelible Welsh memories. They had not won at Twickenham since 1933, but the middle-brow art of *A Run For Your Money* proved as effective as Cynan's high-flown stanzas in inspiring real-life imitation. Bleddyn Williams, who had led Wales in a Victory international, was Tanner's logical heir as captain, but began his series of Twickenham mishaps by injuring a thigh and withdrawing on the morning of the match. So leadership descended, at extremely short notice, on No. 8 John Gwilliam, formidable in physique, intellect and personality, a former tank commander with a Guardsman's erect stance and deep religious convictions, who invariably inspired the adjective 'Cromwellian'. Vincent Griffiths, a rare selector who had also played at the top level, offered advice that was to the point: 'Don't use any of those long wild passes, don't flip the ball back from the line-out, don't hold the ball in the scrum – otherwise play your own game.' Gwilliam, whose forbidding appearance conceals an acute sense of humour and a most un-Cromwellian chuckle, recalled that 'these were the sum of the ideas I had for winning a rugby match'.

It was reasonable to assume that England would play on the presumed first-time nerves of eighteen-year-old full-back Lewis Jones. He was certainly anxious, remembering in his memoirs 'that sinking feeling in the pit of my stomach as I stood with the rest of the lads for the playing of the National Anthem', but recalled the reassurance that came with the first penalty, Gwilliam's words – 'Far downfield as you can, Lewis' – and a sound thump into the England twenty-five. Even so, England scored first. J.V. Smith, of Oxford, later the RFU president, intercepted and charged forty yards for a try that was converted by full-back Murray Hofmeyr, one of the four foreign legionnaires. Gwilliam lost his voice after ten minutes, a blow for a skipper who liked to lead by winding-up his forwards, but whispered to such effect that Robins afterwards wondered why his captain had taken such a dislike to him.

In any case, the encouragement Wales wanted was forthcoming before half-time. Jones fielded the ball deep in his own half, prepared to kick, then 'noticed that the England follow up was neither as speedy nor as collective as I had expected. Taking advantage of this, I moved quickly infield, dummied left to decoy a couple of later arrivals, switched right, and raced through a gap right up to the England twenty-five, where I found the supporting forwards at my elbow.' Among them was Newport flanker Bob Evans, who passed to a team-mate 'whom I expected to be wing Ken Jones. To my astonishment I found I was giving the ball to prop forward Cliff Davies.' It may not have been the jaguar-like Jones, but Wales could not have been better served. Davies was a collier who took a size eighteen collar, a fine prop forward, a humorist who convulsed team-mates among the 1950 Lions with his straight-faced contention that his native Kenfig Hill had more history than anywhere on earth, 'except Jerusalem', and was exceedingly fast. He scored with aplomb. England still led but the balance had shifted. Jones landed a second-half penalty then converted the second try, scored after a dribbling rush by Ray Cale, of Pontypool. Cale impressed novelist Alun Richards as 'the most frightening rugby player I ever saw . . . a Dostoevskian figure, the archetypal Russian policeman with that oddly long, flapping hair of his, the glazed eyes and the ominous watchful stance as he stood salivating thoughtfully on point duty at the end of the line-out.' This may explain why the *Illustrated London News's* picture of the score shows four Englishmen well behind the try-line – in no position to intervene, but also out of Cale's reach – but not the reasoning of that year's Lions selectors, who allegedly omitted him as 'too rough for New Zealand'. Wales fell short of their celluloid predecessors by five points, but an 11-5 win resulted in Jones and Gwilliam being carried off the Twickenham pitch and created unstoppable momentum towards Wales's first Triple Crown and Grand Slam since 1911, accomplished with the resounding points difference of fifty to eight.

With eleven Lions, they were expected to dominate again in 1951 and they started accordingly against England at Swansea in their last championship meeting outside London or Cardiff. St Helen's was Wales's first home ground, and the only British venue at which South Africa, Australia and New Zealand were beaten at cricket and rugby. Radio commentator Teddy Wakelam might have regarded St Helen's with mixed feelings, recording that on wet days with the wind from the south-west 'our window then becomes blurred and rain-swept, and it needs the constant attention of an unfortunate engineer, stationed outside in the wet, to keep it clear'. He reckoned, though, that it had the best singing – 'there one meets the true West Walian and the experts down from the Valleys' and recommended that anyone who wanted to understand rugby should 'go down there on an international day and leave the rest to his own personal observation. The whole town is literally rugger mad on these days, and, whoever you meet, there is only one topic. Everyone knows the "name, age and fighting weight" of each and every other, everyone has a theory, and usually a pretty good one, as to why X or Y should win.' It also routinely produced good playing surfaces as the *Daily Post* noted in capitals when arguing that a rain-sodden match would have been 'TEN TIMES WORSE' on any other Welsh ground.

The demise of St Helen's as an international venue was part of the centralisation on Cardiff that gathered pace from its designation as capital from 1955 – the first year it hosted both Wales's annual games. St Helen's went out against the old enemy with a bang as Wales won 23-5, their biggest win since 1922. Gwilliam took advantage of the contrast in surfaces, having Wales practise on a swampy Cardiff Arms Park the Wednesday before. England fielded the same half-back pairing as the previous year for the first time since 1899 and much good it did them, except that Rimmer and Ivor Preece – a classic Coventry product who had come through the school in working-class Broadstreet and its old boys club, and who was respected by journalist and former international Clem Thomas for his 'composure on and off the field and strength of character' – were almost the only players to escape criticism. They also picked ten new caps, including Bedford centre Lionel Oakley, who contributed little after a ferocious early tackle by Matthews. John Christopher, in the *South Wales Evening Post*, thought England's forwards 'like a flock of spring lambs, and just as innocent'. Gwilliam, 'with a coolness born of perfection, hurled out 20-yard passes directly from the line-out'. Glyn Davies played as well as two years earlier and Lewis Jones set up three of the five tries, all scored by threequarters. Matthews scored twice, as did wing Malcolm Thomas — an unobtrusively excellent presence, in three different positions, throughout the 1950s — with Ken Jones scoring the other. In retrospect it was, Lewis Jones recalled, a misleading result. England would evade losing all four matches only by virtue of a narrow win over Scotland. Jones argued: 'I don't think a weaker back row . . . has ever appeared on an international field in post-war years.' Philip Moore, of Blackheath, later Sir Philip and secretary to HM The Queen, won his only cap on the flank. Wales got their comeuppance only a fortnight later in one of the great shocks of rugby history, beaten 19-0 by a Scotland team destined to lose their next 17 matches – including a 44-point shellacking by South Africa. For England, by contrast, a long-awaited upturn was coming.

CHAPTER EIGHT
ONLY TWO CAN PLAY 1952–58

Most of our people have never had it so good.
Harold Macmillan, 1957

There are still parts of Wales where the only concession to gaiety is a striped shroud.
Gwyn Thomas, 1958

Harold Macmillan's famous claim was fated to be thrown back at him as evidence of complacent disregard for Britain's real, continuing problems. Yet it was true. Britain was strikingly prosperous by all previous standards in the 1950s. It enjoyed full employment and an unprecedented range of consumer goods, such as washing machines and televisions – the number of licences grew in ten years from from fewer than 200,000 to 10 million. What were once luxuries were accompanied by the security of the National Health Service and full-scale National Insurance. If the 1950s look dull to modern eyes, Peter Hennessy points out: 'For people who had come through the slump and the war in the previous twenty years, there was nothing dull about the first small signs of mass prosperity.' Those signs spread so wide that they even reached South Wales. Unemployment was down to around 25,000 in 1953. Developments such as the cold-reduction plants at Trostre and Velindre, the giant Abbey Works at Margam and Usk power station made the region once more an industrial powerhouse, productivity growing well above UK averages.

This sense of well-being extended to English and Welsh rugby. If the most effective rugby of the decade was played by South Africa in 1951-2, and the most intense was between the Springboks and the All Blacks in 1956, England and Wales dominated in the northern hemisphere. Wales beat New Zealand in 1953, but much the same team lost to England a few weeks later. These were the years of the second Anglo-Welsh duopoly. Between 1952 and 1958 England won three Five Nations Championship titles outright and shared another while Wales won two outright and shared two more. Only France, who shared their first titles in 1954 and 1955, interrupted their private party. Wales and England lost only seven out of forty-two matches against the other three teams, drawing three more. Yet neither country recalled this as a golden age. Head to head, they cancelled each other out, three wins apiece and a draw. Wales were serially tantalising, winning three of their four matches every season from 1953 to 1956, but no Triple Crown or Grand Slam. England began a three-yearly cycle of excellence – 1954, 1957, 1960, 1963. Home advantage did not exist, with four away wins in seven meetings.

The mid-1950s had great players and sublime moments, but little rugby that excited for its own sake. Matches were close and exciting – no side won by more than five points – but low scoring, with no team reaching double figures. Trends established pre-war – notably the unchecked rise of the wing-forward – continued apace. The 1953 All Blacks were horrified by the liberties permitted to British back rows. Wales's Clem Thomas remembered 'having a licence to kill outside-halves', a freedom that another ruthlessly intelligent operator, England's Peter Robbins, reckoned made Thomas, a butcher, the only player to practise his profession on the field of play. Nor were conditions, particularly at Cardiff, much help. It is no coincidence that Wales started pressing regularly for fixture rotation at the same time as moving all their fixtures to the endemically swampy Arms Park. Bleddyn Williams, a devoted Cardiffian, remembers: 'It was used all the time – by Cardiff, by the Athletic XV and by Wales – probably 70 matches a season. The ground never had a chance to recover.' The wonder is that an elusive side-stepper like Williams, even if blessed with 'a torso like a tree-trunk and the muscular thighs of a Renaissance sculpture', in Gareth Williams's evocative phrase, prospered so often there.

Wales did not lack brilliance. The years 1952 to 1958 were Cliff Morgan's span in the fixture, although his most memorable contribution, after a spectacular scissors with Ken Jones in 1952, was a brilliant but essentially defensive display of tactical kicking six years later. Jones played until 1956, but did not score after 1952 – or against anyone in his last 17 games for Wales. His lack of opportunities became a national issue – A.A. Thomson suggested that he wear plates reading 'running in, please pass' – but was not resented by Jones himself. When quick young centre Gareth Griffiths provided a succession of passes against Scotland in 1954, Jones told him after fifteen minutes: 'For **** sake Gareth, either have a go yourself or kick it.' Bleddyn Williams played until 1955, as unfailing in his class as he was in getting injured every two years, just before Wales went to Twickenham.

This was a rare period in which Welsh forwards resonated as loudly as the backs. Cliff Morgan recalled the rumbustious Thomas as a manageable club opponent, but a colossal international colleague. Thomas played alongside men such as the vast athletic lock Rhys Williams, Neath's Rees Stephens – a Victory international commended as late as 1957 as 'a remarkably vigorous veteran' of 'robustness and ferocity' – Navy stoker turned steelworking trade unionist W.O. Williams and Bryn Meredith, a hooker so mobile that Bleddyn Williams likened him to having 'another blind-side flanker'.

England's selectors could still mystify. As Thomas said: 'The leading forwards in Wales used to fall about laughing every time England picked a team. All of us could have picked a far better team.' Recognising an adversary of comparable power and ruthlessness, Thomas would always have picked Northampton flanker Don White, who in his turn recalled having 'some awful captains. The best of them were no better than so-so.' Even so, the kaleidoscopic changes of the immediate post-war years gave way to greater stability. Twenty-seven new caps in six games with Wales as their first opponent of the season was well below England's usual average. Naming a single newcomer – Harlequins outside-half Ricky Bartlett – in 1957 was the greatest restraint displayed in curtain-raisers against Wales between 1881 and the introduction of fixture rotation in 1974. Northampton's elegant Jeff Butterfield, who introduced Loughborough University's then revolutionary ideas on training and conditioning into the changing rooms of club, country and the 1955 Lions, is remembered by fellow Lion Gareth Griffiths as 'one of the best – with brains and talent, a great thinker about rugby'. He formed a centre partnership of contrasts in the Williams and Matthews mould with powerful Harlequin Phil Davies, possessor of the widest shoulders in that Lions party and a fearsome outside swerve. Lancastrian Eric Evans was a fixture at hooker, while solid citizens like Bill Holmes, of Northampton, and George

Hastings, of Gloucester, were given time to develop into international props. There was also greater social inclusiveness, with a quarter of England players in the 1950s educated at grammar school, compared to forty per cent from the private sector, although men like Coventry lock Stan Adkins, who played in 1953, a council school-educated capstan operator, remained a minority.

The best day's work by the England selection panel may, though, have been reverting to type and despatching ten debutants to Cardiff in 1956. England were beaten and, true to form, dumped the half-backs. Oxford outside-half M.J.K. Smith, who told his partner 'don't put the ball too far in front of me, I don't see very well without my glasses' and recalled recently that 'I consider myself exceedingly fortunate to have got a cap', was gone for good, settling instead for fifty England cricket caps, half as captain. His partner did return. Dick Jeeps was peculiarly well named as he was an all-surfaces operator who excelled in the mud, a relentless competitor 'apparently built out of India rubber'. He was hardly an England discovery. He went uncapped with the Lions to South Africa in 1955 and displaced incumbent Johnny Williams from the Test team – not least because Cliff Morgan preferred Jeeps' ability to put the ball in front of him to Williams's bullet-like pass. Williams returned for England for the rest of the 1956 season, but Jeeps was back with that year's other rookies the following season, becoming the fixture's greatest individual influence for several years.

England also found a captain. Eric Evans was nearly thirty-five, had won his first cap as a prop in 1948 before moving to hooker and was suspected of 'having passed his best' by the 1955 *Playfair*. Jeeps recalls 'little spindly legs, he was about 8st soaking wet' – Evans claimed he was 12st – and his 'getting a lot out of the word "enthusiasm"'. Modern ideas on physical preparation – Evans trained with Manchester United – cohabited with a disdain for formal coaching, 'the only place for a coach is transporting the team', and a firm philosophy of leadership. 'The most important work is nearly always off the field,' he said. 'It is up to the captain to instil a spirit of playing for the team.'

Nor did England's selectors contrive anything as crass as their Welsh counterparts managed at Twickenham in 1952 after another Bleddyn Williams injury. Wales had a contingency. Reserve Alun Thomas was no fragile novice but a seasoned twenty-six-year-old, who had been close to selection for some time. He was told on the Friday that he would play. Yet a call was made to Cardiff, where Jack Matthews was looking forward to playing at Bath. 'It was always the same day as the England match, so I'd never played there,' says Matthews. 'On Friday night I had a call from Brice Jenkins, the Cardiff secretary, who told me that Bleddyn was out and they wanted me to go up. I said: "That's daft, Alun Thomas is already there," and he told me: "No, Alun is still the reserve, you're playing. See the man on the gate at Twickenham."' He travelled on Saturday morning, meeting journalists who said: 'You're on the wrong train. Aren't you going to Bath?' 'I told them that I had been until the previous night.'

By the time he reached Twickenham, there had been another change of plan. Thomas, although excluded from the team talk, was now playing and Matthews was surplus to requirements. He remembers: 'The selectors had gone into the toilets to talk about it, and they wouldn't come out to tell me. They made John Gwilliam, the captain, tell me that I wasn't playing. I went into the toilets, found Enoch Rees, the chair of selectors, and told him: "I should never have been asked to come here. Never ask me to play for Wales again."'

Williams, from his own experience as captain, says: 'You could never rely on the selectors. We were never consulted. They were hopeless.' Even the warmly charitable Cliff Morgan told how 'selectors were a law unto themselves in those days and extremely inconsiderate. They did not feel that they had to explain or apologise.' He told of meeting three of the five selectors the evening after the 1953 England match, in which he and Cardiff club-mate Rex Willis were displaced at half-back by Newport's Billy Williams and Roy Burnett. 'They said: "Where were you today? We voted for you to play, you know?"' It was, Morgan drily noted, the only case he knows of three selectors being outvoted by the other two.

The same match led Labour MP, rugby Blue and sports essayist Jim Mallalieu to observe that international rugby's supreme moment came every two years – the crowd singing 'Land of My Fathers' immediately before Wales v England at Cardiff. 'It sings best against England for, against England, there are old scores to be paid off, scores which were notched against "My Fathers", long before rugby was first played,' he said. Mallalieu noted that in singing other tunes the crowd showed 'its independence by keeping one beat behind the bandmaster, but these are only working-up exercises in preparation for the supreme moment that is to come. Then at last the teams emerge, England in white jerseys, Wales in red, and there they stand while the crowd gives out its resentments of the past, its joy in the present and hope for the future.'

Huge numbers of Wales supporters still travelled to Twickenham. John Morgan described the journey of pitman 'Davy Jones': 'Up and over the hill into the dawn: cadge a ride to the station on the only bus travelling that early; the workman's; then the excursion train at seven. Two mackintoshes . . . sandwiches enough for a small army; a bottle of orange juice, a small tin full of home-rolled cigarettes; two apples, an orange, a banana and, in the pocket of his navy-blue suit, an old scarlet beret.' While some went 'by hired bus, with seats booked for the beer', the rail excursion remained the majority experience. 'Corridors full, sitting on newspapers . . . flagons coming out as the sun warms a little, talking a lot, singing especially loudly if we stop at an English station, arguing so that before we reach Paddington we have each acquired the name, as nickname, of a player dispute has forced us to deify.'

The train was noisy but 'scarcely anarchy. The violent despair, the prancing rollicking delight is for later, for Piccadilly and the incredible midnight train back to where we belong.' At the match, though, 'Davy Jones is a different man; his face a bright red, his blue scars brighter; his beret is on his head at last. He is an experienced soldier in an expeditionary force that will not surrender until the last gasp.'

He and 25,000 others like him followed Wales to Twickenham in 1952, when there were 73,000 people in the ground and thousands more outside. Hoping to prevent the huge crushes that were as predictable as leek-wielding post-climbers, the RFU made the 1954 match all-ticket. Morgan reported that Davy Jones did not obtain one of Wales's allotted 10,000 tickets, yet 'he was on the train, was at the gates of Twickenham, hoping, listening to the noise, the band, the singing and, in the end, at a barber's shop beyond the ground, the radio commentary'. Two years earlier, John Billot recalled: 'Hundreds of Welshmen watched . . . on television sets within a quarter-of-a-mile of the tall Twickenham stands, taken in by sympathetic householders who watched them standing forlornly in the streets.' For many it may have been a first sight of television, not widely available in Wales before the Wenvoe transmitter began operating in 1955.

Although England v Scotland was televised as early as 1938, rugby regarded television with the distrust it accorded most symptoms of modernity. Fear of its impact on club attendances was given far greater weight than the possible benefits of taking the game to new audiences. The BBC paid the RFU £150 to broadcast the England v Wales match in 1952, the same for games against Ireland and South Africa and £50 less for the Varsity match. That year the four home unions responded to BBC outside broadcast chief Seymour de Lotbiniere's request for regular coverage by resolving that 'since the advantages . . . for Rugby Football are greatly outweighed by the danger of the game as a whole, facilities for "live television" should not be permitted . . . having once yielded in the matter of "live" television it would be impossible to withdraw the facilities granted.' By 1956, though, opinion was shifting. 'England was prepared to televise at any place at any time; Ireland was in doubt, Wales wanted modified television and Scotland did not want any at all.' Wales, paid £600 for a match the previous year, was mollified by a much improved offer – and by 1960 the broadcast fee was more than £2,000 per match.

Those Welsh travellers of 1952 were left talking not only of technological but sporting wonders, having watched one of the most exciting matches in the fixture's history. Wales's fourth consecutive win over England, hailed by Haydn Tanner as 'a victory as good as any that has been obtained by a Welsh XV', was much tighter than the previous three. Wales led 8-6 in the final moments of a match that lasted ninety-seven minutes including half-time – a marathon by 1950s' standards – when England's Gordon Rimmer broke down the right wing and cross-kicked for Bath wing-forward Alec Lewis to cross by the posts. Gwilliam recalled Wales 'moving resignedly into position behind the posts when we realised that the whistle had gone for offside'. Gwilliam remains the only Wales captain to win twice at Twickenham and victory presaged a second Grand Slam in three seasons.

Such a triumph looked unlikely in the first twenty minutes. Lewis Jones, playing on the wing – his third posting in as many matches against England – 'felt an excruciating stab of pain in my thigh' and staggered off for treatment on a pulled muscle. Wasps wing Ted Woodward, a 6ft and 15st former sprint champion winning his second cap, cut a Jonah Lomu-like figure as he capitalised on the one-man advantage, charging 'down the Welsh right flank like a Sherman tank, the first time slipping the ball inside to Agar, who scored, and on the second crashing over himself'. Jones returned strapped up but virtually immobile. Flanker Len Blyth was sent out to cover for him and the seven-man Welsh pack struggled, with Don White – recalled at last and described by *The Times* as operating 'on the blind side of the whistle' – creating havoc. Cliff Morgan remembered that 'he was breaking very fast and hitting lumps out of me'.

Before half-time, Wales turned this to their advantage. Rex Willis, the tough, selfless successor to Tanner at scrum-half for Cardiff and Wales, showed why Morgan called him 'my better half'. He held the ball until Morgan had run past White, then passed to him. From just outside his own twenty-five yard line, Morgan broke past the opposing centres and into the English half, where, Gwilliam recalled, 'Ken Jones . . . cut inside and took a perfect pass. He thus wrong-footed the whole of the opposing team, and no one laid a hand on him as he sprinted forty yards to score.' The skipper described how this giant scissors move 'bewildered both sides and could only have been executed by players of exceptional speed and acceleration'. Malcolm Thomas's conversion – England had missed both theirs – made the half-time score 6-5. Wales's second-half score also involved deception and lethally quick execution. Lewis Jones could not run but he could still take and time a pass – making the extra man to send Ken Jones unstoppably towards the corner. Morgan, seized post-match by fellow Rhonddaites from Treorchy male voice choir, ended standing on a bar counter conducting the singing – a role he reprised for the possibly less tuneful 1955 Lions – missing the team bus and hitching a lift to the dinner with a policeman.

Wales had to make the most of those celebrations. The subsequent six matches divide neatly into pairs, starting with English victories in 1953 and 1954 that fulfilled the promise of 1952's flying start and fighting finish. Wales had six new caps to England's two at Cardiff in 1953, including nineteen-year-old full-back Terry Davies. Mallalieu reported that there had been 1,800 ticket applications from Davies's home village of Bynea, population 3,000, 200 of which had been successful. Davies gave Wales the lead with a first-half penalty before England retaliated. One of their debutants, quick Liverpool outside-half Martin Regan, broke and centre

Lewis Cannell scored. Nim Hall, moved to full-back to accommodate Regan, converted but then struggled with the boot, eventually handing over to Woodward, who landed a long-range penalty. *Playfair* thought that the half-back struggles of Billy Williams and the stylish Rodney Parade idol Roy Burnett were mostly the fault of 'inefficient scrummaging, which has been such a strange feature of Welsh international sides in recent years'.

Mallalieu felt that Bleddyn Williams was no longer the force of old, save one late flash of brilliance when Wales were trailing 8-3. 'A shake of one hip, the twist of one shoulder, and his immediate opponent was grasping the January air while Bleddyn was wisping himself towards the English line,' he wrote. 'On the twenty-five line he passed to Thomas who drew the full-back and passed to Ken Jones . . . but as Thomas's perfect pass came to him, Ken Jones lifted that experienced head, dropped the pass and gave away a certain try and all hope of victory. I could have cried. Thousands of Welshmen did, not from bitterness, but just from sadness that this one last flash from their golden lad could not have brought one glorious triumph before the post-war glory of Welsh rugger crumbled to dust.' It was the decisive moment of that season. England won the title but were deprived of a Triple Crown and Grand Slam by a 9-9 draw in Dublin. Mallalieu's obituaries for Welsh rugby and Bleddyn Williams proved a little premature. Wales won their remaining championship matches before Williams led both club and country to victory over the All Blacks in the autumn of 1953.

Wales went to Twickenham four weeks after beating New Zealand but could not field the same team because of injuries to centres Gareth Griffiths, who had dislocated his shoulder against the All Blacks, and, inevitably, Bleddyn Williams. Debutant Glyn John, of St Luke's College, was a former league player reinstated because he had left union before he was eighteen and had repaid his earnings. There were echoes of 1952, with Wales suffering injuries, Woodward rampaging and a tight contest building to a thrilling finish, but a different outcome. England's six debutants included four forwards, two of them RFU presidents-to-be. One of them, Peter Yarranton, was struck by 'the roar of indignation from a horde of crimson berets in the ringside seats' when he tossed a large leek towards the touchline, and by a pre-match handshake with Wales full-back Gerwyn Williams, a Middlesex county colleague, who told him:

'Don't forget, even if you're carried off one minute after the referee's whistle, you'll still be an international.' Rosslyn Park wing Chris Winn recalled 'six or seven thousand Welshmen standing on Twickenham's South Bank . . . a continuous roar. We couldn't pass instructions on to each other.'

Wales scored first through wing Gwyn Rowlands, the England triallist of 1949 who had made his debut against the All Blacks. It was his only try for Wales, but not an entirely happy memory. 'I fell over in the corner, but I'm very dubious that I touched it down,' he has confessed. 'I told Ivor Jones, the touch-judge, that I wasn't sure I'd scored and he told me not to say anything. I've always felt rather guilty about it.' It was that sort of day. Wales forward Rees Stephens was denied a legitimate try and Woodward only deprived by having the ball kicked out of his hands. The powerful wing did score before half-time, using his weight to crash through Gerwyn Williams, who still winced at the memory half a century later. 'I knew my shoulder had gone as soon as it happened,' said the Welshman. The dislocated shoulder was to end Williams's career, but he returned to the field, having little option with Willis concussed and Stoker Williams also off for part of the match. Wales were down to thirteen men and in disarray, with Morgan playing at scrum-half – Rowlands recalled that 'the front row said he was putting the ball in on the wrong side'. John, described as 'submerged' by *The Times*, went to outside-half while Rowlands had spells at centre and full-back and was understandably hurt when criticised for poor positioning in these unfamiliar roles. Woodward crossed again, but five minutes from time Yarranton was penalised for barging 'right in front of the committee and selection box . . . it seemed a no-risk penalty as Rowlands (an RAF colleague) teed it up – out on the touch-line and at halfway,' said Yarranton. 'To my horror his kick sailed between the posts. I could feel hostility everywhere and resigned myself to becoming a one-cap wonder.'

Rowlands had kicked the equalising penalty for Wales against New Zealand, then converted Ken Jones's winning try. This time the late winner was England's. Yarranton recalled England loose-forward John Kendall-Carpenter driving to within five yards of the Wales line. 'Four of us piled into the loose scrum. I heeled the ball back.' Winn remembers Kendall-Carpenter being tackled. 'He just threw the ball at me. I was lucky. I picked it up on the half-volley. There were only ten or fifteen yards to go . . . Anyone to beat? Oh yes, there were two or three.' Winn forced his way over for the decisive try. Yarranton took comfort in the justified belief that, penalty or not, he would not be dropped after a victory, while Rimmer – omitted in 1953 – won at last after four consecutive defeats by Wales. Gwilliam, Roy John, Gerwyn Williams and Dai Davies did not play for Wales again. Again they lost to no other country. This time England won the Triple Crown but lost a Grand Slam and the outright title by losing to France, who claimed their first title in a three-way tie with their victims and Wales.

Two English wins were followed by two Welsh ones. If Gwyn Rowlands took little pleasure from his try in 1954, his Cardiff club-mate Bleddyn Williams derived still less from Wales's Arms Park victory a year later. 'We shouldn't have played,' he says, 'and probably would not have done if it had not already been postponed for a week because of snow.' It was no way to finish his international career – he was dropped, and retired at the end of the season – or for Ken Jones to overhaul Dicky Owen's Welsh record of 35 caps. Snow was followed by rain, creating waterlogged conditions that *The Times* reported 'kept everyone on tenterhooks up to midday'. Thirty penalties were awarded in the match, but only two in a kickable position. Both fell to Wales in the first half-hour, during which England failed to reach their twenty-five. Ten minutes into his debut, London Welsh full-back Arthur Edwards landed the first, recorded by *Playfair* as 'the high price paid by England for falling offside in trying to start a relieving rush in front of their own posts'. Edwards, like Terry Davies a native of Bynea, was an Army education officer who rose to the rank of colonel before becoming the principal of South London College of Further Education. They were his only points for Wales but, with the venerable Hall, playing his penultimate match for England, denied even a single shot at goal, were sufficient for Wales's 3-0 victory. Wales lost at Murrayfield – their first championship defeat except against England, and Scotland's first win against anyone, in four seasons – but still shared the title with France. Rees Stephens, the Wales captain, earned the label *ce vieux renard*, the old fox, from a disappointed but admiring home press as defeat by Wales at

Stade Colombes denied France a first Grand Slam. England finished fourth, their one poor season in this period.

Twelve months on, there was little talk of the Twickenham jinx. Wales won for the third time in four visits to London, 8-3. England picked nine new caps then added a tenth, Coventry wing Peter Jackson, apparently against the wishes of chairman of selectors Carson Catcheside who, after a bibulous eve-of-match, encountered Jackson in the gents and told him: 'Ah yes, the right wing. You should never have been selected.' Tries for Pontypridd lock Russell Robins, following a break by Clem Thomas, and wing Lynn 'Cowboy' Davies were decisive. For *The Times,* the Davies try exemplified the 'almost tragic prominence' of England outside-half Mike Smith, whose drop-kick attempt was charged down by Wales flanker Brian Sparks. When England full-back Fenwick Allison failed to gather, Malcolm Thomas picked up and fed Davies – who, with Morgan, was one of two Cardiff men in an otherwise all-Newport back division – and he ran in from halfway, Smith just failing to catch him.

There were, though, strong hints of an English revival. Wales captain Cliff Morgan recalled a fortunate win. 'For the most part we were outplayed,' he admitted. 'England, particularly at forward, were the better side. My memory is of playing most of the match going backward and of being taken through the rugby curriculum by this "upstart" from Oxford University, Peter Robbins. The ten-yard line had not yet been invented and at the line-out he was, I swear, no more than six or seven yards away from me.' Those line-outs were dominated by England's new pairing of David Marques, who had an Australian father and a Welsh mother, and John Currie but, as Jeeps recalls, they were not yet the finished operators they became. 'There was too much knock-back ball,' complains the scrum-half. England still enjoyed more possession and pressed for most of the thirty minutes between Robbins's try and half-time. Jackson proved Catcheside resoundingly wrong with several darting runs but was denied a try that he swore for the rest of his life was legitimate. 'I was penalised for not playing the ball with the foot after the tackle as the law required in those days. The way I saw it, I was not tackled. I tripped over someone's hand, but I was not held.'

Redemption was forthcoming in 1957 at Cardiff as England took precise revenge for Wales's 3-0 win two years earlier. Only Smith of the previous season's debutants was missing, his place going to Harlequin Ricky

Bartlett, fondly remembered by Jeeps as sharing Morgan's taste for passes in front of him, and a fine kicker who made particularly effective use of the cross-kick. Arthur Edwards's role as match-winner with a single penalty went to Coventry full-back Allison, that of fall guy to Neath wing Keith Maddocks. He was winning his only cap eight years after his first trial, but was ruled offside while a line-out took place on the far side. It was, wrote Roy McKelvie in the *Daily Mail*, 'the traditional dogfight, dominated by spoiling'. None spoilt more vigorously than Robbins, recalled by Morgan as 'born offside' and by Jeeps as a 'sharp, astute, bloody good player'. Together with Lancastrians Reg Higgins and Alan Ashcroft, he formed a formidable back row. Ashcroft said: 'We thought about the game a lot, worked out our individual roles, tightened everything up as a unit and the trick was to get Peter to fly out, harass the opposition half-backs and drive them outside to Reg Higgins and myself. That game in Cardiff was perhaps the best we ever had . . . we didn't let Cliff get across the advantage line in the entire match.' They also had some Welsh assistance. When Higgins, just back from a year out with a smashed knee, dislocated his elbow in the first minute, Wales physiotherapist Gerry Lewis had him back in action within two minutes.

Even though Welsh prop Courtenay Meredith was reported to have had opposite number George Hastings 'bucking like a steer', and the Wales forwards harassing Jeeps were 'not averse to bouncing this fiery little man when he did not possess the ball', England won what *The Times* said was 'a not very edifying Rugby football match'. It was a first step towards their only Grand Slam between 1928 and 1980. Evans, the captain, remembered his team as having 'no big-heads in the backs . . . they all knew their jobs'. It was also broadly representative of the strength of English rugby, with three players coming from Northampton, two from Coventry and one from Gloucester (the mandatory Bristol full-back was forthcoming when Bob Challis replaced Allison after the Wales match). There were four northerners – of whom Higgins and Ashcroft came from league-playing families – three Oxbridge students, a Harlequin and a medical student (albeit an unusual one as Lewis Cannell had been an international since 1948). Their feat added to the game's vocabulary, *The Times* first referring to their 'Grand Slam'.

Evans was dropped by Lancashire but retained by England in 1958 and led his country to another title, although hopes of another Triple Crown or Grand Slam ended at the first step, a 3-3 draw with Wales at Twickenham. They crossed the Welsh line for the first time since 1954. Headingley wing Peter Thompson, who Jeeps thought of as 'a great big strong fellow, and a good footballer as well', completed a move initiated by the scrum-half's dummy and pass to the side-stepping Butterfield and continued by a 'perfectly timed' pass from the omnipresent Robbins. The try equalised a 45-metre penalty by Terry Davies, who in the second half struck 'a stupendous kick into the teeth of the wind and saw the ball veer into an upright in the last second of its flight'. A group of Welsh fans celebrated his feat by breaking into Twickenham overnight to saw off around three feet of the crossbar over which he kicked the first-half penalty. It was taken to a Cotswolds café, which, by extraordinary coincidence, Terry Davies happened to visit the next day. He signed the stolen artefact and, in his professional capacity as a timber merchant, offered to replace the crossbar.

Geoffrey Nicholson and John Morgan noted, in their fine combination of historical sketch and state-of-the-game snapshot *Report on Rugby*, two views of the match. 'Many Englishmen finding it dull, perhaps with reason, because their backs had not been given an opportunity to demonstrate the attractions of open rugby . . . most Welshmen were prepared to make a rare concession in favour of the defensive game.' It was not the only Welsh rarity. They played in trial jerseys, without the Prince of Wales feathers badge. It was the wrong kit but was discovered only when unpacked in the changing rooms, too late to change it. Wales escaped with a draw thanks to the superbly judged second-half kicking of Davies and Cliff Morgan who, *Playfair* reported, 'cleverly avoided as far as possible the open eastern side of the ground, now pumping the ball with unerring precision into the south-western corner'. England had, by contrast, 'kept on kicking into the teeth of the wind'. There was also, appropriately to this Welsh era, a fierce forward effort. Hooker Bryn Meredith and Neath prop Don Devereux played on with heads bandaged. Skipper Clem Thomas, whose public school education at Blundell's bequeathed a plummy accent, cherished the memory of being embraced at the end by demotic Pontypool prop Ray Prosser – who previously seemed wary of him – with the words: 'I thought you'se was one of them blew bastards, but I'se just discovered you'se one of us.' Had Davies's second-half kick gone between rather than into the posts, Thomas might later in the season have been acclaimed for leading Wales to a championship and Triple Crown. Instead they were second, an appropriate end to this time of near-misses, while England retained their title. The third outright one-two finish for England and Wales in seven seasons (under modern rules, with points difference deciding ties, it would have been the sixth) would be the last for thirty-six years.

CHAPTER NINE
WRESTLING IN THE MUD 1959–68

Something is happening, but you don't know what it is, do you
Mr Jones?

Bob Dylan, 1965

Free Wales! . . . with every four gallons.

Graffiti in petrol station toilet, Brecon, late 1960s

In 1959, France at last won the championship outright. Wales could have
thwarted them at Stade Colombes in Paris, but went down 11-3. No matter
that the breakthrough came in a year of grimly defensive rugby, scores
falling below ten points per match for the first time since the late 1930s.
Nothing in the Five Nations Championship would ever be quite the same
again. Following France's remarkable win in South Africa the previous
summer, it was, as hooker turned *Observer* journalist Bert Toft observed, 'like
finding the All Blacks or the Springboks on your doorstep'. In the fifty
seasons since then, France's overall playing record has been substantially
better than the other four countries'. They have been outright champions
sixteen times, shared the title another six and been out of the top two – if
you count shared second places – only thirteen times.

Despite the progress of France, Wales v England has continued to
matter. As a report of their 0-0 draw at Twickenham in 1962 observed:
'Somehow England are *the* enemy of Wales at this game, and England in
their turn are inclined to mention Wales with bated breath.' Its
importance, though, has rested more on innate cultural and social
rivalry and desire to outdo – and not to be outdone by – the old enemy,
than the belief that it will decide the championship. When Wales and
England took the top two places, albeit four points apart, in 2008 it was
only the second time that had happened in half a century. Welsh players

of the 1970s and Englishmen two decades later readily admitted that France were now the opponents who really mattered.

The duopoly gave way to comparative Welsh ascendancy. Between 1959 and 1968 Wales beat England five times and England won twice – and not at all after 1963 – with three draws. The draws typified a low-scoring era. England have drawn 48 matches in 137 years; a quarter of these, twelve, came in ten championship seasons between 1959 and 1968. Yet this period lives more vividly in English memory than in Welsh. In the topography of Welsh collective recall it is a low-lying region concealed between the giant figures of Bleddyn and Cliff and the Himalayan heights of the 1970s. For England, for whom much worse was to come in the 1970s, it looked like the last of the good times. Their two victories were particularly memorable – 1960 for the sheer brilliance of the play while 1963's long-term currency rested firmly on it being the last time England beat Wales anywhere until 1974 and in Cardiff until 1991. None of the 117 meetings has been replayed more often in match programmes. Losing captain Clive Rowlands was too patriotic a Welshman to have been pleased when England finally broke their twenty-eight-year duck at Cardiff, but nevertheless welcomed the cessation of interview requests. 'Every two years I was asked what it was like to captain a Wales team that lost at home to England,' he said. 'Mind you, I always pointed out that I'd started the winning sequence in 1965!'

After the comparative stability of the late 1950s, English selection rediscovered old vices. Six new caps were dispatched to Cardiff in 1959, with Jeeps and Robbins being discarded. A year later Jackson, whose performances on the 1959 Lions tour stamped him as the best English wing since Lowe, was left out. Steele-Bodger, a selector since he was twenty-eight, explained: 'We may not always have been right, but things were done for a reason. The player who replaced Robbins [A.J. Herbert of Wasps] was much quicker and a hell of a tackler. When we left out Jackson we had such a fast back line we did not feel that he could get to it.' It was, he points out, extremely difficult to select the right England team. 'We had so many players compared to the other countries, and they were spread around a lot of clubs. County football was supposed to provide the next step up towards international level, but really did not.'

Without a strong club structure, the annual trials became disproportionately important. As Jeeps says: 'You had to start again each year and fight your way back into the England team.' Gloucester lock Peter Ford, a reserve against France in 1953, did not hear from England for another decade, then played the entire championship season in 1964. 'I was very surprised. I was over the top really,' he says. 'But it was nice to get the chance and I'd been around for a while and played against Welsh clubs, so I knew most of the tricks.' In retrospect he reckons there was a hint of a comeback when he was chosen for the Barbarians in 1963. 'It went well and Brigadier Glyn Hughes, who ran the Baa-Baas, asked me: "Where have you been all these years?" I looked about fifty and I'd played 500 games for Gloucester.' Don Rutherford, capped while playing for Percy Park in Northumberland in 1960, says: 'We didn't play Gloucester, Coventry or the London clubs. The County Championship was regionalised and we couldn't beat Yorkshire and Lancashire, so the only time you played against top English players was in trials, where you didn't know anybody. When Richard Sharp was called up I'd never heard of him and never seen him. You'd meet up, shake hands and introduce yourselves.'

Once the selectors had settled on their team for the opener against Wales, they usually gave players a reasonably extended chance. If one oft-quoted English archetype is the rugby player with one cap against Wales, there are many more like Ford who played one complete season, four matches, no more and no less. Twenty-one players appeared in 1959, only seventeen in 1960. England were hampered not only by structural difficulties and the International Rugby Board rules, which prevented teams from assembling more than forty-eight hours before a match. Asked to lead England in the final trial in 1960, Jeeps took the post seriously. 'Since we were asked to assemble at Richmond the day before, I wrote to every member of that England team to come to a training session, which I took myself,' Jeeps said. 'Thirteen of them were picked, but I got a fearful bollocking.' This will not have surprised his erstwhile Northampton team-mate Don White, who had been told 'that is a professional approach' when he gave a trial team tactical directions. The selectors were not, though, totally inflexible. They did appoint Jeeps captain in 1960 and acceded to his urgent demand, when a prop was ruled out before the Wales match, that they recall Northampton veteran Ron Jacobs. 'He was still the best around,' says Jeeps, 'and they got another three or four seasons out of him, ending up as captain.'

Jeeps recalls preparation as being wholly amateurish. 'You'd meet up on the Friday and if it was freezing, as it often was, you'd go for a walk. If the ground was fit you'd go to Rosslyn Park for a little practice and the selectors, who were all a good ten years older, were the opposing pack.' Rutherford, a full-back, remembers being told by chairman of selectors Carson Catcheside: 'You must catch the ball, never let the ball bounce, put it back into touch.' As captain, Jeeps did not take Catcheside entirely seriously, recalling pre-match team-talks consisting of essentials such as: 'OK, you're playing Wales today. It is always a hard game. Good luck lads, go out and get on with it.' There was also the time when a roaring drunk chair of selectors climbed on to a Paris nightclub stage with dancing girls. At least, Catcheside's advice to Rutherford was based on having played full-back for England, albeit half a lifetime previously. Ford later saw Tom Berry, who had been capped three times as a flanker, telling England's scrum-half how to put the ball into a scrum.

There was little improvement in England's preparation across the decade. Loughborough-educated Colin McFadyean, an England player from 1966 to 1968, told a seminar at Twickenham in 2008 that his club Moseley were more organised than England. 'There was more preparation and discussion about tactics,' he said. 'Practice used to include set-pieces, which was not the case with England.' England's preparation was confined to a run-out on the Friday led by Jeff Butterfield and 'limited to moves like scissors and dummy scissors and line-out practice. As the squad changed frequently, it was like meeting strangers every week.'

This mattered more by the late 1960s because Wales had moved on. They had experienced some of the same problems. J.B.G. Thomas, usually a friend of officialdom, complained in 1961 that 'the Welsh selectors are still picking teams as they did thirty years ago', and pointed to 'the lack of a tactical policy in the selectorial approach'. Clem Thomas found that he had no support as captain in 1958 and 1959. 'You were in entire charge of the team,' Thomas said, 'you decided all the tactics and it was usually too big a task to mould a side into single-minded thought and cohesion.'

At least Wales's players usually knew each other and, as the decade advanced, benefited for the first time from organised coaching – the nearest that rugby got to the 'white heat of the scientific and technological revolution' proclaimed by Harold Wilson in 1964. By the time Wilson became Prime Minister in October that year, Cliff Jones was leading a coaching working party. This followed a shattering 24-3 defeat on the summer tour of South Africa. Captain Clive Rowlands remembers the Springboks piling on scores in the final minutes as Welsh players became so dehydrated in the heat that their shorts were turned pink by sweat rolling down their shirts, but points out that this showed how little was understood about physical preparation. In 1967, Ray Williams became national coaching organiser, a decision described by Thomas as 'the best appointment made by the WRU in my lifetime' and regular squad sessions started under David Nash, Wales's first coach. The new structures owed much to English methods. Williams was Loughborough-trained, played for Northampton and East Midlands and worked for the Central Council of Physical Recreation. He and his team adopted coaching manuals first devised for the RFU.

This technical awareness ran in parallel with the development of a more conscious Welsh identity. Symbolic advances like the formal recognition of the Red Dragon as the national flag in 1960 and the appointment of the first Secretary of State for Wales, Llanelli veteran Jim Griffiths in 1964, came at a time of rising attendances at the National Eisteddfod, the Welsh Language Society campaign of sit-ins and road sign painting from 1963 and Plaid Cymru's first Parliamentary by-election victory, at Carmarthen in 1966. Appropriately enough, Wales wing Dewi Bebb was the son of Ambrose Bebb, who was a founder of Plaid Cymru. The best North Walian player since Wooller, Bebb erupted into top-flight rugby in 1959 in a similarly spectacular manner. 'When I came out of the Royal Marines, Swansea were short of a left wing and later that season as the Welsh trials progressed it was obvious that Wales also had need of a left wing,' he said. His debut was his sixth senior match in Wales. True to his nationalist roots, his best games were against England, scoring six tries in eight matches. His last was in 1967, the year when the Welsh Language Act secured a significant nationalist objective.

Declining religious influence in Wales was shown in 1961 when ten districts out of seventeen voted to end compulsory Sunday pub closing, but choral traditions still echoed from the terraces at the Arms Park and Twickenham. In 1959, as Wales attacked in the final minutes of a narrow victory, *The Times* reported '60,000 voices, in spontaneous harmony and uninterruptedly, without punctuation even by applause, the matchless strains of 'Land of My Fathers' swelling in crescendo each minute. It was a rare, instructive and unforgettable expression of relief and gratitude.' Vivian Jenkins, whose memories went back to the Twenties, said it was the 'first time I have known the closing stages of a match set to music'. Ray French, later best known as the BBC's rugby league commentator, was an England debutant at Cardiff in 1961. He immediately recognised something more akin to the rugby league of his native St Helens. 'It brought an instant recall of the scarves, flags and bunting, the silver hip flasks, the miners clutching their sons and the extra payment for transfer to the "posh paddock". Amid the cheers, boos, jeers and singing, I thought to myself "this is rugby league under rugby union rules". Twickenham, by contrast, had 'a rather sedate and "olde worlde" feel', car park luncheon parties providing an air of the grouse moors. England fans were, though, becoming more vocal. Political journalist Alan Watkins, a rare observer with anything to say about English followers, thinks that they started to shout for England in about 1967 – which suggests rugby support was a by-product of the football World Cup victory a year earlier, which had been accompanied by uninhibitedly vocal support.

Other social trends left a more limited impact. Most rugby officials probably thought that counter-culture was something to do with shops, but England's selectors picked Harlequins scrum-half Jeremy Spencer in 1966. The match-day programme said that Spencer 'spends evenings weaving fashion fabrics on a handloom . . . lives in a converted air-raid shelter and says this accommodation (is a) big improvement on the engine shed and double-decker bus'. Spencer recalled later that it was not only his long hair, earrings and a 'Trotsky moustache' that differentiated him, saying of team-mates: 'I could pee further than most of them could pass.' He lasted one match but fellow debutant David Powell, a Northampton prop who 'keeps fit by humping hundredweight sacks of corn across ploughed fields', proved more durable. A degree of social change was evident, though, in England teams of the 1960s. They had more grammar than public school products (thirty-five per cent to twenty-six) for the first time. Despite this, Ray French still felt inhibited about declaring his true hobbies as 'snooker and rugby league' when quizzed for a programme profile. In spite of doing neither, he claimed 'squash and skiing' in an effort to seem more in line with his team-mates. Catcheside, when collecting the answers, asked where he skied. French answered 'the Bergi', and was relieved that no further information was sought. The Bergi was, in fact, a St Helens landmark, a vast spoil-heap created by glassmakers Pilkington. Wales fielded four striking steelworkers in 1964, but more collective militancy was present four years later when players threatened a strike in order to get travelling reserve Phil Bennett a full ticket allocation.

The rugby of the 1960s echoed its politics, being less radical than popular memory suggests. It was more entertaining than the hand-to-hand battles of the previous decade, particularly once midfields were decongested when the offside law was changed in 1964. Touch-kicking, though, remained unlimited until 1968, when kicking directly into touch on the full from outside your twenty-five was outlawed, and the 'cricket catch' knock-on rule was not introduced until 1972. Clive Rowlands, the Wales scrum-half and captain from 1963 to 1965, remembers how he took full advantage of the old kicking-to-touch law. 'If it wasn't good ball you would put it away.' He argues that his own preparedness to do precisely that – most famously at Murrayfield in 1963 in a match of 111 line-outs – has been exaggerated and cites film of the final ten minutes of that match in which he kicks very little. Part of a remarkable Swansea Valley scrum-half tradition that extends through Owen and Tanner to Gareth Edwards and Robert Jones, Rowlands was perfectly in tune with his times – a sharp-witted pragmatist who led Wales on all fourteen occasions he was capped. 'I suppose I always was the bossy type,' he admitted. His incantations to his forwards reminded Dai Smith and Gareth Williams of 'a Welsh Sergeant Bilko' while his doggedness led novelist Alun Richards to see him as 'a reflection of ourselves, and our immediate past . . . a workman whose confidence, aggression and guile raised him above the level of his fellows.' Richards praised him as 'a virtuoso bad-weather player', an invaluable quality in an era whose signature tune was nothing by Bob Dylan or Jimi Hendrix but Flanders and Swann's 'Mud, mud, glorious mud'. Cardiff produced rugby swamps in 1959 and 1965 and, by way of variation, a polar icefield in 1963. When the fixture was moved to April in 1967 to accommodate that season's Australian tourists, the remarkable attacking brilliance shown that day made Wales's case for fixture rotation better than any verbal advocacy. Twickenham, not to be outdone, offered swirling winds in 1962 and sub-zero temperatures four years later.

The stars of the early Sixties were Bebb and England's Richard Sharp. Wales did not exceed six points in eight matches from 1957 and 1964, scoring six tries in all – five by Bebb. England were only a little more effective with eight tries but reached double figures points-wise in 1960 and 1963, both matches, for different reasons, associated with Sharp. Bebb was the defining figure in 1959, 1961 and 1964. Bebb was a footballer until his late teens. Even so he and Rowlands had already become friends, despite coming from opposite ends of Wales, after meeting at festivals run by the Welsh-language youth movement Urdd Gobaith Cymru. 'We met when we were thirteen, were at college at the same time, played for Wales together and were even dropped together!' says Rowlands. It was, he remembers, typical that Bebb, 'the nicest of all players, totally unassuming', presented him with the England jersey he swapped with Peter Jackson in 1963, knowing that Rowlands, wanting his own Wales shirt from his debut, would not have swapped with his opposite number.

Don Rutherford remembers Bebb as being 'like Gerald Davies. He never swerved a huge distance, but he could beat you through the eye of a needle, never losing pace as he did so.' Rowlands adds that 'he had a beautiful change of pace and outside swerve, could see a chance and take it, and would chase every ball'. The first Trinity College, Carmarthen student capped since Ronnie Boon, Bebb also emulated, on his 1959 debut at the Arms Park, Boon's habit of match-winning scores against England in conditions spectacularly soggy even by Cardiff's standards. John Morgan and Geoffrey Nicholson recounted 'a man whose experience was wide . . . said that more than anything else for him the match had freshened up an old memory of the wrestling in the mud at a Hamburg night club'.

Wales prospered in these conditions. The pack 'rushed and wheeled like characters out of the 1890s', Rhys Williams was 'a terrible sight to see' and Clem Thomas was 'leading them in rushes or frequent wheels or in tackling the English backs with great enthusiasm. Clem Thomas is a great believer in allowing the other side to have the ball on a wet day: no day was wetter than this and no side has been allowed to have more of the ball than England were.' *The Times* noted that Terry Davies 'handled a loathsome ball like a cricketer and kicked with the crispness of a sweetly timed drive'. Jeeps would have loved it. Unfortunately for him, England had preferred Stephen Smith, an Indian-born Cambridge scrum-half remembered by his half-back partner Bev Risman as 'the first of the great long passers', who would later return to India as an educational missionary.

Bebb's score showed his opportunistic qualities. Morgan and Nicholson reported: 'Not many tries have been scored at internationals ... from the device of a wing-threequarter throwing the ball to the front of a line-out, taking it back and running over.' The only try, it was one of only two scored in twenty internationals by the opposite number to Peter Jackson, whose attacking genius obscured great competence in defence. While Bebb was the hero, an England debutant could feel unlucky. Risman, son of the rugby league great and wartime union cap Gus, had turned down a Wales trial two years earlier, citing his exclusively English union experience including two years playing for Lancashire. Like many sportsmen, he remembers his debut as 'a bit of a blur; it went very quickly', but he has crystal-clear recall of one early incident. 'I saw a chance, chipped into the gap behind a line-out and got there before anyone else. I'm convinced to this day that I scored, but about half a dozen bodies piled on top of me and the referee was unsighted, so could not give it.'

The Cardiff pitch was merely 'heavy' in 1961, according to *The Times*, although French remembers 'a good game in a monsoon'. Wales's 6-3 win owed much to Terry Davies, who was 'his usual cool dependable self at full-back', and lively Bridgend outside-half Ken Richards, who was 'always scheming and contriving'. Cardiff centre Cyril Davies sparkled briefly before suffering a career-ending injury that forced Wales to move flanker John Leleu into the backs. The seven remaining forwards inspired John Morgan to quote twelfth-century poet Peryf ap Cedifor: 'We were seven men, faultless, indispensable, in attack irresistible; seven men, unshakeable, who would get stuck-in until the last trump; seven men, like the heroes of the past, who would not let them pass.'

Bebb, though, was the executioner, scoring in each half after moves involving several handlers and deft switches of direction. French, replacing the unwell John Currie, had played for Leeds University only three days before. 'It was an important match for us,' he recalls, 'they'd said: "Come on Ray, we need you", and I was only twenty, when you don't think about getting injured.' The first St Helens player capped, he discovered the extent of club pride in his achievement shortly after playing against Wales when he was approached by a committee man. 'He kept on looking round to make sure nobody was listening and said: "Ray, we're very proud of you. To show that there's a free pint for you every Saturday – but don't let anybody know. Have one now – ordinary bitter, mind, not best. That's 1s 2d a pint."'

French did not ask if this professionalised him. He was destined to play league. 'In St Helens the only way to be respected as a rugby player, international or not, was to play league,' he said. He and Risman were league players by the end of the season. So, too, were opposite numbers Ken Richards and Danny Harris, although Welsh losses never again reached inter-war levels. French's departure occasioned controversy when Loughborough University withdrew its offer of a place.

Bebb's third tour de force was at Twickenham in 1964, when he scored both Welsh tries in a lively 6-6 draw. Rowlands says: 'We were two tries down before the anthems had finished.' Outside-half Phil Horrocks-Taylor, whose appearances in 1958 and 1964 bracketed the Risman and Sharp era, created scores for wing John Ranson and flanker David Perry. Bebb rescued Wales with a try in each half – the first from a lethal outside break, the second well remembered by his outside-half, David Watkins. 'As the England players stood momentarily to watch my [drop-goal] shot just past the post,' he recalled, 'Bebb sprinted through to pounce on the ball before it could bounce across the touch-in-goal line.' Rowlands tells of how one score so excited Welsh touch-judge Mal James that 'he was waving his arm in the air and the ref might easily have assumed he was signalling that it wasn't a try'. As captain, Rowlands was criticised for giving a kickable last-minute penalty to full-back Grahame Hodgson, who had already missed several shots, rather than debutant Keith Bradshaw, a prolific scorer for Bridgend. 'A selector asked me afterwards why I didn't take it and I said: "If I'd known he was going to miss I would have done". You have to make a judgement – Keith didn't look keen, but Grahame did.' *The Times* reported that Hodgson 'shaped for the kick in deadly silence. Nine times out of ten it would have been a sitter for him.

But this time, poor fellow, with everything in the balance and no-side's approach measured almost in seconds, he missed with a horrible slice.' Welsh spirits were not completely deflated. Watkins, flanker John Mantle and lock Brian Thomas went dinner-jacketed from the banquet to the Strand Palace Hotel, which was packed with Welsh fans. They were mistaken for waiters and played up to the misapprehension, 'plying with trays between the Welsh fans and the bar, even picking up a few tips'.

Post-match toasts four years earlier had been devoted to Sharp, who made his debut after Risman was injured. Sharp was twenty-one, Indian-born, an Oxford undergraduate and former Royal Marines national serviceman. One telegram he read in the Twickenham changing rooms was from a services friend: 'Congratulations on your selection. PS Are they short?' while a Welsh friend wrote: 'Hope you play well for the losing side.' Sharp complied with one of those desires, but not the other. The running of this tall, elegant blond figure, 'in his white shirt positively albino-like', inspired a 14-6 victory. A Welsh debutant was centre Geoff Windsor Lewis, son of the 1920s outside-half, who grew up in Cambridge, played for England Schools and rejected an English trial two years earlier. He said: 'At practice on Friday the talk was "Stop Risman". Then Bev dropped out.'

Sharp was also helped by the wiles of Jeeps. As Risman recalls: 'Dickie was terrific to play outside. He never gave you the ball unless you had the chance to do something. If there was nothing on he'd take any punishment himself.' Rowlands appreciated a fellow scrum-half of comparable craft and competitiveness. According to him, Jeeps was 'brilliant at using the gap between forwards and backs'. Those qualities were evident in the opening minutes. Peter Robbins had suggested to Jeeps that he make a couple of breaks to draw Welsh attention from Sharp. 'It wasn't what they were expecting and it worked very well,' said Jeeps. Welsh open-side Haydn Morgan, a red-haired former Paratrooper and British Lion, was both flu-ridden and unsure where to direct his formidable attentions. Lewis recalls Welsh defensive disarray. 'England got the ball and we were all supposed to go up hard, but Sharp went sailing through a huge gap and Roberts was in under the posts.' Debutant wing Jim Roberts, of Old Millhillians, 'who had his hair swept back as if permanently on the break' and was one of England's last old boys players, scored twice before half-time when England led 14-0. Sharp recalled that

Wales did not help themselves. '[They] made it easy for outside-halves in those days. They expected the wing-forward to tackle the opposing fly-half, their fly-half never came up in defence, and their centres were under the surprising illusion that they should tackle their own man and not the man with the ball who was running at them.'

England had no such problems. Full-back Don Rutherford, another debutant, says 'You can see from the back whether your team is well organised and if people are tackling. In 1960 the people in front of me were doing their jobs.'

The crowd noise was such that Jeeps and Sharp could not hear each other and resorted to 'hand signals, semaphore instead of morse' to communicate. An England victory that was appreciated even by Welsh observers – Clem Thomas called Sharp 'the most exciting thing seen in rugby for years' – led on to a Triple Crown. The championship was shared with France, the outright title and Grand Slam being lost by the width of a Stade Colombes goalpost from which Rutherford's conversion attempt rebounded. The memory still pains captain Jeeps.

By 1963 Sharp was captain, the immediate successor to Jeeps. Wales were led by Rowlands, who was both captain and debutant. England's seven new caps included the entire front and second rows, with Simon Clarke, of Cambridge, who was 'quite small and a typical English player – did everything correctly' according to Rowlands, inheriting Jeeps's shirt as scrum-half. Welsh newcomers included the darting David Watkins at outside-half, athletic Ebbw Vale prop Denzil Williams and Neath lock Brian Thomas. As Mike Burton pointed out, Thomas was that most dangerous of rugby beings, an intelligent hard man, with a Cambridge degree.

Cardiff in 1959 had reminded Morgan and Nicholson's acquaintance of mud-wrestling. Four years later, with the coldest winter since the 1740s capping England and Wales with snow for several weeks, *The Times* thought of polar bears. The *Guardian's* well-named David Frost reported on a match that was 'easy to remember, much harder to explain with the motley collection of farm implements, three tractors, harrows and other assorted paraphernalia – parked throughout the match between the West goal and the River Taff. Then, too there were high banks of straw encroaching to within a few yards of the goal-line.' 'We shouldn't have played, but I was glad we did,' says Rowlands. 'If it is your first cap and it gets called off you don't know what might happen – you might break a leg and never win a cap.'

While the RFU wrote to the WRU congratulating it on getting the match played, Welsh team preparations were ad hoc. Driven inside by the extreme cold, Rowlands and Watkins were forbidden to use a ball in the Newport gym and practised with a rolled-up tracksuit tied up with cord. Home-based players still travelled to the game on match days. Watkins, promised a lift from Blaina by flanker Dai Hayward, panicked when he was late and hitched a lift with travelling fans. He was deemed an impostor by an Arms Park security man and had to 'await the arrival of the better-known Alun Pask to bear out my story'. Wales issued players with woollen underwear. Rowlands thought the clicking sound of thirty pairs of boots on the frozen surface was 'like a herd of cattle' and recalls 'a disappointment verging on rage' when told that, because of the cold, the players would not run on until after the anthems. 'We couldn't hear them in the changing rooms and the anthem is a big moment for a player winning his first cap.'

It was not the last disappointment for Wales on an afternoon that another debutant, Roger Michaelson, said was 'so cold that even Clive Rowlands stopped talking'. Rowlands thought that 'we should really have won. Robert Morgan scored, but it was disallowed. Dewi Bebb had a clear run, but dropped the ball. We created enough chances to win.' Those not taking chances could scarcely be blamed. Watkins recalled Morgan dropping an early scoring pass. 'I could see the wide, raw frost weal that began at his temple and disappeared under his jersey. "It goes down to my hip," he continued, refraining from adding that his fingers were frost-bitten.' England, according to Rowlands, 'made two chances and took them both'.

The first would have been exceptional in any conditions; on an icefield, it was little short of miraculous. Wing Jim Roberts threw long at a line-out on the England twenty-five. Mike Weston collected the ball and passed to Malcolm Phillips, his partner in England's best centre pairing since Butterfield and Davies. Phillips took up the story: 'I scissored with my wing, the inimitable Peter Jackson, who drew the nearest Welsh defenders on to him like a magnet. Though normally he mesmerised the opposition before releasing the ball, on this occasion "Jacko" gave a surprisingly quick return pass which put me into an outflanking position on halfway. Into the freezing wind it was a long haul at the Welsh line at the river end of the ground, but fortunately for me the defence was suffering as well and I was able to round off a move in which the ball must have travelled some hundred yards.'

The second score, after half-time, owed more to the conditions. Sharp fly-hacked ahead, Phillips and Welsh full-back Hodgson both skidded past the ball and Coventry lock John Owen followed up for a debut try. Sharp converted both tries and added a drop-goal as England began their march towards another title. Wales finished bottom for the first time since 1949. Sharp so inspired a fan by the name of Bernard Cornwell that he borrowed the name, added an extra 'e', and gave it to the hero of his Napoleonic-era historical novels. Sharp did his best to win the 1962 match at Twickenham, which ended in the second scoreless draw in the history of the fixture. Sharp said it was 'one of those games which the players rather enjoyed . . . but it seems nobody else had'. One reporter, misattributing Alfred Tennyson's words to Francis Thompson, reckoned it 'faultily faultless, icily regular, splendidly null'. Amid eighty-eight line-outs, Sharp made four drop-goal attempts, one reported by the *Sunday Express* as having 'floated towards the post and then dipped and swirled around it on the wrong side like a swerving snooker ball'. Welsh full-back Kel Coslett had five penalty shots, taking up to seventy-five seconds while trying to gauge the wind. All were well struck. The last 'soared up into the air, only to be carried away from the posts by the currents of blustering wind which swept up one touchline and down another'. Coslett's kicking abilities were shown in rugby league, as he became St Helens' all-time leading scorer. Rutherford, similarly unlucky with his goal-kicking in 1966, says: 'There are days when it seems you can't miss, others when it doesn't matter what you do, it still won't go over.'

Playfair thought that Coslett had had some compensatory luck when he was not penalised in the final seconds for impeding Budge Rogers. The scrum-capped flanker, who Rutherford remembers 'could keep going all day, he'd just run and run' and would eventually chase down Wakefield's ancient England caps record – was pursuing a kick across the Welsh line.

The wind blew again at Cardiff as Wales began their winning run there in 1965. England's oddly assorted team included seven new caps, an entire Oxbridge-educated threequarter line and two players who might have thought their international careers were over. Rutherford, back after four years, was a familiar figure compared to scrum-half Johnny Williams, who had last played in 1956. Opposite number Rowlands says of Williams: 'He was a very good player, but not on a wet day.' In Rutherford's opinion: 'The team had changed almost completely from 1960 and wasn't nearly as good.'

Conditions described by *Playfair* as 'near farcical' provoked Wavell Wakefield, elevated to the House of Lords two years earlier, to write to *The Times* complaining that 'nine times out of ten in the last fifty years, because of adverse conditions, what ought to have been one of the highlights of the season has been markedly interfered with'. Noting the better conditions usually prevailing for the England v Scotland game in mid-March, Wakefield suggested reorganising the season to run from mid-September to May, with the Five Nations Championship taking place on five weekends in March and April.

As England had done two years earlier, Wales showed that rugby can be played in atrocious conditions, scoring three tries to nil to win 14-3. As Rutherford points out, that was 'quite a hammering in those days'. Rowlands says: 'It was a really good day for us, when everybody played well.' Bounding Newport wing Stuart Watkins scored twice, the first after Denzil Williams 'charged down the left touchline like a mad rhinoceros', and then Rowlands initiated a passing movement involving the entire Welsh threequarter line that he rates the best score he was ever involved in. The other try was Haydn Morgan's belated revenge for 1960, scored from a deft kick by his Abertillery colleague Alun Pask, a No. 8 of such extraordinary footballing skills that Rowlands chose him rather than a back as an emergency full-back in Dublin later that season. Rowlands says: 'He wasn't very happy but he did it superbly, as I knew he would. He was so good, he could have played anywhere. He was probably ahead of his time as a back-rower.' *Playfair* said the true hero was full-back Terry Price, grandson of 1922 hero Dai Hiddlestone, who showed composure and power rarely seen in nineteen-year-old debutants. Wales went on to win the Triple Crown and championship, a point ahead of France despite losing heavily in Paris. Rowlands was voted Welsh Sports Personality of the Year, and promptly dropped, ending his international career. England could finish only fourth.

*

The following year, 1966, offered an echo. Wales again won the title by one point from France, squeezing past them in the dying minutes of the final match when Stuart Watkins intercepted and ran seventy-five yards for a try. England finished bottom of the table, only a draw with Ireland averting their first whitewash. Both trends were set on the opening day at Twickenham. Gordon Ross complained in *Playfair* that 'there is too much hanging on the result of an England v Wales contest to expect much more than a forward battle'. Wales won 11-6 with Pask, Rowlands' successor as captain, 'going like the wind' on an afternoon of near-hurricanes, as he came up in support to fling himself over in the corner. England, said *Playfair,* had their 'poorest side in years' and promptly dropped three of their six debutants, although Bristol hooker John Pullin and Northampton No. 8 Bob Taylor both had international futures.

By 1967, though, it was Wales who looked like record-breaking failures. Because of Australia's visit, the fixture was moved from the beginning to the end of the championship, on 15 April, in Cardiff. Wales had lost all three matches up until then. Flanker John Taylor, the Watford-born and raised son of Welsh parents whose appreciation of his heritage was reinforced by uncles visiting the family en route to Twickenham in the 1950s, says: 'We were terribly aware that Wales had never lost all four matches. We couldn't even contemplate it – and England were a decent side.' They arrived in Cardiff pursuing a Triple Crown, fresh from a 27-14 beating of Scotland at Twickenham, their highest score between 1938 and 1980. England's team, again including a Bristol full-back, Roger Hosen, was drawn from the West and Midlands – three players coming from Bristol, Coventry and Moseley, two apiece from Bedford and Northampton, along with Birmingham-born Bradford scrum-half Roger Pickering and Stephen Richards, the Richmond hooker who was born in Cheshire.

As in 1965, Wales had a teenage debutant full-back. Then, Terry Price, who later played league for Bradford Northern, kicked for the Buffalo Bills and died young, knocked down when helping another motorist, had been a schoolboy international with rugby in his genes and senior experience at full-back. Two years later, it was Keith Jarrett's turn. Jarrett's school, Monmouth, where he was taught by Glyn John, the former league player capped in 1954, did not send players to national trials. His grandfather was a classical pianist of Polish-Jewish descent named Jarewski. His Johannesburg-born father Hal played cricket for Glamorgan in the 1930s and was groundsman at Rodney Parade, home of Newport rugby club. Jarrett made his debut for Abertillery as a schoolboy under the minimum age for senior rugby. He played under the 'nom de scrum' of Keith Jones, and was smuggled out of the ground to evade press attention after scoring a match-winning try. He had been persuaded to leave Abertillery for Newport by David Watkins. 'Dai came to see me at the school,' Jarrett recalls. 'He was such a star, it was like having George Best come to see you.' He was also, like Vivian Jenkins, a centre. He was spotted in December 1966, his last month at school, when chairman of selectors Cliff Jones watched his son captaining Llandovery against Monmouth. Jarrett says: 'I scored a couple of tries and kicked some goals. Afterwards the coach said: "There's somebody who wants to talk to you." It was Cliff Jones, who congratulated me and told me that I'd be playing in the final Welsh trial. I couldn't bring myself to tell the coach, I was wondering: "Did he really say that?".' Jarrett played in the trial and, although not chosen, kept himself in mind by scoring heavily for Newport.

Jarrett was called up, at full-back, after Price kicked badly against France. By way of preparation, the selectors asked for him to play full-back for Newport against Newbridge. Jarrett denies the story that Watkins told him at half-time: 'You will never make a full-back', but he was moved back to centre after the interval. On the following Tuesday, Cliff Jones asked him to come to Rodney Parade. 'He told me: "You can't learn how to play full-back in five minutes. What you must do on Saturday is watch David Watkins and make sure you're about thirty to forty yards behind him. That way you shouldn't have to do the most difficult thing for a full-back, turning to take a ball going behind you, but should always be running forward on to it.'

He still recalls leaving the Wales changing room. 'We walked up towards the Taff, around the West Stand, down the stairs and out through the tunnel. I was struck immediately by the noise. I couldn't believe that anybody could play rugby in that din. But when the game started it stopped, as though somebody had turned a switch off.' Both that, and the performance that followed, sound like the sportsman's state of grace known nowadays as 'being in the zone'. *Playfair* said it was 'the most remarkable rugby international of all time'. Jarrett eclipsed another Newport man, Jerry Shea, in providing the most astonishing one-man display in the history of the fixture. His nineteen points equalled the Welsh record set by Jack Bancroft in the 1910 thrashing of the French and Wales won by a barely credible 34-21.

This tour de force had two key moments. Jarrett may have looked 'full of confidence' to skipper Watkins, but did not feel it. He remembers: 'When I was given my first kick at goal I hit it so weakly that it barely reached the goal from thirty yards, hit the post and just crept over. The second one was not much better, but after that I started to feel more confident.' He remains puzzled that 'England did not test me more. You'd have thought that they'd have peppered me with high balls. But they did not do it more than two or three times.'

The truly defining moment came with about fifteen minutes to go. Enough had happened already to lift this out of the run of unremarkable recent matches. Wales led 19-15, the highest aggregate score since 1922, but Jarrett admits 'England's forwards were well on top and we were living on scraps.' Colin McFadyean kicked towards the Taff end. It was, he reasonably argued, 'not a bad percentage kick'. He also bemoaned that, after a career incorporating a Lions tour and the England captaincy, it is the only thing he is ever asked about. Jarrett describes what happened. 'I'd had a ball like this one before. It bounced straight up and hung there, and the difficulty was timing it right. I couldn't possibly have timed it better. I took the ball going flat out between halfway and our ten-yard line. Keith Savage, the England wing, was the only player near me and because of the angles we were at it was quite easy to brush him off – then I just kept going. The big problem was staying in play, as I was close to the line, but from halfway I didn't see anyone else.' The lack of English cover has always puzzled Jarrett, and he thinks that David Watkins' explanation made the most sense. Jarrett says 'England were going forward, McFadyean kicked and suddenly I was going very fast in the opposite direction. They had no time to react and adjust, and it doesn't take very long to run sixty yards.'

Jarrett's fame was sealed by that single run. 'The fuss went on for a long time because it was the last game of the season. So I couldn't [then] have a bad game and nobody else could do anything to deflect attention,' he said. Sadly for lovers of rugby legend, Jarrett denies the oft-repeated story that later that night a South Wales Transport inspector reprimanded a driver who had taken out a bus specially to take Jarrett home to Newport. 'Certainly not,' the inspector is supposed to have said. 'Take it back – and get a double decker. He might want to smoke.' Jarrett says: 'I've always wanted to know who started that story.' When Phil Atkinson, a teenage spectator at the 1967 game, met Jarrett in 2008 he congratulated him as being 'the only rugby player to have made a physical impact on me as a spectator. I was shouting so much that I dislocated my jaw. My sister couldn't understand why I'd suddenly gone quiet. My jaw clicks to this day. It is all your fault!'

England were similarly awestruck by Jarrett and conceded two more tries – both inevitably converted by the new full-back – in the next few minutes, the four-point gap becoming a yawning 34-15 before they rallied with a late try and penalty. So spectacular was Jarrett's performance that he obscured several other significant performances. Scrum-half Gareth Edwards made his home debut for Wales. Gerald Davies, then a centre, has no recollection of his own two tries – the first of nineteen he scored for Wales. His first was a passing of the torch between great attackers as Bebb, playing in his last match for Wales, cut inside to send Davies on a forty-yard run to the line while the second, created by John Taylor, celebrated a new generation. Bebb scored his sixth and last try against England in the final minutes before John Barton, of Coventry, completed the rare feat for a second-row forward of scoring twice in an international. England's full-back Roger Hosen then completed his single-season record of forty-six points. The match aggregate of fifty-five points was only two fewer than the total scored in eight meetings between 1955 and 1962.

It could, Jarrett recalls, 'only ever be a one-off'. And it was. He did not play full-back for Wales again, winning his subsequent nine caps in his preferred position of centre. Two seasons and a Lions tour of South Africa later he moved to rugby league with Barrow. He was about to join Wigan when a stroke ended his league career. Looking back aged sixty, he said: 'If I had the chance again I probably wouldn't go, but I certainly don't regret it. You've no way of knowing what is going to happen.' He remembers forgetting that he had a meeting with officials from Barrow, being summoned, hungover, from his bed by his parents and naming a sum he didn't think they could possibly offer – only to be told that they would happily pay up.

The 1967 match had significance far beyond being the single most crowded hour experienced by any England or Wales player in their countries' historic rivalry. The brilliance of some Welsh play was a harbinger of the next decade. Averting an unprecedented fourth defeat insured the still nascent international careers of players such as Gareth Edwards, Gerald Davies, John Taylor and Dai Morris against interruption or worse.

The extent to which fortunes can vary even over the space of a single year was evident in 1968. Jarrett, struggling with the boot, missed several penalties at Twickenham. England fielded eight debutants, among whom the one-eyed Bristolian Bill Redwood was rated by Gareth Edwards as the best of the many English scrum-halves he faced, and Harlequins full-back Bob Hiller proved the most enduring of the new boys. The night before, Hiller and another player went for a late-night drink and, to their horror, found the England selection committee in situ. 'They didn't seem to mind and rather generously bought us a couple of drinks before we all pushed off to bed at closing time,' said Hiller. Asked forty years later, he said: 'What do I remember about that match? I remember dropping the ball under the posts for one of Wales's tries!' It was the second time that a Jarrett miss was followed immediately by an England knock-on and a try. Hiller's error created an opportunity taken by a Welsh newcomer, Aberavon No. 8 Bobby Wanbon, whose pleasure was qualified by the comment from coach David Nash – also in his first championship match. 'You may have scored, but you shouldn't have been standing in that position at all,' said the coach. After trailing by eight points, Wales recovered to draw 11-11, Wanbon's try and Jarrett's conversion were capped by a drop-goal from outside-half Barry John. England were disappointed to have let slip a clear chance of victory. Much worse would happen to them in the decade to come.

CHAPTER TEN
THE DRAGON THAT SLEW ST GEORGE
1969–79

We can trace almost all the disasters of English history to the influence of Wales.

Evelyn Waugh, *Decline and Fall*, 1928

The English have a remarkable gift for turning wine into water.

Oscar Wilde

That Twickenham draw in 1968 was as good as it got for England – one year excepted – between 1964 and 1980. The subsequent decade saw Wales attain heights only previously reached in the first ten years of the twentieth century, while England plumbed depths associated with the same period. For Wales, it was a second golden age, but this time with colour pictures and a soundtrack provided by the television commentaries of Bill McLaren and the humour of Max Boyce. For England, analogies included the Great Depression and Black Death.

The pattern was similar to six decades earlier: hammerings in Wales alternated with much closer matches at Twickenham. In eight matches at Cardiff from 1965, Wales scored 186 points. England replied with 64, only once keeping the margin to single figures. Wales won five times at Twickenham between 1966 and 1978, but by a combined margin of thirty-one points. Only the 1976 win there was by double figures, and even that followed a spirited English opening.

While Jarrett's match was a foretaste, most date golden age number two as starting from 1969. Over eleven seasons, Wales won six outright titles, sharing another with France, six Triple Crowns and three Grand Slams, while most observers outside Ireland believe that not travelling to

Dublin because of security worries after Wales had won their first three matches in 1972 prevented another title, crown and slam.

Wales lost seven championship matches over those eleven seasons, and none in Cardiff. Over the same period, England won eleven matches, and never more than two in a season. There was, technically speaking, a shared championship in 1973 – every match was a home win and all five teams were deemed to have tied on four points. Under rules adopted in 1993, Wales would have been top on points difference and England bottom. If the truncation of the 1972 season thwarted Wales, it could not save England from losing all four matches for the first time – an unhappy precedent that was repeated in 1976. Their high point, in moral terms at least, was going to Dublin the year after Wales and Scotland had declined the trip. They lost but skipper John Pullin won immortality in the annals of English self-deprecation by starting his speech: 'We may not be much good, but at least we turn up.'

England had turned up in Cardiff with considerable hope for the last match of the 1969 championship, following victories over France and Scotland. A win would have given them a share of the title. There was, as Wales wing Maurice Richards confirms, a strange atmosphere at the game. The rebuilding of the Arms Park, transforming the old club ground into what would bcome the National Stadium, was under way, with the former's main stand demolished and the new North Stand just beginning to rise in its place. As Richards says: 'The ground was a building site. The changing rooms were temporary sheds on what is now the Cardiff club ground. It felt slightly odd and perhaps took something away, although you did not notice much once you started playing.'

There were fewer than 30,000 spectators there. England full-back Bob Hiller recalled that the temporary changing rooms had advantages over the usual quarters under the stand. 'It was just possible,' he said, 'by putting your fingers in your ears and covering your head with a towel, to pretend that there weren't 50,000 Welshmen outside singing and baying for blood.' Certainly, England did not seem intimidated, taking the lead with a penalty by Hiller, whose meticulous preparatory routine was once described with comparable care by journalist John Reason. 'Hiller kicks off a tee. This has to be kicked out of the ground with his heel and then constructed like a horseshoe. If the ground is fairly firm, obviously it takes him some time to disturb enough divots to build a tee which is high enough to meet his requirements. Having done that, he cleans the ball, just as a golfer would clean the ball and dry it most carefully before putting. Then he examines both ends of the ball and studies its four panels. He says that one end of the ball is always better than the other for kicking and that one panel is always truer than the others and therefore better for holding the ball on course through the air. Having selected the rounder of the two ends to kick and which panel to place uppermost, Hiller settles the ball into the tee with as much care as a hen thrush placing an egg in a nest. He clears his nasal passages by spitting a couple of times, too. Then he stands up, with the toe of his right boot behind the ball, and walks back six paces, shaking his right leg to loosen the muscles as he goes. He makes the minimal adjustment he feels necessary to his position to put him on exactly the line he wants to run up to the ball and cleans the toe and side of his kicking boot on his left sock. If it is very muddy, he also cleans his studs. That done, he squares his shoulders and takes three deep breaths. It is at this time that he builds up his concentration and it is at this time that the unknowing louts in the crowd usually give him the worst of their ribaldry. Once Hiller is ready to kick, he moves into the ball slowly and hits it with a sharp stabbing action. He does not use a big hip swing and a big follow through. In his judgement, this makes for inaccuracy. His results seem to prove his point.'

Hiller's penalty was neutralised by a try from Richards, who remembers: 'An England attack broke down. Stuart Watkins broke away and got to within five or ten yards of the English line. Barry John followed up and I followed him. I had been slightly caught behind our attack but when I got there all I had to do was take Barry's pass and go over.' Nobody had scored a hat-trick in the fixture since Jehoida Hodges in 1903. Now Richards, of whom Gareth Edwards, a Cardiff and Wales team-mate, wrote: 'When he wanted to play, nobody could stop him', went one better, matching Willie Llewellyn's four tries seventy years earlier. Wales open-side John Taylor says: 'It was the most incredible display of running wing play. I was outside him for two or three of those scores, thinking like a greedy loose forward: "I'm going to fill my boots here", but he never needed me.'

Richards reckons he touched the ball 'four times that day, five at the most' and remembers his scores as coming from 'great team play' by 'players who could do something exceptional and were always alive to every possibility'. His three second-half tries came in a late fifteen-minute deluge after a typical run by Barry John, whose 'ethereal quality' was admired by the *Observer*, and accurate kicking from Jarrett had taken Wales into a 14-3 lead. 'One score came from following John Williams,' Richards says. 'Trying to stop him was like stopping a tank. He made a break from halfway and got to within a couple of yards. I was backing up and over I went. John Dawes was a wonderful centre to play outside – he always knew exactly what he had to do to put you into space. We were about ten to fifteen yards out and I was accelerating on his outside. John timed and placed his pass perfectly so I was able to run past Ken Plummer and score. The last one was a set move we had rehearsed. A line-out was thrown long and I came in between the centres. If it worked you had only the full-back and anybody covering to get past and it was my day.' Wales clinched title, Triple Crown and their first Grand Slam since 1969 by the resounding score of 30-9.

Like Llewellyn, Richards came from the Rhondda Valley. The two were later introduced. Richards found Llewellyn, in his nineties and the last survivor of the first golden age, 'still pretty lucid', although he remembers nothing of their conversation. His celebrations were low-key – 'I never developed a taste for beer or anything like that' – and it proved to be his only appearance against England. Following Wales's miserable summer tour of New Zealand, where acerbic local critic Terry McLean thought Richards 'pretty well the complete wing-threequarter', he joined Salford, and like many a Welshman before him, made a permanent home in the North of England – becoming Salford's all-time top try-scorer and living to this day in the Manchester area.

If the star of 1969 was of the shooting variety, other elements in the Welsh victory had more lasting significance. Not least was the construction work. It was part of the process that transformed the Arms Park into the National Stadium – the programme contained the fund-raising scheme that made the phrase 'debenture holder' a term of respect in 1970s Wales – and created a separate home for the Cardiff club on the former cricket ground next door, with Glamorgan's cricketers decamping to Sophia Gardens. There was one more epic mudbath against South Africa in late

1969, but the easing of the pressure on the playing surface along with the rotation of fixtures from 1974 ensured that foul conditions became occasional ill-fortune rather than routine.

Wales lacked two first-choice players – lock Brian Price and Gerald Davies. That their replacements, Delme Thomas and John Dawes, fitted so seamlessly into the team was, reckoned Geoffrey Nicholson, a tribute not merely to their individual quality as players but to the effectiveness of the squad training sessions permitted by International Rugby Board regulations from 1968. 'They had remained in training with the squad and so fitted into the team and its strategy at once,' said Nicholson. 'Each man might have his unique value, but nowadays nobody was irreplaceable.' John Taylor has recalled 'that dreadful feeling on a Sunday morning after a heavy game and a heavy night when they realised they had to report by 10 a.m. or risk the wrath of the selectors. For London Welsh players it was particularly traumatic . . . the 5.30 reveille at John Dawes's house in London [he was the only one with a car] was almost enough to persuade some of us to argue against the squad system in principle. Nobody did, we were all far too worried about keeping our places.'

Those training sessions were run by Clive Rowlands, who took over as national coach when David Nash resigned the post after a single season. Rowlands was thirty and had retired as a player only at the end of the previous season, but rapidly established both authority and a modus operandi based, in Taylor's words, on 'a mixture of jokes, impassioned pleas and a fair amount of bullying'. Gareth Edwards recalled his ability to 'convey his message to individuals who had previously contributed on different wavelengths', while Clem Thomas wrote that 'aside from being a master of emotive appeal, Clive was also the shrewdest judge of a player'. That talent for pre-match rhetoric, invoking 'calon' (heart) in team talks that, as Taylor recalled, 'invariably left him soaked in sweat', was such that England prop Mike Burton still recalls a talk from half a lifetime ago before an England and Wales v Ireland and Scotland match. 'It was done beautifully,' said Burton.

Rowlands did not find the change in role difficult. 'As captain of Wales I had been in effect the coach,' he says. He likens his role to that of the mother of a Welsh family. 'In Wales, the mother is the boss. If any of the children does well, the world knows very quickly. If they do something wrong, the mother knows very quickly, keeps it within four walls and makes sure it is sorted out.' He was undoubtedly fortunate in the remarkable quality of his players, but operated in a manner that made the most of his luck. 'I let them play. I'd say to Gareth Edwards: "If it is bad ball put it away, don't pass the buck on, while if it is good, use it – but you decide how good it is."' Edwards himself wrote of Rowlands: 'He saw how we had so many possible points of attack that he tried to reduce the game to simple concentration on the basics. He may not have been the greatest coach in the world, but he cared very much for the family and its motivation.'

Wales's growing strength at this time is underlined by the quality of the second-choices who played in 1969. Llanelli lock Delme Thomas was, according to Richards: 'Someone who could play anywhere in the pack but more than anything a great line-out player – not through lifting like nowadays, but by his own unassisted ability to jump and win possession.' Dawes's fame is so fixed by his leadership of the successful 1971 Lions in New Zealand that it is easy to forget that, although the central figure in London Welsh's brilliance, he came late to international captaincy and spent much of his career as an under-appreciated centre. Rowlands, though, was never among those who underestimated him. 'Even in 1965, when he first came into the team, he had the gift of making the right decision at the right time,' he said. 'He was a perfect passer of the ball, defensively brilliant and hugely knowledgeable.'

The 1969 match also saw the first appearance of two men who added a significant dimension to Wales and changed the way their positions were played – full-back John Williams, not yet known by his initials of J.P.R., and No. 8 Mervyn Davies. Both played at London Welsh and were part of a voluntary diaspora, in which teachers like Davies, Taylor and Dawes were prominent. The exiles' club made full advantage of natural talent, the progressive liberation provided by law changes and the more relaxed atmosphere of London rugby to produce play of often dazzling virtuosity. Davies, who was instantly recognisable with his moustache and headband, rose with Bebb-like rapidity from London Welsh seconds to the national team, his talents recalled with gratitude by Taylor, his back-row colleague. Taylor, whose early clean-shaven look gave way to the abundant facial hair that earned him the nickname 'Basil Brush', possessed sufficient moral courage to risk his international career by declining to play against South Africa as a protest against apartheid.

Rugby-wise, Edwards recalled that he was 'first to the loose ball and always setting up the next move and thinking about the one after that', while Wales's other flanker, Dai Morris, had qualities associated more recently with England's World Cup-winning blind-side Richard Hill. Mike Burton wrote of Morris that 'spectators and journalists thought he was a good player, but other players thought he was bloody brilliant'. Taylor remembers him as 'dogged, never stopping and incredibly strong for his size'.

Morris and Taylor's speed, intelligence and footballing skills made the Welsh back row a genuine attacking weapon. Neither, though, was physically imposing. Taylor happily acknowledges that 'Merv was the catalyst. He was the only reason Wales were able to play both of us. He was such an extraordinary ball-winner in every phase – such an athletic jumper that he won quite a few middle-of-the-line balls by leaning forward from the back and picking them off.' Previous No. 8s, Gerald Davies pointed out, were either a third flanker or grafters in the tight. 'Merv the Swerve', who was 'always in the forefront of all the action, wherever the ball was', combined the two.

John Williams's arrival in international rugby was timed as perfectly as the thunderous incursions into the threequarter line that would come to characterise his play. The introduction of the 'Australian dispensation' in 1964, which outlawed the practice of kicking into touch from outside the twenty-five, freed full-backs to become attackers as well as sure-handed defenders. A medical student, he had been presented with a rugby ball by Dr Jack Matthews, a colleague of his father's, when only six months old and was already a low-key professional sportsman, a former British junior tennis champion who won £20 at the first open tournament, at Bournemouth in 1968. It was a toss-up as to whether he had more impact as an attacker coming into the line with the unstoppable force of his 14st frame or as a tackler who, as his English opposite number Alastair Hignell recalls, 'launched himself at you in a way that was new for full-backs and left the attacker much less time to consider his options.' In an era when Wales were spoilt for greatness, Williams was the supreme hammer of the English, never a loser and often the match-winner against them.

*

Wales's golden decade divides into two parts — the 1969 to 1972 period when thirteen out of fifteen championship matches were won along with two outright titles, a shared one, two Triple Crowns, a Grand Slam in 1971 and only one defeat — a 14-0 disintegration in Dublin in 1970 that was almost as shocking as the Murrayfield debacle of 1951. The next two seasons formed an interregnum — the five-way tie of 1973 being followed by Ireland's title in a similarly tight championship the next year — before a renewed team began a run of four titles in five years, with two Grand Slams and four consecutive Triple Crowns. The pack was almost entirely rebuilt during the transition. If the earlier years were characterised by the Morris-Davies-Taylor back row and Delme Thomas's dominance of the line-out, the later period was the era of hugely powerful Swansea lock Geoff Wheel, known as 'The Ripper' for his extraordinary effectiveness in loose mauls, and the Pontypool front row of Charlie Faulkner, Bobby Windsor and Graham Price, celebrated in song by Max Boyce as the 'Viet Gwent' and in prose by Clem Thomas as Wales's version of The Three Musketeers. The Monmouthshire valleys club had always had a tough reputation. When the future England cricket captain Tony Lewis was injured playing for them in the early 1960s, Wilfred Wooller said that while he was stupid to be jeopardising his cricketing prospects by playing rugby, at least he hadn't been daft enough to play *against* Pontypool. In the 1970s and 1980s they rose to become a formidable force under the direction of former Wales and Lions prop Ray Prosser. Fearsomely rugged, they were not universally popular. Llanelli and London Welsh were among those who suspended fixtures against them, while Gerald Davies and John Morgan recalled hearing cheers in a West Wales clubhouse for, of all things, a Cardiff win because it had been at the expense of 'Pooler'. At national level, though, the rugged durability of players like Faulkner and lock John Perkins, Windsor's astute competitiveness, the sheer class of Price and former Newport back-rower Jeff Squire, were warmly appreciated.

Mervyn Davies bridged the two periods, returning from London to help rejuvenate his home-town club Swansea and to take on an unexpected role as Wales captain in the style later associated with Martin Johnson and England. Gerald Davies said of Mervyn: 'He did not say very much off the field and the few words he did say were straight and to the point so that no one could mistake or misunderstand them. He simply led by example on the field and showed a total commitment to winning a game.' His career was to end prematurely, however, when he suffered a brain haemorrhage during a Welsh Cup semi-final in 1976 when he was only twenty-nine.

So continuity was represented by three backs – centre turned wing Gerald Davies, scrum-half Gareth Edwards and full-back John Williams. Davies, Edwards and outside-half Barry John – an elusive talent who, when asked what he intended to do in certain circumstances on the field, replied: 'How can I tell you? I don't know myself until I get the ball' and, alarmed by the pressures of becoming British rugby's first authentic superstar, retired when he was only twenty-seven – were born within two years of each other in West Wales mining communities. Like their East Walian forebears Bleddyn Williams and Cliff Morgan, they were white-collar sons – all three trained as teachers – of fathers who worked with coal and were determined that their sons should not. Edwards followed Williams's path to the extent of winning a public school scholarship. But where Morgan and Williams were products of depression and war, who played amid the mudheaps and crowded midfields of the 1940s and 1950s, the later trio grew up amid the unprecedented security brought by the welfare state and coal nationalisation. After learning to play in the same confined circumstances, they reached maturity with perfect timing to enjoy the space, freedom and better playing conditions brought about by the rule changes of the 1960s and early 1970s and the replacement of the battered Arms Park by the sparingly used National Stadium.

John Williams was the product of upward mobility a generation earlier. His father was a miner's son who was successful enough as a doctor to own, as Cliff Jones's father did in the 1930s, a Rolls-Royce and pay much of the costs of sending John as a sixth-former to Millfield, England's most expensive public school. Awareness of his privilege, though, gave Williams 'an extra incentive to prove to my mates that I was tough, and one of them'. Men like Morris, a colliery face worker, and Phil Bennett, the diminutive, darting outside-half who succeeded Barry John and worked alongside his fans in the Llanelli steel works during the week, represented Wales's still considerable heavy industrial base. They played rugby with an audacity and panache that still draws smiles from middle-aged rugby fans, whether Welsh or not. Historian Adrian Smith, a native of Coventry, says: 'English disappointment in defeat was not resentment as Gareth, Phil the Boot, J.P.R., J.J. etc. were clearly so magnificent, and by virtue of being so transcended normal rivalry . . . one consequence of this, based on observation in pubs, is that long-standing rugby fans of my generation don't revel in Welsh defeat and we welcome Welsh wins . . . we have a respect for Wales rooted in nostalgia for the 1960s or 1970s.' It helped, Smith points out, that 'the Welsh gave us Englishmen the chance to be winners via the Lions'. Wales supplied the core of the Lions sides – and in 1971 both captain and coach – who attained unprecedented success in New Zealand and South Africa in 1971 and 1974, compensating in part for the single, substantial asterisk against Wales's own record in this period – failure to beat the All Blacks.

It was not all attacking brilliance. Wales were also highly proficient at containing opponents. Alastair Hignell recalls as an opponent being aware not merely of talent. 'If you looked at the team-sheet it was hard not to be impressed,' said the England full-back. 'They had some fantastic players.' But there was also an underlying mental strength. 'There was an implacability about them. We were always up for it and felt that if we got a few breaks we had a chance. We'd win ball and perhaps go ahead early on. But there was always a sense that Wales would absorb the pressure and sort things out.'

It was not as if England lacked talent. The Harlequin Hiller and Bristol's Hignell, one of the last top-quality cricket and rugby players, were full-backs of genuine quality. David Duckham and John Spencer formed a centre pairing that Geoff Nicholson thought 'simply unravelled the Welsh defence' at Twickenham in 1970, before their partnership was dissolved by injury to Spencer and Duckham's move, emulating Gerald Davies, to the wing where he played well enough for Mervyn Davies to include him in a notional Rest of the World XV: 'A magnificent sight in full cry for the line, with his flowing blond locks and long-striding thighs.' John Taylor was a fan of Duckham. 'When you went on a Lions tour with him, you realised how exceptionally good he was.' Similar in build, hair colour and shoe size, Duckham and Spencer did nothing to disabuse England team-mates of the theory that they were twins separated at birth by wearing identical, brightly coloured underwear to a squad session. Each showed an affinity for Wales. Duckham was, with the arguable exception of Peter Jackson, the greatest single talent to emerge from the remarkable post-war Coventry production line, but called his autobiography *Dai for England*. Spencer, on tour with the 1971 Lions, enjoyed joining Wales players on visits to expatriate groups and trying out Welsh phrases, unaware that what his team-mates said were greetings were in fact unprintable expletives.

England might have paired goal-kicking outside-half Alan Old, elder brother of England fast bowler Chris, with either Moseley's Jan Webster or the younger Steve Smith. Forward options that were generally not taken included a prop pairing of Mike Burton, born in a caravan on a Gloucester council estate, and Smith's Sale team-mate Fran Cotton, the formidably strong son of a rugby league international, a destroyer on either side of the scrum. Both Burton and Cotton were to enjoy hugely successful rugby-related business careers. John Taylor recalls: 'You saw Cotton and thought "now here really is a player".' At hooker, the durable Bristolian John Pullin, farmer of land in the shadow of the Severn Bridge at Aust, was succeeded in the second half of the decade by Leicester's Peter Wheeler. As for the back row, Mervyn Davies once told Terry O'Connor of his relief that England never combined Tony Neary, Roger Uttley and Peter Dixon, all players he admired as Lions team-mates, against Wales. One reason was the unorthodox talent of Rosslyn Park's engagingly bonkers Andy Ripley at No. 8.

Duckham revealed that: 'Even the Wales guys would say to us "what's the matter with your team? You've got a lot of very good players, but you don't win anywhere near often enough".' Frustration was compounded by two remarkable results for which, Mervyn Davies admitted, 'we Welsh would have given our eye teeth!' – away wins over South Africa in 1972 and New Zealand a year later. The memoirs of leading players are unanimous in blaming the selectors. Uttley wrote: 'I never understood what the selectors were trying to do; I am not sure the selectors did either.' He believed that the treatment of Old, whose sixteen caps were spread over seven seasons, was 'criminal when you consider how desperate England were for a controlling influence', and felt that Dixon, too, suffered for his forthrightness. Hignell concurred. 'An almost inevitable feature of England sessions,' he said, 'was Alan arguing with the selectors – and he could always run rings round them intellectually – about the choices they had made. He'd tear them to shreds.'

In eleven consecutive matches for Wales, Gareth Edwards faced eight English scrum-halves, while the 1975 and 1976 seasons saw them cap forty-six players, taking five more who were never capped to Australia and losing nine of their eleven matches. If Old's reaction was anger, other players took to satirising the precariousness of an England career. Smith wrote: 'The lads used to make up such games as "Golden Guillotine" in which they staggered around the dressing room pretending to clutch gaping wounds at the back of their necks.' Burton describes himself as 'the only life member of The Rest', routinely a Possible at trial time whether or not he had played for England the previous season. The outcome was a bizarre international career in which he played alternate seasons – four times against Wales at Twickenham, but never at Cardiff – and won twelve of his thirteen Five Nations caps in even-numbered years.

Duckham, first capped in 1969, noticed the inhibiting effect of endless changes. 'It was evident to me . . . that players were generally unwilling to take the law into their own hands on the field and assert their own authority, using the individual skill and flair at their disposal,' he said. Little had changed by the time Hignell made his Five Nations debut against Wales in 1976. 'I was sharing a room with Duckham and his advice to me was "play safe and don't make a mistake, or they'll drop you". I was shocked. Even senior players felt insecure as the selectors were so inconsistent . . . There was no point in building for the next game or the next season, since you might not be there.'

England were, Gareth Edwards has recalled, 'always hard to beat because they deprived us of so much ball, but somehow they could never put their whole game together'. As John Dawes argued in 1975: 'They have a great capacity for winning the ball, but not much for using it.' There was also some acceptance of failure. This was not necessarily true of all players. Sharing a dressing room with David Duckham for the Lions, Gareth Edwards thought him if anything over-intense. 'Clenching his fist in the corner muttering "come on, we've got to do it", building himself up. I wanted him to relax, because that is what his game needed.' A degree of fatalism does, though, appear to have crept in. Uttley, disappointed by losing his first international against Ireland in 1972, was told by team-mate Chris Ralston not to worry – it was his tenth match and he was still waiting to win. Brian Moore, who epitomised a very different attitude in a much more successful England era, saw the Twickenham defeat by Wales in 1978 and recalled: 'There was no real depression that England had lost. England supporters didn't really feel that way at the time; they were never overburdened with expectation.' There is something to be said for not fixating on success. Gareth Edwards thought that 'more Englishmen have got the game in proper perspective than Welshmen. The game is for winners, but it is also for enjoyment. The element of physical exercise and a few pints afterwards should always exist at club level. I have seen the game in Wales, even at minor level, destroy families. I have seen players crying, shouting and threatening when they lose. From the man in the street to the international players at the top, there builds up a huge rugby pressure: sometimes it is like a quicksand and we are sucked into endless rugby talk. Then Welshmen are boring; the game is removed from its proper position in life. It eats us up.'

In some respects these were spectacular years for the English game. The RFU had 971 affiliated clubs in 1965 and 1,769 a decade later, a growth partly attributable to the way that the Wales team in particular were showing television audiences – 91 per cent of households had a TV by 1971 – the possibilities of the game. England's administrators, though, continued to see the spectre of professionalism in any improvement in organisation. They appointed a coach, Don White, in 1969 but insisted on calling him manager and did not initially allow him to call squad sessions. That same year Rutherford began a long career as technical director, a euphemism for coaching organiser. He could count on encouragement from Ray Williams, whom he recalls beginning phone calls with a jovial 'Hello, God speaking', but the contrast in circumstances with Williams, who was able to tell the 1971 WRU AGM that 'Welsh rugby has been transformed', was striking. Rutherford recounts how 'I started with a blank sheet of paper, the odd coaching course but really nothing else. We started courses for PE advisers, teachers and team captains – I remember Ian McGeechan [the future Scotland and Lions centre and coach] coming on one of those. But there was no real system. We had to develop coaches and a playing system and the problem was that all the committees were based on RFU's constituent bodies who were reluctant to see the County Championship downgraded in any way.' Alf Wyman, of Coventry, a club whose pre-eminence was reflected when, thinly disguised as Warwickshire, they won seven county titles between 1958 and 1965, led the push for an expansion of club competition. The RFU finally acceded in 1972, creating a Knock-Out Cup in the same year that the WRU introduced their own competition. Four years later came the further concession of regional merit tables – not, it was firmly emphasised, leagues.

Uttley moved from Gosforth, who won the English cup in 1976 and 1977, to join Wasps in 1979 and found London rugby 'everything I had been led to believe it was . . . sociable, uncompetitive, soft and inconsistent'. Hignell, at Bristol, observed the epidemics of 'Welsh flu' that afflicted less resolute team-mates when a midweek trip across the Severn Bridge to Pontypool or other forbidding destinations loomed on the fixture list. By the end of the Seventies, Devonian No. 8 John Scott had joined Cardiff, saying: 'Welsh players have a much harder attitude . . . they are far better prepared for international rugby because the gap between club and country is not the yawning one which exists in England.'

On the Welsh side, John Taylor says: 'We always felt we could beat England. We played against England's best clubs and players at London Welsh and while we occasionally lost, there was nobody we feared. The Welsh clubs were better organised and played their rugby in an environment where we got much more out of people. English players weren't developed as well as they could have been. Ripley, for instance, took up rugby late and was a very good athlete but didn't have all the rugby skills – he was a poor passer and knocked on too much.' One consequence, says Taylor, was that 'we regarded playing France as the real challenge in our season'. Not losing to England, though, remained important. Gareth Williams and Dai Smith wrote that 'not since the early twentieth century had Wales been so self-conscious or so aware of her expression of identity', but a successful rugby team was perhaps the most significant single symbol of that awareness. This created pressures. Edwards wrote of going to Twickenham for the last time in 1978, recalling that Gerald Davies 'looked his usual tense self, whiter than white' and that 'fear of failure set in. Losing at Twickenham is more than coming second in a rugby match. It is a national disaster.' Davies asked him: 'Why do we keep on doing this Gareth?'

Not losing at Twickenham was accomplished four times in five visits in the 1970s. Those games can be divided into those particularly associated with Edwards and those defined, either by his presence or absence, by J.P.R. Williams. The 1978 victory, by 9-6, was the first match since 1964 in which neither side reached double figures, and was played in conditions all too reminiscent of earlier, low-scoring days. It was, though, a personal triumph for Edwards on the day that he became the first Welshman to reach fifty caps. Still routinely top of any 'greatest ever rugby player' polls, Edwards loomed massively in this period. He was, his most famous half-back partner Barry John wrote, 'an explosion waiting to happen', possessing as he did the 'perfect physique for a scrum-half; he's heavy for his shape and his body has a low centre of gravity'. Steve Smith admitted: 'The England players were quite paranoid about him and their sole topic of conversation used to be how to stop him . . . you might finish a game and be able to claim that he had never made one break against you, only to concede that he had probably won the game with his kicking instead.' Burton particularly admired his ability to shine in adversity. 'His performances were superb on the days when it was hard to be good,' he said.

This was never better illustrated than at Twickenham in 1978, a foul day on which not all the liquid coursing down the open terrace largely populated by Welsh fans had fallen from the grimly black skies above. The *Observer* headlined a 'Welsh elegy in an English graveyard'. England dominated the forward exchanges and led 6-3 at half-time but, recalled Burton: 'Gareth Edwards controlled the match like a conjuror, thereby rendering all our muddy efforts in our little twilight world utterly useless and irrelevant. It didn't really matter who was on top, Gareth kicked the ball down behind us and broke our hearts. We could win two or three balls in succession, batter our way up field and be poised for an attack on the Welsh line, then Gareth would send the ball rolling . . . into our twenty-five and we had to start again.'

Edwards might have crowned his day with a try but, when a single opportunity occurred, 'in I went, down went the arm and scooped, but there was nothing there. It had gone because just as I was about to lay a hand on it at a hundred miles an hour, dear old Charlie Faulkner bent down and hauled it back into the pack. "Sorry, Gar, didn't see you coming," he admitted so simply.' Even this, though, would not have topped his supreme moment of virtuosity – the image of his moving to within a few feet of the touchline from a scrum in the shadow of the East Stand before rifling an extraordinary kick sixty-five metres down the line lives on vividly thirty years later.

The match finally came down to two penalty attempts. With eight minutes to go, debutant flanker Bob Mordell, the only England player born in the district of Twickenham, was penalised at a ruck. John Taylor said: 'He later made a great fuss about the decision being wrong, but he was the only person at Twickenham that thought so.' Phil Bennett landed the kick to give Wales a 9-6 lead. Minutes later Hignell, who had defended superbly but had an afternoon of near-misses with the boot, had his chance. As he says: 'Twickenham was difficult, either huge long grass or a quagmire. It was incredibly mucky and difficult under foot. There were no kicking tees, so you had to dig a castle in the mud then keep your left foot steady as you kicked a ball that was like a piece of soap. Other people managed it, but I didn't front up so well. When I struck the final kick I thought it was OK. It was struck well but didn't go straight enough and missed by a few inches. There's a great picture of me with my head in my hands immediately afterwards.'

The sole asterisk against Edwards's greatness is that, though he captained Wales fourteen times, beginning at the age of twenty, he was not a very successful skipper. In Taylor's opinion: 'He was thinking too much and robbing himself of his greatest asset, his intuition as to when to pass and when to go himself.' He had been captain eight years earlier at Twickenham when Wales, as J.P.R. Williams recalled, were 'being totally hammered' and he was forced off with an injury. He was not the first to leave – referee Robert Calmet got himself in the way of an Edwards surge before half-time, possibly preventing a try but suffering a leg injury that meant the second half had to be refereed by English touch-judge Johnny Johnson. England had led 13-3 at the break after debutant wing Tony Novak, who was 'built more like a No. 8 than a wing' according to John Taylor, set up a try for Duckham with a thumping tackle on J.P.R. Williams then scored himself. Barry John reduced their deficit to 13-6 with a typically ghosting run for a try, but the departure of the feared Edwards with twenty minutes left seemed the final confirmation of an English triumph. On came Ray 'Chico' Hopkins, of Maesteg, the first replacement in eighty-nine years of England v Wales matches, and he nearly performed a do-it-yourself vasectomy as he jumped the gate into the tunnel. Duckham later admitted: 'We relaxed, totally under-estimating Ray's ability.'

As at the Stade de France in 2005, a Welsh captain's departure proved the catalyst for a revival. Hopkins remembered recently: 'Things just went right for me. There was a scrum and I wanted to get it to Barry John on the left of the posts but it came out too far. So I'm going towards the touchline when along came J.P.R. – and everyone thought it was a planned move, but it wasn't – and over he went. Then England threw a long throw-in, and it bounced up and over Dai Morris and – here's fate again – into me behind him. All I had to do to score was just dive over.' That made it 13-12 to England, with the conversion to come and injury time already being played. Jarrett's departure to rugby league had left Wales without a full-time goal-kicker and the job was divided between Edwards and the reluctant J.P.R. Williams, who 'never liked it because I felt it affected my concentration on other aspects of full-back play'. He and Edwards missed several kicks, and Hiller was landing everything for England. But J.P.R. made up for the earlier misses. 'I got my head down, struck the ball well and watched in relief as it sailed through the posts to a great roar from the Welsh contingent in the crowd.' There was still time for Barry John to land a forty-metre drop-goal and for Duckham to evade several tacklers on a surge into Welsh territory before perishing through lack of support. It was the first time that either team had come back from a ten-point deficit. Hopkins told of how 'tough front-row boys like Denzil Williams and Jeff Young were coming off crying, it was such an emotional game'. He added, pointedly: 'A lot of people think this is the only bloody game I ever played because I sat on the bench to Gareth Edwards about twenty-one times.' There are worse things to be remembered for.

Goal-kicking was not the only thing that J.P.R. Williams disliked. He was not keen on Twickenham. 'The grass was kept so long there,' he said. 'It was like running through a field and especially so on the damp days.' He was far from the only player to make this complaint; Harold Day blamed the luxuriant growth on Twickenham having previously been a market garden. England could be forgiven for fearing what J.P.R. might have accomplished had he liked the place. If his efforts in 1970 were overshadowed by the ebullient Hopkins, there was little doubt about the star of Welsh victories in 1972 and 1976. The first match followed a pattern familiar in this period – a slow start, with England taking the lead and raising supporters' hopes before a steady, ultimately irresistible Welsh revival. England debutant Burton found out what playing for Wales could do for a player. 'I'd played against John Lloyd before when we played Bridgend. He was a strong and capable loose-head, but I had no great difficulties with him. But put him in a Wales shirt and he was a very different proposition.' Alongside Burton was hooker John Pullin, who did not like Twickenham either, although it was the crowd that irked him. 'Ninety per cent of the people were there because it was Twickenham. They were not really there to watch the rugby, whereas in Wales it was ninety per cent the other way. If you took one against the head at Cardiff Arms Park, a big noise would go up from the crowd because they understood and appreciated what was happening. If you took one against the head at Twickenham, nobody would know. They wouldn't have a clue what was happening.' It seems likely that Pullin developed this view in 1972 since in that year's Wales match he took eight strikes against the head, but his complaint was hardly unprecedented. As far back as 1944, Sewell, admittedly a world-class harrumpher, compared fans at different international grounds and concluded that 'Twickenham is the most ignorant – the futile kick when it was the game to keep the ball in play – the senseless reverse pass by a wing when he ought to have risked his all going for the line – these things *always* bring down the Twickenham house. Never is that the case when it happens at Cardiff Arms Park or St Helen's, Swansea. There the crowd ticks off the sinner quite impartially.'

Interest in the England-Wales match of 1972 was so great that, with stand tickets costing £2, the RFU refunded £75,000 to disappointed applicants. With debutant Jan Webster 'snapping and darting with the energy of a Jack Russell' at scrum-half, England took a merited early lead with a penalty by Hiller. Wales, though, were ahead by the break as Barry John, a harbinger of the shift in kicking duties from straight-ahead kicking full-backs like Hiller to instep-using outside-halves landed two penalties with the insouciant ease he brought to everything else. Peter West, reporting for *The Times*, reckoned that England spent only seven second-half minutes in Welsh territory. Yet they hung on, thanks not least to Duckham who, like his Coventry forerunner Jackson, was a player whose sublime attacking skills concealed stout defensive competence. English resistance lasted until J.P.R. Williams thundered up to take a short-side pass from Gareth Edwards at a five-yard scrum.

Team-mate John Taylor had an excellent view. 'He brushed aside Keith Fielding and dived triumphantly over the line as Peter Dixon managed to tackle him. It was a classic J.P.R. intervention, a sudden surge of pace which caught many a defence unawares and then a dive for the line making full use of his fourteen stone.' He could have been stopped, thought Clem Thomas, by 'nothing short of the West Stand collapsing on him'. The fixture's first four-point try was converted to make Wales 12-3 winners before the team were collared in the tunnel for the filming of Barry John's episode of *This Is Your Life*.

Four years later Williams was even more compelling. It was his year, helping seal a Welsh Grand Slam with a shuddering shoulder-to-shoulder challenge on French wing Jean-François Gourdon that served as the defining image of the man, matched perhaps only by his playing brilliantly against England with blood streaming down his face and socks rolled down around his ankles. England again started the match well, with Hignell prevented from scoring on his Five Nations debut by a J.P.R. tackle the physical impact of which he can still recall. 'He used all his weight and exploded into things. Instead of scoring, I hurt my nose!' Wales took control following a mix-up between No. 8 Ripley and scrum-half Mike Lampkowski, who, Burton recalls, 'was tough and brave but couldn't pass, which is a bit of a problem for a scrum-half'. Gareth Edwards seized the opportunity to score. Hignell says that England's defensive worries went beyond their inability to keep Edwards quiet. 'We couldn't decide if we were drifting or closing down or blitzing and we got stuck in between,' he said. 'We didn't get much chance to play together or formulate plans. Nowadays you would have practised, but I don't think we ever practised defence. You might say "let's do a drift defence", but you'd have people who were doing something different at their clubs.' The bleeding Williams went over for two tries, the second from a stunning scissors with Bennett, to take his total to four in three matches at Twickenham. Wales's 21-9 victory was their largest ever at Twickenham, but skipper Mervyn Davies said it was 'not a good win' and Nicholson thought that 'only in one respect was it the best; the phenomenal performance of J.P.R. Williams'.

He made an impact in 1974 as well, albeit with his absence through injury. His replacement, Roger Blyth, was a fine full-back but, as Burton put it, 'the scourge of England wasn't around'. Williams, watching from the steps in one stand after failing to get a ticket, thought Blyth played well but said that he himself might have stopped Duckham's first-half try. 'Having played with and against Dave so many times, I knew he tended to go off his left foot,' Williams said. Wales's other John Williams, Llanelli's former Commonwealth Games sprinter known as J.J., was also adjudged to have lost out to Duckham after a trademark kick and chase towards the English line in the second half. Today it would have been awarded following review by television match officials – journalist Barry Newcombe recalled Duckham telling him that it was a try, a view reiterated in Duckham's book *Dai for England* – but no such facility was available to referee John West, who did not give the try. This and a less defensible decision to call back Bennett, who had an overlap outside him and a try begging, in order to give Wales a penalty, earned Mr West his dubious place in Welsh legend as a leading inmate in Max Boyce's 'Sunshine Home in Dublin for Blind Irish Referees'.

Wales might have guessed before the kick-off that it was not to be their day. The only anthem played was 'God Save The Queen'. Welsh fans either booed resentfully or began an a cappella rendition of their anthem that the *Western Mail* reported 'was still being sung by sections of the crowd with the game in motion'. RFU secretary Bob Weighill straight-batted post-match questions on the subject. 'My committee is firmly of the opinion that when all of the countries of the four home unions play at Twickenham, we play the "Queen" only. As far as I am aware, we have never played any other anthem of the home countries.' He added that a selection of Welsh tunes including, he understood, the anthem had been played by the band during a programme of music before the match. J.B.G. Thomas reported that an instruction had been given by the 'match committee' of the RFU, although there is nothing evident in the minutes retained in the Twickenham archives. Welsh opinion rather suspected retaliation for the increasingly hostile response given to 'God Save The Queen' – notably at a match against Japan the previous autumn – in Cardiff, fans resenting an anthem perceived in a sporting context as English, rather than British, at matches where England were not involved. Steele-Bodger, the RFU president at the time, remembers the occasion with acute embarrassment. 'There was certainly no committee decision. If anything, it was a unilateral action by the band. I remember we had Elwyn Jones, the Lord Chancellor, as a guest in the committee box and he was furious. It was terrible.' It was Clive Rowlands' last match as coach and he remembers England's 16-12 victory as 'second only to losing to the All Blacks in 1972 as a disappointment'. That, too, was controversial, with Wales having a try by J.P.R. Williams ruled out – television footage was inconclusive, but suggested that it was at least as legitimate as the first-half score by All Black prop Keith Murdoch – and the All Blacks cynically obstructing Welsh kick chases in the later stages.

Anger over the anthem and the J.J. Williams 'try' rather obscured the reality that England's win was both foreseen – Rupert Cherry wrote pre-match in the *Daily Telegraph* that 'it seems strange to write that England have a good chance of beating Wales at Twickenham, but I am going to do just that' – and largely merited. England also had a possible score ruled out, after their dominant forwards had pushed the Welsh scrummage over the line, but scored two further tries. The second, after half time, was the highlight of perhaps the best display Andy Ripley ever gave in an England shirt. Ripley has been cast variously as 'England No. 8, author, church warden, triathlete, British Superstars champion, city banker, 400 metres hurdler, motorcycle enthusiast, British canoe instructor, lecturer at the Sorbonne and the youngest ever president of Rosslyn Park'. That list was compiled by *Telegraph* journalist Brendan Gallagher, who reckoned that the placing of *Ripley's Rugby Rubbish* in the philosophy section of a Galway bookshop was more inspired perception than classification error. Even that list missed out 'pilgrim on the hippie trail to Kathmandu' and the role forced upon Ripley in recent years as an inspirational battler against prostate cancer. Ripley, his high-stepping run an echo of that past as a hurdler, charged over for a try from the back of a five-yard scrum shortly after half-time to give England a lead they never subsequently lost. Webster, the scrum-half, was the common factor in England's best performances of the first half of the 1970s, yet he won only eight championship caps – four against Wales. John Taylor described him as 'a real livewire and strong as well, but the way he was in and out was extraordinary'. On this day he combined to huge effect with the similarly maltreated Old, who ensured that forward ascendancy was not wasted and matched Phil Bennett as a goal-kicker.

*

If England were competitive at Twickenham, they suffered persistent misery in Cardiff. The margin of defeat was exactly the same, sixteen points, in the three matches between 1971 and 1975. Gerald Davies scored in all three, claiming two tries in 1971, and his fellow wingers also prospered; the robust and direct John Bevan scoring in 1971, then twice in 1973, before his departure to league with Warrington created the vacancy filled by the lightning-quick J.J. Williams, who crossed in 1975. Davies was the third, and certainly not the least, of Wales's holy trinity of backs – possessing the rare gift of being able to side-step without losing pace, and being so deceptive that one international referee reckoned him the most challenging player he encountered because 'when he gets the ball he seems to disappear'. Would-be tacklers often thought that they had Davies in their sights, only to find themselves ignominiously clutching air, a fate that befell the young Alastair Hignell when he played for Cambridge University against Cardiff. Physical gifts were complemented by footballing and personal intelligence. J.P.R. Williams wrote: 'I played with him for a decade and I can never remember him dying with the ball – he either scored or passed back inside.' No great player has written more capably about the game or its context; his description of his native village of Llansaint in his memoirs bears comparison with any account of Welsh childhood.

England managed only two tries, both from line-outs, in these three matches. In 1971, John Taylor and Mervyn Davies got in each other's way at the back of the line early on and Gloucester flanker Charlie Hannaford flopped over. Taylor remembers: 'It was terribly embarrassing but it did not feel like a catastrophe. It was early in the game and I was confident that we would beat England. Merv just shrugged his shoulders.' By the half-hour mark Wales were 16-3 up, their pack driving 'through their opponents like an armoured division through cavalry' according to Nicholson, and were 'content just to control the game' after the break, according to *Playfair*. The other try was scored by lock Nigel Horton at the end of another Welsh stroll in 1975. The result was not in doubt once Wales had run up a 16-0 interval lead, with England having to wait sixty-six minutes to produce their first threequarter move. Gerald Davies and J.J. Williams both scored tries from breaks by Ray Gravell, a powerful, straight-running centre whose partnership with the similarly rugged Steve Fenwick epitomised the bludgeoning style that characterised the later 1970s, as defenders worked out how to close down the space opened by rule changes over the previous decade. Gravell's warm, voluble and bilingual emotionalism also personified Llanelli as nobody else has done. In between these two matches was the 25-9 Wales win in 1973, year of the quintuple tie in the championship table. *Guardian* reporter David Irvine commented on how Wales were 'as usual building slowly to their climax' and he also picked out Webster for showing 'courage and resource' behind a badly beaten England pack. England also singled him out – dropping him for the rest of the season in favour of rising star Steve Smith.

By far the best English performance – the only time between 1963 and 1981 that they confined Wales at Cardiff to a single-figure margin, 14-9 – came in 1977. The difference, according to David Frost of the *Guardian*, was that 'if you have great players on your side . . . and can find the opportunities to use their gifts – you will win even against a team prepared to give their all as England did'. Gareth Edwards scored unstoppably from an early five-yard scrum. England lock Bill Beaumont said: 'Although from the dark murky depths of the second row you cannot see exactly what is going on behind the scrum, I could tell from the roar exactly what happened.' Yet England led 9-7 at half-time through three penalties by Hignell, who had one of his best matches at full-back, and were only forty minutes from a Triple Crown. It was Wales, though, who would claim the crown – their third in an unprecedented sequence of four. The decisive score came, again, from J.P.R. Williams, his fifth and final try in the fixture. Carwyn James wrote that he 'sensed that the cover so feared [Gerald] Davies's pace that he dummied his pass and straightened his run to score the winning try'.

England were hopeful again in 1979. They had just beaten France; Wales were without Davies and Edwards, who had retired along with Bennett and Terry Cobner, the astute flanker who led Pontypool for much of the decade. Grey-haired lock Mike Roberts was recalled after a four-year absence. England hooker Peter Wheeler said that he 'cringed when I look back at some of the pre-match comment'. Yet England were apparently in contention after an hour, trailing by only 7-3, and might have taken heart when J.P.R. Williams, playing what was assumed to be his last international, went off injured. Once again Wales were galvanised rather than demoralised by losing an iconic captain, scoring twenty points in the final quarter to transform a tight contest into their most resounding victory in the fixture since 1905. Roberts scored 'with a stunning six-inch dash' from a line-out and the final try came from a remarkable counter-attack launched by J.P.R.'s debutant replacement, Clive Griffiths, of Llanelli, who was just beaten to the touchdown by wing Elgan Rees. By the end, wrote Clem Thomas, 'England were in rags'. It was their fifth consecutive defeat since that isolated triumph in 1974, and their fourth without scoring a try. Hignell had played in all four and had the distinction of being England's only scorer, with a total of nine penalties. It was to be his last international as the following season was disrupted by an injury that occurred during the cricket season, but was blamed on rugby. He retired at the age of twenty-four. 'I still felt I had a lot to learn,' says Hignell, 'but I was being paid to play cricket, so that had to take priority.'

In spite of England's defeats in Cardiff, Hignell says that he still 'loved playing there, because it was full of people who were as passionate about rugby as I was'. And it was there nearly thirty years later that he reported on his last international as a BBC correspondent, receiving a framed Welsh jersey from the WRU in recognition of his services.

In 1979, another distinguished player turned journalist, Clem Thomas, reckoned that Edwards and Bennett's successors, the Cardiff pairing of scrum-half Terry Holmes and outside-half Gareth Davies – a product, as Carwyn James and Barry John had been, of Gwendraeth Grammar School – 'look like gracing the scene for another decade'. The 1980s, though, would be a disappointment – and not only for Wales.

CHAPTER ELEVEN
RECESSION 1980–89

O God, Grant me mediocrity!

Honoré Mirabeau

My first contact with the Welsh was as a small child, sitting with my parents in the members stand at Welford Road, Leicester. I recall father going purple in the face and I asked: 'Mummy, why is Daddy waving his fist at that man in the white shirt?' Mother gently replied: 'Because he's a Swansea player, dear.' Since then I have discovered more about Welsh rugby. I am also able to appreciate why my father was waving his fist.

Michael Green, *The Art of Coarse Rugby*

Shortly after the post-match press conferences following the England-Wales match at Twickenham in 1980, winning captain Bill Beaumont was asked to go out to the committee box in the stand. He recalled: 'When I got there I was flabbergasted at the amazing scene in front of me. Thousands of delirious, almost hysterical supporters were chanting my name and when I waved and gave them the thumbs-up sign they screamed and cheered their approval. They had patiently waited a good many years to indulge themselves in such celebrations and I was really delighted that at last we had given our followers something to cheer about.'

England had won 9-8 – the last time that neither side reached double figures. They scored three penalties to two tries by opponents who played for more than an hour with fourteen men. It was, Clem Thomas wrote, 'obviously not the way England would have wanted it, not that they will care too much'.

This was the year when England finally got it right, winning a Grand Slam after sixteen consecutive seasons in which they had failed to win more than two matches and had become entrenched in the championship's lower reaches. As the flamboyant French captain Jean-Pierre Rives put it: 'We have always known that there were a lot of Lions dotted around your country, but it seems to me that this is the first time you have ... played so many of them together in the same England team.' The pack included the last four England captains – Beaumont and predecessors Uttley, Cotton and Neary. All four were Lancastrians, as were scrum-half Steve Smith – restored after being out of favour for so long that he and Hignell, a fixed point for four seasons, had played together only once – and wings John Carleton and Mike Slemen. All seven had taken part in one of the best recent performances by an English team, the North's 21-9 victory over the All Blacks at Otley three months earlier. A second axis of familiarity was provided by a Leicester quartet – full-back Dusty Hare, centres Paul Dodge and Clive Woodward and hooker Peter Wheeler. The line-up was completed by Bath outside-half John Horton, two Englishmen abroad – John Scott, of Cardiff, and Maurice Colclough, of Angoulême – and the latest thing in tough Gloucester props, the grey-haired twenty-nine-year-old Phil Blakeway, survivor of a broken neck two years previously, who played against Wales with a fractured rib.

Neary, in particular, had suffered selectorial capriciousness. As England's captain in 1976, he paid for a championship whitewash with his place on the flank, was omitted completely from the trials in 1977 and capped only once over the next two seasons, even though he went on the 1977 Lions tour of New Zealand. His qualities were particularly appreciated by other open-sides, such as John Taylor. 'In his early days he was a bit flash, but he developed and by the late Seventies he was really a very good player.' So good, that Ireland's Fergus Slattery considered him 'far better on the open side than Jean-Pierre Rives, of France. A complete footballer – athletic, superb support player and excellent worker with his line-out forwards.' Uttley, his successor as captain in 1977, whose features were as homely and characterful as Neary's were conventionally handsome, had suffered both injury and indecision over whether his best position was No. 8, blind-side or lock, and now brought the grafting qualities of the tight forward to the flank, while Smith's talent and ebullience were increasingly complemented by mature decision-taking.

Hare, a Nottinghamshire farmer, made his debut in the win over Wales in 1974, played well – and was promptly forgotten for four years. Hignell perhaps had the edge in all-round football skills, but both had the reliability under a high ball of the serious cricketer. Where Hignell was a good goal-kicker, Hare was exceptional, piling up more than 7,000 points in senior rugby. They had also found, in Beaumont, a leader who fitted the role better than anyone since Evans and Jeeps. He was, reported journalist Stephen Jones, 'so popular that nobody resented him being given the job.' To Clem Thomas, his attributes were 'honesty, integrity and courage . . . he was like a St Bernard, a loveable, bulky, gentle old thing, possessing great strength under the gracefully floppy exterior, someone who would always come to your rescue'. Alan Gibson called him 'the tubby walrus'. The Grand Slam, captaincy of the Lions and evident amiability transformed him in the space of a few months from a well-liked sportsman into something closer to a national treasure.

Amiability, though, was the last characteristic associated with this particular match. England had won against Ireland and France and were evidently stronger than they had been for years. Wales had beaten France. Both context and pre-match coverage provided more heat than light. A steel strike played to traditional Welsh resentment. No. 8 Eddie Butler says: 'There was a lot of silly stuff about downtrodden little Wales.' Welsh social and economic resentment had a rugby-based mirror image in England. Years of defeat and the feeling that Welsh delight in victory too often slipped into triumphalism and a lack of respect meant that Englishmen felt as oppressed on the field as Welshmen did off it. The much-loved heroes of the 1970s had gone, and rugby was taking a more physical turn. Peter Robbins, a candid friend to Welsh rugby, said: 'The Welsh en masse can be horrid, for they present an image of having lost the art of losing gracefully, and there is no doubt in my mind that the Welsh have become arrogant because of their success.' Richard Sharp, another player turned journalist, reported 'an antipathy towards the Welsh when one is among Englishmen, and it is shared by the Irish and the Scots', although he personally found this inexplicable. John Reason argued that 'physical intimidation . . . has become far too big a factor in their game'.

Pre-match analysis of this apparently excessive physicality was backed by footage from the Wales v France match, which Butler – who was making his debut – recalls as 'a dirty, spiteful game. The French thought they'd been ill-treated, which we thought was a bit rich from them, and there was a build-up of coverage about Welsh skulduggery.' This focused particularly on the abrasive Llanelli flanker Paul Ringer, while Graham Price, the leonine Egyptian-born Pontypool prop, was accused of collapsing scrummages. As one international referee told me, Price could do pretty much anything he wanted in a scrum, so any occurrence was probably his fault, although England's Fran Cotton was a rare opponent against whom this presumption could be suspended.

The atmosphere at Twickenham that day was rivalled for concentrated venom, in my experience of nearly 300 international matches, only by the France-England World Cup quarter-final in 1991. Butler says: 'It was pure evil. As a player it was spellbinding. There was a crackle of something that went well beyond sport.' Geoffrey Nicholson was reminded of a Conservative Party conference, much further down the scale of fear and loathing until one remembers that he was writing for the liberal *Observer* less than a year after Margaret Thatcher became Prime Minister.

Butler was one of the many England v Wales participants down the years who qualified for both teams. He was born in Wales and attended Monmouth School, which regaled pupils with the exploits of Keith Jarrett, but had English parents. Butler is a highly unusual international sportsman in that he has 'not a nationalist bone in my body. I don't believe in flags, anthems, kings or queens. I'm utterly without emotion on the subject.' He was not, though, immune to the Twickenham atmosphere. 'You couldn't help be affected by it. The occasion does it, and on that day the atmosphere was everything. It was the perfect arena for something to go spectacularly wrong.'

A contest described by Nicholson as 'almost sickeningly exciting' went wrong very quickly for Wales. After fourteen minutes Ringer was sent off for a late tackle on Horton – the first dismissal in this fixture, the second in a Twickenham international after All Black Cyril Brownlie in 1925. Ringer's was not a particularly lethal challenge, but referee David Burnett had already responded to a rough start by warning both captains. Fran Cotton watched Ringer's challenge, and thought: 'He must be a head-banger.' Butler feels that Horton went down a little too willingly, but says: 'We'd all had a warning, so Paul was foolish to go anywhere near him.' Roger Uttley thought that Ringer played 'like a man who believed totally in his own publicity'. The sending-off made, as

Barry Newcombe reported, 'little difference to the general tone of the contest. The warfare continued.' It did, though, change the match. While Wales scored shortly afterwards, as Smith and Scott lost control of the ball at a scrum and Wales captain Jeff Squire dived in for an opportunist score, it was tough to play for so long with fourteen men. That they nearly won owed much to Gareth Davies, producing in adversity the best performance of an ultimately unfulfilled career. His half-back partner Terry Holmes agreed: 'He was brilliant and his tactical kicking out of his hand was flawless. Wales had no right to dictate territorially, but they did so because of Gareth who kept rolling them back with masterly kicks. I don't think he failed to find touch once.' His single failing was taking three of the seven missed goal-kicks that ultimately cost Wales the match.

Uttley was kicked in the head by Geoff Wheel – Smith thought it an accident – and replaced by Mike Rafter at half-time. That was enough for him. 'Go back to play in that? You must be joking!' he said. 'Scared? Too right. That first forty minutes had knocked the stuffing out of me. Coming off the field to take a detached view made the whole affair look like a brawl. There was very little rugby in this crazy game; everybody was at each other's throats and growling, instead of watching the ball.' In all, thirty-four penalties were awarded.

Englishmen had little doubt, then or since, who to blame. Cotton wrote: 'None of the incidents which took place that day resulted from English violence; the real culprit was the over-motivation of the Welsh players and their win-at-all-costs attitude. The ridiculous thing about the whole affair was that they might very well have won had they concentrated on playing rugby.' Holmes, playing his first match at Twickenham, thought differently and cited the first maul as evidence. 'A huge powerful hand had grabbed me, fingers clawing at my eyes, and I thought that I was going to have my head pulled off,' he said. The hand belonged to his Cardiff club and flat-mate, John Scott.

Uttley argued: 'Any confrontation was bound to lead to a duel because we were not prepared to bow to Welsh intimidation as England teams had done in the past . . . we were physically prepared to commit ourselves the way the Welsh do: totally and without consideration of life or limb – theirs or their opponents.' Carwyn James saw it as 'the kind of rugby one would expect the Mafia to play; the accusing finger, with some justification, is pointed at the Taffia. But their opponents, let it be said, were no innocents.' Butler accepts that Wales were more sinning than sinned against. 'England were not a particularly dirty side,' he said. 'Welsh rugby is much, much dirtier and with a far greater potential for violence than the English game. Wales, and Welsh teams, will be as dirty as they are allowed to be.'

Wales's fourteen men played with spirit and greater enterprise. Hare kicked England ahead at 6-4 with fifteen minutes to go, but Wales struck back with three minutes left. Smith had his kick charged down by Wales hooker Alan Phillips, who sent wing Elgan Rees over for a try. Smith recalled: 'I have never in all my life felt as I did at that moment. It is the only time when I could hold my hand on my heart and say I had lost my bottle. As I trooped back over the England line I couldn't bring myself to look my team-mates in the eye. I felt I had betrayed them all.' Davies, however, missed the conversion. Butler says: 'We were caught up in the euphoria of the moment after the try, thought we had won and perhaps relaxed a little.' England were offered a chance of redemption when Holmes was ruled to have prevented the ball being released after tackling Dodge. Hare, kicking from near the right-hand touchline around thirty yards out, was not overawed. 'I'd come to terms with the conditions and was confident of the ground and of making the kick . . . only watching it later on TV did I start to feel my stomach churn.'

Exultant fans penned the England team coach in, Cotton recounted, for 'a full hour and a half as thousands of fans surrounded it, shouting "England, England"'. The Welsh coach was also surrounded, but with less good humour. As Holmes said: 'By the time we were all in our seats, they had assembled in hostile clusters around the bus. Taunts soon became insults, nastier ones, including the questions of our fatherhoods and a flurry of Harvey Smiths [V-signs].' Ray Gravell, as patriotic a Welshman as there was, was dissuaded from 'getting off the bus to discuss the matter with them'.

The players mixed sociably afterwards. Wheeler tried, along with Derek Quinnell, to raise the devastated spirits of Ringer, formerly a club-mate of his at Leicester. The repercussions, though, rumbled on long after the game, with Ringer's eight-week suspension the least of them. Clive Rowlands says: 'That was the game in which Wales started to go into decline.' Butler concurs, saying: 'We had no idea what would be unleashed. The backlash was utterly excessive and left a lasting scar. It castrated the side. We couldn't go out and play as Wales traditionally played. We were still shaken when we played Ireland at the end of the season. It was the order of the day not to step out of line. Ireland took one look and after thinking "we don't believe this", just ripped into us. They ate us raw. It tore the guts out of us for about three years.'

It would always have been hard for Wales to maintain the extraordinary standards set in the 1970s. One element of that success, thought J.P.R. Williams, was that 'I never felt one bad game would be taken out of proportion' by the selectors. The 1980s were less forgiving. Butler, captain by 1983, says: 'We had six different scrum-halves in the sixteen matches I played. They were all good, but nobody got a clear run. When you're trying to build success, particularly with a young team like 1983's, you have to give people a chance to bed in and get experience together. We never had that. There was a sense of desperation about everything and we never played with real freedom. There were good games, but they were fragmentary. It was difficult to shake off the shadow of the 1970s and the expectations created, and there was unrelenting negativity in the media, particularly the *Western Mail.*'

Delighted at becoming captain in 1983, Butler admits to relief at losing the job a year later and was one of several Welsh players who retired early from international rugby. 'All the enjoyment I had out of playing for Wales just vanished,' he said. His Pontypool team-mate Price went in 1983, complaining about the 'totalitarian methods' of coaches and selectors, while Gareth Davies's disillusionment was complete in 1985 when A.N. Other was named to play outside-half against England. Movement to rugby league, which had all but ceased after prop Glyn Shaw and wing John Bevan departed in the mid-1970s, resumed a decade later.

Renewed losses to league reflected not only international disappointment, but a much tougher social and economic environment. If the overwhelming rejection of a devolved Welsh assembly in the 1979 referendum was Wales showing confidence in its ability to prosper and maintain its identity within existing structures, the subsequent decade demolished much of that self-belief. Margaret Thatcher, elected Prime

Minister in 1979, had bigger targets in mind than Welsh rugby – even if she was able to take advice from husband Denis, a former referee and highly aware of what Wales had done to England of late – but its social base of unionised heavy industries and public services was in her line of fire as the gains of the 1960s and 1970s were rapidly destroyed. The Welsh workforce declined by more than 140,000 between 1979 and 1983. Steel lost 38,000 jobs between 1980 and 1982 and Welsh unemployment rose from 5.5 per cent to 13.2 per cent in the first seven years of Conservative government. In his 1985 study *When Was Wales?*, historian Gwyn Alf Williams characterised the modern Welsh as 'a naked people under an acid rain'. If the miners' strike of 1984-85 displayed traditional collective loyalty, South Wales remaining solid as other districts splintered, it was still a shattering defeat. In 1984, Wales had thirty-one pits. The last, Tower, closed in 1994, later reopening as a worker-run co-operative.

Large parts of industrial England also suffered. It is no coincidence that Coventry lost their place among England's top clubs in the 1980s, Liverpool merged with St Helens, and Merseyside's other club, Waterloo, also slid out of rugby's top rank. Success shifted southwards with Bath, long established but previously subordinate to local rivals Bristol and Gloucester, beginning a long hegemony – their cup win in 1984 was followed by nine more over the next dozen years. Economic miseries and a government caricatured in 1987 by *The Times*, one of its most enthusiastic supporters, under the banner 'Cry God for Maggie, South-East England and St George', gave an edge to Anglo-Welsh relations reflected in the 1989 declaration by the North Wales Free Church Council that 'Wales's premier tragedy is that it is so far from God and so near England'. It was little wonder that matches in the 1980s were often charged, particularly since Wales fed England's more specifically rugby-based resentments by winning most matches and celebrating noisily.

The English promise of 1980 was not fulfilled, however. Rutherford, who spent the decade working on England's coaching infrastructure, remembers the Grand Slam as 'a blip – we won a championship and nothing came of it'. The Lancastrian heart of the team stopped beating. Uttley and Neary, who had won a record 43 caps, did not play for England after 1980, Cotton was forced to retire in early 1981 and Beaumont a year later. England's administrators went on earning the distrust of players. Even in 1980 lock Nigel Horton was reduced to tears after the 24-9 victory over Ireland when brusquely informed that he would be dropped. Three years later, Hare recalls the chairman of selectors, Budge Rogers, telling England captain Steve Smith that he would take the press conference, rarely a favourite chore of captaincy, after the 13-13 draw in Cardiff. In his absence, Rogers then blamed Smith and half-back partner Les Cusworth for England's failings. Clive Woodward, who later presided over a very different era, wrote: 'The environment of England rugby was wrong. It didn't challenge us as players. It didn't give us the preparation we needed. It didn't give us every chance. The selection system was inconsistent. The coaches insisted on a style from the stone age, focusing almost exclusively on forward play.' The outcome, Butler says, was that: 'However much we may have declined in the 1980s, England were worse, and we always felt that we could deal with them. They might outmuscle you, but there was no danger of them taking you by surprise.'

The Eighties were better for England than the Seventies, if only because they could scarcely have been worse. Thirteen matches were won, with four drawn, in nine championship seasons following the 1980 Grand Slam. Only two of those wins were against Wales – in 1982 and 1986. Cardiff continued to be impregnable, creating in English minds a complex similar to Wales's Twickenham fixation of the 1920s. Wales were no longer vastly superior, so England believed that they had a chance before every visit to Cardiff. They drew in 1983, lost to a late penalty in 1981 and by three points in 1989. Their widest margin of defeat was nine points – but still the breakthrough eluded them. As Rob Andrew, the outside-half who made his England debut in 1985, wrote: 'Nineteen sixty-three was a millstone around our necks. This was true for both teams.' Yet England's worst defeat took place at neither Twickenham nor Cardiff but Brisbane, in the quarter-final of the inaugural World Cup in 1987. At the time – and for a couple of years afterwards – it seemed to confirm a pattern of Welsh dominance, even if, in wider rugby terms, it echoed the Argentinian writer Jorge Luis Borges's description of the Falklands war in 1981 as 'two bald men squabbling over a comb'. Both England and Wales were also-rans for most of the Eighties. Previously, the longest spell since 1900 without either winning or sharing the title was three seasons from 1925 to 1927. The English Grand Slam of 1980 was followed by seven years in which France, Scotland and Ireland shared the titles. Wales's 1988 championship was shared with France. While England were getting their act together by the late 1980s, they still took until 1991 to win a championship.

Most matches were exciting, but only because they were closely fought and played in front of large crowds who cared desperately about the outcome. If the 1970s saw rugby sparkle because players were given unprecedented space and freedom, the Eighties were when defenders learnt how to stop them. The most consistent performers were forwards such as England's Peter Winterbottom, a blond flanker and former farmer who became a dealer in the City when he joined Harlequins, and Wales lock Bob Norster. Higher scores were largely the result of a proliferation of penalties. Wales crossed the English line in every match but only once, at Brisbane, managed more than two. England scored only five tries in eleven matches between 1980 and 1989, and none after 1984.

England were, though, conspicuously the better side at Twickenham in 1982. They, they completed their first back-to-back home defeats of Wales since 1939 and the result, 17-7, was also their most conclusive in more than two decades. John Reason, of the *Telegraph*, wrote that: 'The old assumptions about Welsh rugby no longer apply. The idea that their backs are bound to win any game in which their forwards are winning ball is no longer valid.' Holmes had to go off five minutes after half-time, a loss which Reason reckoned 'neutralised the half gale blowing at the back of Wales'. The match had been settled long before. England led 11-0 after 26 minutes with tries from their Lancastrian wings. Slemen crossed after build-up work from half-backs Cusworth and Smith, before some typically fast-moving, quick-thinking opportunism from Carleton. With Smith engulfed at a ruck, Carleton played acting half-back and, in Reason's words: 'All Wales expected him to pass but instead he skipped around the forwards and ran through the Welsh centre-field defence as if it did not exist.' Wales, he wrote, 'had given up the ghost so long before the end that their supporters did not even bother to start singing'. If further proof were needed that the Seventies were gone, Wales and France shared the wooden spoon, with Ireland the champions.

England's other victory four years later followed a more familiar pattern. It was won 21-18 by a last-minute drop-goal from outside-half Rob Andrew, a Yorkshireman who followed a beaten track from an exceptional Cambridge University team by using his degree in land economy, the archetypal rugby player's course, to join upwardly mobile

Wasps and work in the property trade. His long international apprentice-ship was punctuated by periodic losses of selectorial confidence in him as he evolved from youthful dasher to conservative tactical kicker. This was one of his happier days as he kicked six penalties – one wind-assisted from beyond halfway – before in injury time he 'checked, thought about his right foot, switched to his left and then dropped the goal'. The media impact was registered by Wales's debutant scrum-half Robert Jones, a twenty year old filling the massive boots of Holmes – who had joined Bradford Northern. 'I turned on the television a few days after the match, and there was Rob on *Wogan*,' said Jones. The *Telegraph's* John Mason thought that 'many international opponents will notice the presence' of Jones and fellow debutant John Devereux, 'a strapping lad of nineteen'. Possibly happier than either was a third rookie, Newport lock David Waters, who had been picked twice for matches postponed by bad weather the previous season, who finally played for Wales at the age of thirty. Wales scored the only try – a sharp break by the effervescent Jonathan Davies setting up centre Bleddyn Bowen, a native of the same village, Trebanos (population 1,611), as Robert Jones.

The plethora of penalties had the *Guardian's* Frank Keating imagining a TV highlights editor's job: 'You have to show the foul that leads up to the kick that leads up to the kicker's celebrating trot back. Repeat each passage at least thrice from varying angles and there is no possible room to show anything else.' Mason said that Wales 'performed miracles with limited possession', but two distinctive locks – the towering Blackpool policeman Wade Dooley, who chose to stay with junior club Preston Grasshoppers, and Maurice Colclough, who after playing in France had joined Swansea – won England two-thirds of the line-outs.

The Twickenham match bracketed by those two England victories was very different. In 1986, Wales were without Cardiff lock Bob Norster. In 1984, when Wales won 24-15, Norster, the fixture's most influential player of the 1980s, was there. Brian Moore, England's hooker later in the decade, was a thoroughly admiring adversary: 'He was only about six-foot-five, by no means massive by today's standards, and he was not massively well-built either. But he had great hands, his timing of the jump was brilliant, and for all but the very tallest players, he was a nightmare.' Butler agreed: 'He had the most incredible standing jump. When he was in the mood he was the best in the world. He was a mood player, not the typical tough second row, but a pure athlete with something of the temperamental thoroughbred about him.' England's misfortune was that he generally was in the mood against them. In 1984, says Butler: 'Bob jumped at four with Dick Moriarty behind him, and me at six. I took John Scott out, Bob kept the other English jumpers fully occupied and Dick won a lot of possession at five. When England won the line-out there was a huge ironic cheer from the crowd. You know you are doing OK when that happens.'

Butler was also involved in the only try, scored by wing Adrian Hadley. 'Bleddyn Bowen sold a dummy and passed. I nearly dropped it, but just managed to hang on and pass to Adrian.' In spite of Wales's possession, it was a tightly contested match. 'We simply couldn't get away from them until the last few minutes when we scored a couple of drop-goals,' said Butler. Those scores completed a memorable afternoon for outside-half Malcolm Dacey, a Swansea player juxtaposed with Gareth Davies in a classic Welsh outside-half controversy, mixing east-west tension with class and education – Davies was an Oxford Blue, while Dacey came from hard-edged Bonymaen – as well as playing styles. Butler says: 'Malcolm could start the line beautifully if he was given decent ball and he was a very good footballer. About the only thing he didn't do well was drop goals, but he took his two at Twickenham very well.'

Played on the final championship weekend, with neither team in contention, the match was shown live on television only after, as Clem Thomas reported, the BBC were 'assailed by the indignant clamour of public opinion'. The result, as Scotland completed their first Grand Slam since 1925 by beating France, consigned England to fourth place while Wales completed a strange year, winning their two away matches but losing both at Cardiff for the first time since 1963.

That year echoed ever more loudly throughout the decade as England failed to break the Cardiff jinx. England could have won in either 1981 and 1983, with the first particularly tantalising. It was, in Carwyn James's view, 'forgettable, but exciting ... lacking in skill, lacking in respect for the laws of the game and lacking the essence of a handling game' and so typical of much of the 1980s. England lost Cotton to the injury that ended his career in the first few minutes. Beaumont recalled 'a wonderful ovation by the crowd . . . that while among the most passionate and vociferous in the world . . . is also one of the most knowledgeable. Perhaps they were glad to see the back of him!'

Had England won, this would have been remembered as Hare's match. The prolific full-back scored all England's points, nineteen, including a try. England led 19-18 with a few minutes left when Wales were awarded a scrum thirty yards from the England line. England centre Clive Woodward wrote: 'I watched the Welsh scrum-half, Brynmor Williams, with one eye and my Welsh opposite number with the other. Williams fed the ball into the scrum and then moved around the back of the scrum to wait for it to emerge, poised to race off for one final attempt at the try line. Out of the corner of my eye, I saw him bend over for the ball. He lunged towards his backs to start the attack. I raced off with a single focus of preventing their scoring. As if looking for me, Williams rounded the referee with his two hands held out, begging the call. The ref instantly blew his whistle and raised his hand to indicate an offside offence. I turned around in shock to see fourteen of my team-mates all standing behind the offside line, a couple of yards away. All behind, but me. All onside, but me.

'"Shit!" I screamed in complete frustration and exasperation. I'd fallen for the oldest trick in the book. Brynmor Williams was famous for dummying to scoop up the ball and moving away as if to attack, drawing the opposition offside.'

Woodward was right about the antiquity of the ruse, which was outlawed not long after. Dicky Owen had used it seventy-nine years earlier to break Wales's losing run at Blackheath. Now it lengthened a jinx as Steve Fenwick, the Bridgend centre, landed the goal to put Wales into a 21-19 lead. There was one final twist. Wales conceded a penalty in injury-time, giving Hare the chance to repeat his match-winning exploits of a year before. Woodward was not optimistic: 'From the look on everyone's face, you could tell it wouldn't come. We knew we had been beaten. We were right.' Hare recalled the kick as being 'just out of easy-kicking range, too far to stroke over, and I tried to kick it too hard.' Smith described Woodward as being inconsolable afterwards. It was not his first unhappy experience in Wales. As a pupil at a North Wales boarding school that he disliked intensely, Woodward was chosen for a Wales Schools trial only to be denied selection, he recorded in his memoirs, because he was English. His misfortune would be repaid several times over.

The 13-13 draw in 1983 was consigned to history by Clive Rowlands' comment that 'the replay is next week and I'm not coming!'. Mark Ring, who was making his debut for Wales at centre after only a dozen games for Cardiff, reckoned that he touched the ball four times while Hare has recalled that Smith and Scott had become obsessed by 'holding the ball in the back of the scrum, which slowed everything down'. There were echoes of earlier meetings. Jeff Squire, a back-rower whose footballing and other skills were so respected that he has been credited with vetoing the selection of Scott for the Lions, took advantage, as in 1980, of an English mix-up to score an opportunist try. Hare, England's try-scorer of 1981, had earlier helped create a score for Carleton, the try-scorer of 1982, then landed the late goal which secured the draw.

Butler captained Wales for the first time that day and was left frustrated at the result. 'In some ways it was more disappointing than 1980. After three years of numbness, we had young talent coming through and I was thrilled to become captain. We were pretty confident, but we played very badly. Dick Moriarty and Bob Norster took a long time to sort out where Bob should be jumping in the line-out and we only just got away with the draw. Losing to England at Twickenham was one thing, losing at home to them for the first time in twenty years would have been quite another. Suddenly being captain, and having to explain how that had happened, didn't seem quite such a good idea.'

Optimism was not entirely misplaced – Wales went to France for the final match with a genuine shot at the championship, losing 16-9, while England's point from the draw served only to avert a whitewash. Even so, reported Frank Keating, the *Guardian's* colour man in succession to Carwyn James, who had died suddenly a month earlier, there was little trace of the old confidence. 'The red-devilled arrogance is diluted now, cockiness is furtive and the *Western Mail's* eight-page morning pull-out is full of insecurities,' Keating wrote. 'Even the Arms Park choral society seems a thing of the glorious past. Patchy stuff now, unharmonious and over-strained.' He quoted John Williams, leader of the St Alban's Band: 'In the old days all the people in the stand had been brought up in the chapel tradition and they could sign off twenty hymns without any problem. Nearly everybody in the ground could sing non-stop for at least three-quarters of an hour. Now they don't have the same religious training and with modern music and pop songs they only remember the choruses.'

Keating made much the same point two years later, but saw a better home performance. Wales won another last-day contest of also-rans, climbing over England into third place in another year of triumph for the Irish, by 24-15 – the same score as at Twickenham in 1984. England led four times but were undone by familiar forces – Norster's domination of the line-out and the power of Holmes, of whom Butler said: 'He was an absolute giant for us. Had he remained injury-free we would be talking about him in the same terms as Gareth Edwards.' Gareth Roberts, an overdue selection on the flank, scored on his international debut. Prop Stuart Evans added bulk and power to the scrummage but made a bigger impression by something he did not do – react in any way to a punch landed with the full weight of England lock John Orwin. The lasting memory, though, was the international unveiling of Jonathan Davies, the explosively quick Neath outside-half and eventual occupant of the A.N. Other slot that had irked Gareth Davies into retirement, who justified the choice with a vivacious display. He dropped a goal before half-time then claimed a try as England full-back Chris Martin fumbled his over-struck up-and-under. England coach Dick Greenwood said the try 'didn't demoralise us, but it moralised them'. Like Woodward, Greenwood would have his revenge.

The nadir of mutual fortunes was reached in 1987. For the first time since 1948, and only the second in the twentieth century, England and Wales occupied the bottom two places – sharing the wooden spoon with one win each. Wales's win was over England, 19-12 at Cardiff, in a match of thirty-eight penalties, twenty-three of them conceded by England. Clem Thomas characterised it as 'ugly, brutal . . . mean, bad-tempered', blaming 'the appalling indiscipline and indiscretions of the English forwards'. England coach Martin Green had proclaimed his team 'good enough to win in Cardiff'.

The second line-out of the match finished with two Wales forwards on the floor. Lock Steve Sutton collided with his second-row partner Norster's elbow, and No. 8 Phil Davies had his cheekbone broken by Dooley, the Blackpool policeman continuing in a similar vein to his apparent audition for work with the CRS riot police in the previous match against France. Dooley recalled seeing a Welshman strike England back-rower John Hall. 'I saw red, literally. It was a gut reaction, totally spontaneous. I lashed out at Hall's assailant, completely unaware of his identity, and the punch landed with a sickening thud on the side of Davies's face. Fortunately, from my point of view, Mr Megson and his linesman had failed to see the blow. Had they done so I think it is a pretty safe bet I would have been asked to leave the field.'

Wales, playing into the wind, took advantage of England's indiscretions with four first-half penalties from Swansea full-back Mark Wyatt, then settled it after the break with the first in a series of Cardiff mishaps by wing Rory Underwood. He explained: 'I tried to collect a kick into the corner from Jonathan Davies and their forwards came rumbling over me for Stuart Evans to score the only try of the match.' Clem Thomas observed 'no sense of guilt in the English camp'. There clearly was within the RFU, with suspensions handed out to Dooley, captain Richard Hill – whom Andrew thought was 'too fiery' to be captain – and the Bath front-row duo of Gareth Chilcott and Graham Dawe. Chilcott, a rotund French polisher with a fearsome reputation, admitted years later that: 'We had been on the back foot against Wales, and were certainly over the top.' Dawe's replacement was Brian Moore, an abrasively intelligent lawyer from Nottingham, who seized his opportunity so firmly that he was England's hooker for most of the next decade. Dooley remained aggrieved that 'not one Welshman was disciplined or, so far as I am aware, even warned about his conduct', while recording his gratitude to one of them – fellow policeman Sutton, who made a point of buying him a drink at a tense post-match dinner. Some Welsh supporters behaved less well. Dooley found spittle on his England blazer after a pre-match walk and full-back Marcus Rose collected £3.50 worth of coins thrown at him during the match, handed them to referee Ray Megson, then spent them in the bar at the dinner.

Memories of that Cardiff match were fresh when the teams met three months later in the quarter-final of the first World Cup, in Brisbane, Australia. England coach Martin Green said before the tournament: 'I wish the Scots and Irish luck in the cup, but I am afraid I cannot say the same to the Welsh.' Neither union had wanted a World Cup – Derek Wyatt, the Labour MP and former England wing, has suggested that it happened only because International Rugby Board delegates from both countries defied orders, and voted in favour of the concept. Nor were events in Brisbane a ringing endorsement of the new competition. Stephen Jones recalled 'a thoroughly bizarre occasion', played on a ground with 'a few rows of benches, a largish stand down one side and acres of grass verges' where 'you could turn up a few minutes before the kick-off and pay on the turnstiles. Only 17,000 watched.'

England had looked the more impressive team in the pool stage and were generally rated the favourites. Wales were forced by injuries to call up teenage prop David Young for his debut. Former Australia coach Bob Templeton called Wales's 16-3 win 'the worst match I have ever seen'. England's hooker Moore remembered 'a horrible match on a horrible day and a truly awful England performance'. He and Andrew implicitly blamed Green – Andrew for a debilitating three-hour training session in the Brisbane heat the day before, Moore for the coach acceding to RFU demands not to have Dooley jump directly against Norster. 'Martin Green said he didn't want the confrontation to develop, forgetting that Test rugby is essentially confrontation.' Wales manager Clive Rowlands did not think it was that bad a game. 'The press said it was because England lost after we hadn't been given a chance. It was a match where psychology mattered. David Young did well against Paul Rendall, who was a good prop. Bob Norster shouldn't have played, but we knew he had a hex on Dooley. He dominated the first twenty minutes. After that his leg had gone, but he still won ball for us.' English disarray was evident when Rendall was injured, but they failed to get a replacement on before the next scrum, from which Gareth Roberts scored an opportunist try. All three Welsh tries came from England errors, the later ones scored by Robert Jones, who would be named the best European player at the tournament, and John Devereux. It was, in the words of the *Telegraph's* John Mason, a reporter with ample experience of England debacles, 'rock bottom'. Wales went on to an entirely predictable semi-final massacre by hosts and eventual winners New Zealand, but recuperated by beating Australia in the third-place match. Asked where Welsh rugby went from there, Rowlands replied: 'Back to beating England every year.' He does not claim it as the wisest statement of a long and loquacious career, but points out: 'We were down in the dumps after being hammered by the All Blacks and it was a joke really. And we did win the next two times.'

For England it proved the catalyst for long-needed reform. RFU president Alan Grimsdell told the 1987 AGM that change was essential. Pressure for the creation of leagues had borne fruit even before the World Cup with the creation of a vast nationwide competition of more than a hundred divisions, extending from champions Leicester to Armthorpe Rovers at the bottom of Yorkshire League Six. Don Rutherford remembers starting to see real progress as he was allowed to bring in specialists such as national athletics coach Tom McNab and Loughborough's Rex Hazeldine. Most significant was the appointment of a new England manager. First choice was Mike Weston, but he declined the post when not allowed to reappoint Green as coach. The job went to Geoff Cooke, who had fewer credentials as a player but had shown himself to be a shrewd selector as long ago as the North's victory over New Zealand in 1979 and, as director of the National Coaching Foundation, was fully attuned to modern thinking in many sports. He said: 'We have to be honest enough to face the fact that we're in the second division.'

Promotion did not come immediately. The first hint of serious improvement came in 1988 when only a late French try deprived England of victory in Paris. Next up were Wales at Twickenham. Wales coach Tony Gray, as wing Ieuan Evans testified, 'believed implicitly in the Welsh way of playing and gave the players a certain latitude to play it off-the-cuff'. He took that faith as far as the calculated risk of dropping full-back Paul Thorburn, a goal-kicker of massive range and great accuracy, in favour of twenty-year-old Tony Clement, one of four outside-halves in a back division packed with footballing talent. Gray was rewarded with the fixture's best rugby of the 1980s. Wales won a contest that exuded life and purpose even during a scoreless first half. Clem Thomas wrote that it 'restored one's faith in this fiercely combative fixture'. Norster's control of the line-out supplied enough possession for the backs to prosper, while Jonathan Davies, 'a force of nature gifted with astonishing vision' according to the *Guardian's* Robert Armstrong, persecuted England's big, tough back-rower Mick Skinner. Wales, wrote Armstrong, 'displayed instinctive fluidity and the sharp sense of each man's position that fashions danger out of nothing'.

Even so, it seemed that they might yet regret the loss of Thorburn's kicking. A remarkable tackle by Bristol full-back Jonathan Webb, the latest and almost last in the great tradition of England doctors, denied Davies before the breakthrough came in the fifty-seventh minute. Cardiff wing Adrian Hadley claimed both Welsh tries, each time finishing off a long-range assault involving multiple hands – the second, an eighty-five-metre masterpiece incorporating a slashing break down the right by the irrepressible Davies. Wales went on to win their first Triple Crown in nine years and, with a young, vibrant team playing brilliantly, could look forward to better times.

That promise was destroyed in New Zealand that summer as perhaps the most formidable team of recent times twice beat them by more than fifty points. Jonathan Davies offered to supply the Welsh Rugby Union with a report on what needed to be done to match the vastly superior power and conditioning of the New Zealanders. Defeat in South Africa in 1964 had set in train reforms that underpinned the success of the following decade. In 1988, the WRU rejected Davies's offer and, instead of accepting responsibility for an absurdly demanding tour schedule, blamed Gray and manager Derek Quinnell, who were fired a few months after winning the Triple Crown.

As a result, gentle decline gave way to, in Butler's words, 'falling off a cliff'. The promise of 1988 was destroyed. According to Robert Jones: 'It was a crazy decision, which did far more damage than the defeats by the All Blacks. Wales certainly did not recover from the shock of it during my career.' The team broke up. Five Twickenham winners, starting with Jonathan Davies at the end of 1988, went to rugby league. By the time Wales played England again, in Cardiff, in March 1989, the balance of power had shifted. Wales had lost all three matches and faced an historic first whitewash. England had had two wins and a draw. Though captained from centre by Will Carling, who at twenty-two had become their youngest leader since Peter Howard in 1931, England had prospered through the dominance of their pack and a relentlessly focused nine-man game. The ninth man was a scrum-half with the resoundingly un-English name of Dewi Morris, a native of Crickhowell. 'I'm often asked why I chose to play for England rather than Wales,' says Morris. 'There never was a choice. I had played all my adult rugby in England. The Welsh selectors didn't know about me and even if they had, wouldn't have been interested – they had Robert Jones.' Now a television analyst for Sky

Sports, working alongside another England player with Welsh connections, Stuart Barnes, he says: 'If I had used my first name and played as Colin Morris, nobody would have said anything.' Instead he has spent two decades having 'Dewi' mispronounced — 'even my wife gets it wrong and the only time anyone gets it right is if we have Welsh lads on the programme. I've had a few variations — John Howe, of West Hartlepool, called me "Doggie".'

English fans were confident. Peter Corrigan, writing in the *Observer*, said: 'They poured off the trains with that same laughing confidence exhibited by arrivals at Las Vegas.' Their players were not received warmly. Lock Paul Ackford, an inspector in an all-police second row alongside PC Dooley, echoed his partner's 1987 report of finding spittle on his England blazer, while Cooke, the manager, was 'taken aback by the obvious depth of hatred . . . it was like going into a war zone'.

Morris sang both anthems. 'Why not?' he said. 'I got a few wry smiles from the England lads, but they understood. It was for the people I'd grown up with and my dad. I didn't do it again, but it was the right thing to do.' Not a lot else went right for England. The early loss of the imposing Gloucester flanker Mike Teague eliminated a line-out option and, as Dooley said, 'to make matters worse Norster played out of his skin'. It was, in Morris's view, 'a day when we couldn't get the shackles off. The crowd were phenomenal for Wales. It was very physical, Norster ruled the air waves and Robert Jones gave one of the great displays of kicking skills, keeping us on the back foot all afternoon.'

Four hours of pre-match rain should have favoured England's powerful pack but, as Carling admitted: 'Our forwards were turned over physically and psychologically . . . and there was no plan B.' Jones noticed early on that 'if I put the ball behind Rory Underwood, he and Jon Webb would struggle to deal with it'. Wales's score came when their thirty-year-old outside-half Paul Turner, playing, as Ieuan Evans wrote, 'like someone who has waited all his life for this one chance', hoisted a kick. Underwood caught it but, under pressure, threw a wild pass to Webb. The Welsh forwards engulfed the full-back and centre Mike Hall was awarded the try, although whether he had grounded the ball properly was debatable. Wales held their 12-9 lead through a mountingly tense second half as Norster, in his last game for his country, went on ruling the line-out and Jones box-kicked with killing precision. As the crowd rejoiced at the final whistle, Wales captain Thorburn gesticulated wildly at the press-box and later used his after-dinner speech to denounce Welsh journalist Stephen Jones as 'the scum of the earth'. Jones had warned in the *Sunday Times* that victory might blind Wales to its undoubted problems but a sub-editor had headlined this as suggesting that he wanted Wales to lose. England captain Will Carling was no happier when he stopped at a motorway service station on the way home. 'Around thirty Wales supporters made a tunnel and jeered and taunted me as I walked back to the car park,' said Carling.

Robert Jones called it: 'A one-off, founded on pride and character,' but he acknowledged that 'you won't win a Grand Slam or Triple Crown that way'. Corrigan warned: 'There's a mighty debt to be paid in mocking laughter from our rivals one day.' It was perhaps the most accurate prediction of a long and distinguished journalistic career.

CHAPTER TWELVE
ANGLO-SAXON ALTITUDE
1990–2003

The race is not always to the swift, or the battle to the strong. But that's the way to bet.

Damon Runyon

'The answer about Wales,' said Malcolm, 'is that nobody in England thinks anything of it.'

Derek Raymond, *A State of Denmark*, 1970

A question always at the back of the minds of thoughtful Welsh rugby fans, even in the golden days of the 1970s, was: 'What happens if England, who are so much bigger and better-resourced than we are, ever get their act together?' Those Welsh fans got their answer in the 1990s and early years of the new millennium – and did not much like it.

Like Wales's first golden age, the second was followed two decades later by an era of English ascendancy. English dominance was far greater in this period than in the 1920s, at last giving the country an era to match Wales's best, with the World Cup victory in 2003 an additional triumph not available to earlier great teams. Over fourteen seasons starting in 1990, Wales and England met sixteen times – the extra two matches, a pre-World Cup friendly in Cardiff and a quarter-final in Brisbane, were in 2003. Wales won two of the fourteen, each time by a single point in contests as tight as the score suggested. Both owed much to Welsh spirit and determination, but were ultimately down to English aberrations – Rory Underwood's defensive inattention in Cardiff in 1993 and Lawrence Dallaglio's over-confidence at Wembley six years later.

Over this period England won seven championships, eight Triple

Crowns and three Grand Slams, overtaking Wales in their overall head-to-head record. Trailing by forty-seven wins to thirty-six after losing in Cardiff in 1989, they regained the overall lead, by fifty wins to forty-nine, with the World Cup quarter-final victory in Brisbane in November 2003. Wales's fate echoed England's in the 1970s. They did not just lose to the old enemy, but to most opponents. In the last ten seasons, 1990 to 1999, of the Five Nations Championship, Wales won only twelve matches, finished bottom three times and twice, beginning in 1990, suffered the unprecedented humiliation of losing all four matches. There was one trophy, an unexpected championship in 1994 won, in spite of losing at Twickenham, on points difference – a tie-breaker introduced a year earlier.

Ieuan Evans, Wales's outstanding captain and arguably their best player across the decade, said of that 1994 triumph: 'Although we had won the trophy and won it deservedly it didn't feel right. The look on our faces could not disguise a feeling that it had a slightly hollow ring to it.' There was perhaps an element of poetic justice. Of the ten previous Welsh sides who had shared titles, nine would have been champions if the points-difference rule had applied. It was about the only moment Wales did enjoy at Twickenham. The 15-8 defeat that preserved the title for Wales was the second smallest English home victory in this period. Previously their biggest win over Wales at Twickenham was the 18-3 beating inflicted in 1921. That record was comprehensively shattered in 1990, and that mark in turn exceeded in three consecutive Twickenham matches between 1998 and 2002. Even allowing for much higher scoring, these were historic beatings. By 2002, hammering Wales was so routine that Paul Ackford, who had moved from the police into journalism, wrote that England's 50-10 win 'somehow never caught the imagination'. It was, he argued, in terms unimaginable to earlier generations, 'impossible to get too excited about the summary execution of mediocre Wales'.

Twickenham itself was transformed between 1990 and 1995. The familiar double-decker stands that had flanked it since the 1930s were swept away, replaced by vaulting grandstands in an all-seat stadium holding 75,000 people. It acquired its own signature tune as well. The adoption of the American spiritual 'Swing Low Sweet Chariot' is usually dated to the hat-trick scored by wing Chris Oti, who was of Nigerian descent, against Ireland in 1988. Once a favourite with Welsh choirs such as Morriston

Orpheus, its association with English rugby success meant that it rapidly became as popular in Wales as the '*Marseillaise*' was with French aristocrats. Welshmen could argue that Twickenham only ever mastered a four-line chorus, but Cardiff's singing had also become more myth than reality due to a combination of low spirits, declining chapel culture and the progressive elimination of standing areas. 'Cwm Rhondda', formerly sung in its entirety, became Wales's 'Swing Low' – with which it shares a reference to Jordan – the 'Bread of Heaven' chorus taking on an independent existence, not least as the title of Ieuan Evans's autobiography. 'Calon Lan' was still sung occasionally, but other traditional hymns and arias were heard no longer, giving way to a much smaller repertoire featuring Tom Jones's 'Delilah' and – ironically – Max Boyce's 'Hymns and Arias'. The best Welsh singing of the decade was at, of all unlikely places, Wembley, during a two-year hiatus when the London football stadium became Wales's home while the Millennium Stadium was being built. England coach Clive Woodward noted: 'The WRU had done a great job . . . turning the stadium into a small outpost of Wales.' While Boyce and Jones were singing their most famous songs, Woodward wondered 'if I hadn't strayed into an open-air pop concert', but the most important Wembley presence was the London Welsh choir, giving prematch singing a coherence that had been lost in the last years at the National Stadium. Since Wales's return to the newly constructed Millennium Stadium, the most consistent performer in a red shirt has been Neath soprano Katherine Jenkins.

It was not only singing that declined in Cardiff. If the venue intimidated anyone in the 1990s it was Welsh teams unable to cope with public expectation conditioned by the results and performances of the 1970s. Robert Jones said: 'The crowd at Cardiff was very quick to get on our backs when things went wrong . . . it was not hard to catch the mood, and a sour one was undoubtedly inhibiting to a struggling team. Indeed, it was becoming easier to play away from home because of the pressure.' Though England hooker Brian Moore was probably right to argue that 'anyone who believes that Cardiff will ever provide easy pickings for an English team does not understand international rugby, or life', some England victories certainly looked easy. They won three of their last four visits to the National Stadium, by a margin averaging eighteen points. The Millennium Stadium saw three consecutive England victories, including, in 2001, one of their best ever performances. It also witnessed one of Wales's worst, in the pre-World Cup friendly between the sides two years later. When Wales lost 26-9 in the championship match in between, it seemed a reasonably successful exercise in damage limitation, while English writers bandied terms like 'below-par', 'anxious' and 'no longer acceptable'.

If the rebuilding of Twickenham was evidence that, whatever their attitude to the inevitable acceptance of professionalism, the RFU possessed considerable commercial sense, the Millennium Stadium did much less for Wales. Its construction, under the deadline pressure imposed by the 1999 World Cup, took ill-afforded income, attention and energy during the immensely difficult transition to professionalism in the second half of the 1990s, while its costs left the WRU with a heavy burden of debt. The transition, following the long-overdue acceptance of professionalism in August 1995, a century almost to the day after the rugby league schism, was tough for both countries. England's playing success was accomplished against a soundtrack of conflict between leading clubs bent on making the game pay and a union dominated by officials and affiliates uncomfortable with professionalism. Previously volunteers, in theory at least, players became employees with con-tractual commitments to club and country, who squabbled over the time they spent on release for international duties. Aggressive recruiting by Newcastle as soon as professionalism was accepted provoked a huge inflationary spiral and heavy losses for most clubs. England, though, ultimately had the resources, both in terms of money and population, needed to fund professional rugby. Wales had fewer ideological qualms, but lacked resources. Wales is smaller and poorer than England and has fewer rich men seeking an outlet for surplus income. Fear of the rugby league scout gave way to worries about free-spending English clubs such as Richmond, who signed several Welsh internationals. While this lasted only until financial reality dawned in England and the less committed owners pulled out, it was a pointer to the future balance of power.

For a century leading Welsh clubs had been stronger than their English counterparts. Their ill-luck was that national leagues – Wales introduced theirs in 1990 – downgraded traditional Anglo-Welsh club fixtures at precisely the time when English clubs became seriously worth playing.

The shift in balance became evident when the Heineken Cup was introduced in 1996. In common with the times, England's clubs were better, while Wales's remained more enthusiastic. English clubs emulated their football counterparts forty years earlier by ducking out of the first year's competition – and later boycotted the 1998-99 season – but have been a force since Bath capped their greatest era by winning the European title in 1998. No Welsh club has matched Cardiff's achievement of reaching the first Heineken final in 1996. Of Wales's traditional powerhouses, only Cardiff avoided severe financial difficulties, but instead they underachieved on the field. Unable to compete financially or in playing terms with the best of England and France, the Welsh clubs were merged into regional franchises in 2003.

Change was similarly dramatic for players. Not least of the hypocrisies of the pre-professional era was that players took on huge commitments in terms of time and energy, but were not allowed any financial return for making them. Regulations were routinely evaded. The Pugh report, which gave the amateur ideology its long overdue quietus in 1995, showed that breaches of the rules on professionalism were rife in every significant rugby country with the exception of Argentina. Players still, though, had to seek a full-time living outside the game. England scrum-half Kyran Bracken said: 'A club used to attract a player by helping him find a lucrative job, and I had been introduced to my law firm by a rugby contact but, even as late as 1994, I was still paying annual subs to Bristol RFC as my contribution to the running of the club.' The subscription-payers of 1994 soon evolved into paid employees.

As well as the club v country conflict, there were battles between nations. England's desperation to fund professionalism while maintaining payments on the building of Twickenham led them to argue – echoing their attitude to the new International Rugby Board more than a century earlier – that their numbers of clubs and players and larger television audiences entitled them to a larger share of Five Nations television revenue. In 1996, they unilaterally signed a contract with Sky Television to show their home matches and came close to expulsion from the Five Nations. Two years later, they were briefly expelled, before a deal was brokered in a Glasgow pub. Some English voices argued that England no longer benefited from playing the Celtic nations and should instead confine themselves to France and the southern hemisphere giants.

This rhetoric reflected the change brought by the first World Cup, in 1987. British and European rugby had previously been defined by the annual championship cycle. Now it moved increasingly on a four-year cycle, defined by World Cups. If that was the ultimate objective, it was possible to argue that the Five Nations was dispensable, even an obstacle to supreme success. Yet whatever its limitations, the Five Nations was invulnerable. Its traditional rivalries remained so compelling that matches were guaranteed sell-outs, generating steady profits for unions increasingly driven by commercial priorities. Longer-term worries about the ability of the Celtic trio to compete against their larger, richer neighbours peaked on the weekend in 1998 when, after more than a century without a single fifty-point score, there were two on the same day – England running up sixty against Wales at Twickenham while French scored fifty-one points away to Scotland.

For England this era is a tale of two managers. First came Geoff Cooke, identified on the field with the captaincy of Will Carling and steamrolling packs that systematically flattened all European opposition, but struggled against the best of the southern hemisphere because of a lack of variation and initiative. Then, after a transitional period under Jack Rowell – one of the architects of Bath's long hegemony – came Clive Woodward. His leader and totem was the giant Leicester lock Martin Johnson, once likened to '6ft 6in of rolled-up barbed wire'. While still fielding formidable forwards, England played with greater variety and imagination. Though making them more vulnerable in Europe, this flexibility enabled them to conquer the world. Weaker opponents, and none were weaker than Wales, became like candidates sitting Sellar and Yeatman's examination paper for medieval kings in *1066 and All That*, with its final question: 'How do you wish to die?'. Neither being bludgeoned to defeat by Cooke's forwards nor dazzled and dismantled by the pace and power of Woodward's team was much fun. Then again, little about Welsh rugby was fun. Wales went through a succession of coaches, each change bringing its concomitant shift in playing style and selection, with two disastrous attempts – under Ron Waldron, of Neath, in 1990-91 and Alec Evans, from Cardiff, in 1995 – to build on the foundation of a single club. Losses to rugby league continued in the early 1990s, with Scott Gibbs, Wales's brightest young back, and powerful No. 8 Scott Quinnell both leaving for spells in the North.

The Welsh game's rulers were in disarray. They were among the collateral victims of the later stages of South African apartheid, their weakness being brutally exposed in 1989 when the WRU advised players not to play in the Republic's centenary celebrations. The ten who went, receiving payments of around £25,000 each, were recruited by Wales's most recent captain, Paul Thorburn, with the assistance of WRU International Rugby Board members Terry Vaux and Gwilym Treharne. Vaux and Treharne lost their posts, along with vice-president Rhys Williams, the Lion of the 1950s. David East, the well regarded union secretary, resigned in protest at union officials acting behind his back. President Clive Rowlands offered his resignation. Commissioning an inquiry from lawyer Vernon Pugh launched his rapid rise through rugby officialdom to the leadership of both the WRU and the IRB. The WRU, though, continued to struggle for credibility and decent results. In 1993, its committee lost a vote of confidence, while Alan Davies, one of the more successful national coaches, was wont to tell his players: 'I've just had a meeting with the WRU committee. Someone take the knives out of my back, please.'

Politics and public expectation were not the only Welsh afflictions. They had some high-quality backs – Robert Jones and Ieuan Evans were the best scrum-half and wing in Britain before 1995, while Jones's successor Robert Howley and the ex-league centre pairing of Allan Bateman and Scott Gibbs enjoyed similar standing later in the decade, supplemented by the prolific goal-kicking of Neil Jenkins. All of them, though, spent their international careers on the back foot thanks to the collapse in Welsh forward play. There were two Lions tours during the 1990s. No Welsh forward played a single Test. Seven of the pack who played the last two Tests against New Zealand in 1993 were English. This followed on from two phenomena of the 1980s: the contraction – and, in the case of coal, disappearance – of Welsh heavy industry and the withdrawal by teachers, subjected by government to increased workloads, central direction, pay restraint and blame for most of the ills of the modern world, of the goodwill essential to running school teams. This was not an exclusively Welsh problem. Tony Collins has pointed out that the proportion of privately educated England players started to rise again, after fifty years of steady decline, in the mid-1980s.

Among these was Will Carling. A product like Wavell Wakefield, John Spencer and more than twenty other internationals of Sedbergh School, he came to epitomise his era. He thought Cooke was winding him up when he invited him, the youngest man in the team at twenty-two and not yet fully established at centre, to become captain late in 1988. A square-set, powerfully built figure, his sharp acceleration, resolute defence and, particularly early in his career, gift for putting the man outside him into space, might in another life have made him a fine league player. In this one he led England fifty-nine times over the next eight years. Those talents were rapidly overshadowed by the celebrity that came with his role and England's success – making news by first marrying a television presenter, then having the marriage break-up over his friendship with Diana, Princess of Wales. Buying himself out of the Army, he took his fame into business as a consultant and motivational speaker. Chris Jones wrote that 'he embodies the new breed of England rugby player'.

He was predictably unpopular in Wales. One reason was given by Robert Jones on a Lions tour. 'You've captained an England side that has beaten Wales, so there is no way you are going to be flavour of the month,' said Jones. 'You are built up to be the arrogant, aloof English git because then the defeat is easier to stomach.' There was, though, rather more to it. Carling himself recognised that international sportsmen 'become a representative of a set of values and those values are attributed to you individually'. Carling's accent, appearance, background, job and air of being pleased with himself – he had, to be fair, much to be pleased about – meant that he appeared both toff and Thatcherite, the epitome of what Welshmen most disliked about the English.

Cooke made several choices that underlined his gifts as a selector, another being the summoning of Ackford almost a decade after his first appearance for England B. At the end of his forty-nine matches in charge, which brought thirty-five wins, two Grand Slams and a World Cup final, he remembered taking over when 'confidence was at a very low ebb. The players were feeling very insecure in their own ability as individuals, in their ability to stay in the team and in their futures in international rugby . . . England went on to the field with a total fear of failure. They were incredibly inhibited and had been tremendous underachievers for years. All I said was: "If you just want to be failures and underachievers, carry on as you are going. But if you want to be part of a successful England team you have to get thinking of yourselves as international athletes, as the elite of your sport, and not traditional rugby players."'

The effects were visible to journalists. Interviews that previously took place over a lunchtime pint now involved players emerging from a gym to demand nothing more intoxicating than a glass of mineral water. Brian Moore recalled: 'He gave the team a level of organisation that it never had before. He also handled the press well.' Morris says: 'He provided stability and continuity, which was what England needed. Previously people had been in one match, out the next. Geoff and Roger Uttley didn't do that.' There was some austerity in personal relations. Moore, a senior player, said: 'I never had a long conversation with him. He was not unfriendly, but exceedingly difficult to get to know well.'

This cultural revolution burst upon Wales in two landmark English victories in 1990 and 1991. The impact of their 34-6 win at Twickenham in 1990 was underlined by Press Association correspondent Terry Cooper, who saw his first Wales v England match in 1949 and recalled this as 'the first time I had seen Wales completely outclassed by the men in white'. The course of the contest was set early. Jeff Probyn, a Wasps prop whose formidable scrummaging tested the boundary between unorthodoxy and illegality, said: 'The first scrum on the Welsh put-in was the best I have ever been in for England. We pushed them back a yard and right off the ball and that really set the seal on the game and which way it was going. I doubted the Welsh heart for battle that day and there were enough wheezing noises to doubt their fitness as well.'

England were twelve points up in ten minutes, two penalties from Simon Hodgkinson followed by a try from Carling, who fought his way through three Welsh tacklers to the line. Rory Underwood took revenge for previous miseries in Cardiff with two tries, the second a seventy-five-yard interception, at the end of which, he said, 'I would have been happy enough to stay there, flat on my back. I walked back all the way and I was out, my head was just buzzing.' The reason was a cold rather than a lack of fitness. Athletics coach Tom McNab, who worked with Cooke's England, reckoned that Underwood's athletic test scores, which showed upper body strength superior to that of most forwards, could have been bettered only by Daley Thompson, the former Olympic decathlon champion. The half-Burmese Underwood was a rare, reserved, rugby-playing teetotaller – Carling wrote that 'I've known him for a long time now, yet have never known him' – appreciated by team-mates as a ruthless finisher apparently propelled by the same fuel as the planes he flew in the RAF. After four tries in twenty-two internationals up to the end of the 1988 Five Nations, he was a major beneficiary of English improvement, claiming thirty-four in his next thirty-eight games and erasing fellow airman Cyril Lowe from England's record books. Another outstanding Englishman, outside-half Rob Andrew, could thank a Welshman for his improvement. In 1989, he missed selection for the Lions party to tour Australia but went out as a replacement. Playing outside Robert Jones, he recalled: 'I have never felt more comfortable more quickly with any other scrum-half.' Given what Stephen Jones called 'that almost agoraphobic extra yard of space that lightning service from the base of the scrum can give', Andrew acquired a confidence and authority that took him into all three Tests and sustained him for the rest of a long career.

Mick Cleary wrote in the *Observer*: 'The spectre of a thousand Welsh victories past was swept away in the rout, roared on by an ecstatic, if slightly disbelieving, crowd who were full of passion.' Wales's heaviest championship defeat since before results were counted in points did not exaggerate English superiority. 'We were probably lucky it was not more,' said Robert Jones, the Wales captain. 'They were simply much better than we were – big, powerful and confident.' Frank Keating and John Reason both thought that England should have scored fifty points. Probyn heard Jones asking: 'How are we going to live this down?' Coach John Ryan could not, and resigned.

Carling's hope that it would be seen 'as a turning point in English rugby' was dashed a month later when England were beaten by Scotland's utter determination and their own over-confidence. Resolved not to be caught out like that a second time, they reined in the style and never recaptured the freedom of that Twickenham performance. Eddie Butler argues: 'The defeat at Murrayfield hardened the English mindset. They became much more focused and single-minded and made a conscious decision that nobody would do them that way again.' There was, though, no doubting English delight at the demolition of Wales.

Carling said a few days after the game: 'Public reaction has been remark-able. I can't walk far down the street before somebody stops me to say "thank you very much" and I know what they are thanking me for. I have to say "well, it's a pleasure". And it is.'

If a thousand Welsh spectres had been chased away, one more remained to be exorcised – the Cardiff jinx. While Carling said, 'I don't believe the problem exists,' English preparations for their visit the following year suggested otherwise. Cooke had the Welsh anthem played as his squad trained at Gloucester on the previous Wednesday, and several more times over the next few days. Most previous English teams had stayed outside Cardiff – Hignell remembers one 1970s team staying in Bristol – and travelled in on the day of the match. This time England arrived on Thursday. Andrew explained the reasoning: 'You need to see the way the Welsh feel about the English. Otherwise, when you drive in on a Saturday, it hits you.'

It did not all go to plan. Scrum-half Hill, unrecognisable as the rational individual who now coaches Bristol so astutely, was asked to give a team-talk on the Friday evening. Andrew said: 'Unfortunately the red mist descended over Hill at the very mention of Wales, rendering normal speech quite impossible. Such was the torrent of outraged abuse which poured from him that we were reduced to uncontrollable laughter and the meeting broke up in disarray.' The next morning, though, Dooley, out for a walk with Ackford, found Cardiff different from previous visits. 'The edge had gone,' he said. 'We were amazed how quiet it was. There were plenty of supporters about, but they all seemed to be English. The few Welsh fans we came across were very quiet and tame; it appeared they knew the writing was on the wall.' England walked from their hotel to the ground and, as Moore says: 'By the time we reached the dressing rooms the process of desensitisation was complete, the bogey had ceased to register; it was just another international rugby match, one in which we had the better team.'

It did not look like that in the first minute. Dean Richards, who later admitted, 'I played like a drain . . . the worst game I had played for England', dropped the ball, Jones box-kicked and England conceded a penalty which Thorburn converted. Andrew recalled: 'We were 3-0 down and the whole of Wales was going potty. I remember running back under the posts thinking "this can't be happening". It was. The spectre of another unexpected defeat began to loom.' This England team, though, was better equipped mentally and physically than its predecessors. What followed was, in the words of the *Telegraph's* John Mason, 'about as exciting as watching the tide turn in Swansea Bay'. Welsh journalist Steve Bale was more appreciative, admiring: 'A heroic effort by one of the most durable and efficient packs assembled in international rugby to squeeze most of the life out of their opponents'. Wales fielded two nineteen-year-olds, Pontypridd outside-half Neil Jenkins and Neath centre Scott Gibbs, both in their first seasons in senior rugby. Neither they nor any other Welshman saw much of the ball. Ieuan Evans said: 'England outclassed us up front, which was not surprising, considering that we didn't have a pack.'

England turned pressure into points via the boot of full-back Hodgkinson, who landed seven penalties, a new international record, between the fifth and sixty-ninth minutes. After his first-minute success, Thorburn had an unhappy day, missing four penalties before giving way to Jenkins, who landed the first of many kicks for Wales early in the second half. By then Wales were reduced to damage limitation. England prop Jason Leonard, a shining exception to English re-gentrification, was an engaging carpenter from Barking who was just beginning an international career of extraordinary length. He was amazed to see grown men crying, 'a different level of intensity that was quite incredible to witness'. Moore has another memory: 'At least ten minutes from the final whistle we could sense people leaving in droves. I could make the line-out calls from the touchline and needed to call only once. Usually at Cardiff you have to scream at your scrum-half, who then walks up and down the line trying to scream the signal against the noise.'

The coup de grace was administered by Gloucester flanker Mike Teague driving off the back of a scrum to score the only try. Morris, a reserve on the day, savoured the importance of ending the 28-year jinx. 'It was the monkey off our back, the fear factor about Wales and Cardiff had gone.' As with Wales in the 1970s, the old enemy was no longer the main one. 'Once we had managed to win in Cardiff, the big game was against France.'

*

England won the Grand Slam in 1991. Later that year they played Australia in the World Cup final at Twickenham, blowing their chances with a tactical brainstorm. Wales were knocked out after being beaten at home by Western Samoa. Another Slam, two in a row for the first time since 1924, followed in 1992, completed with a 24-0 victory over Wales at Twickenham. Fran Cotton cannot have been the only England player of earlier vintage marvelling that 'Twickenham was relatively quiet, yet we've won a Grand Slam by beating Wales 24-0. What would have happened if we'd ever done that? We'd have gone absolutely mad!' Victory was almost taken for granted. As Andrew said: 'We always knew it was a game we were going to win, the only question was by how much.' As if to balance the Welsh-born Morris, Wales fielded Llanelli second row Tony Copsey, who had qualified through six years' residence but was a native of Romford, Essex, and had 'Made in England' tattooed on one buttock. Ieuan Evans, appreciative of a team-mate who was 'all elbows and arms, an awkward customer . . . would willingly give everything for his adopted Wales', suggested he add 'Refined in Wales' on the other.

The most memorable moment was supplied by an opposing lock. England, as commanding as Wales teams had been two decades earlier, scored through Carling within sixty-one seconds of the kick-off and wrapped the match up within half an hour, taking a fifteen-point lead. Dooley, who was winning his fiftieth cap and becoming the third Englishman to do so after team-mates Underwood and Winterbottom, scored his third try in that time. He later recalled: 'Rob Andrew, who never ordinarily passed back inside, for some reason on this occasion did. And for some reason I, who never came up in support, found myself taking his flicked pass. It shocked me. And then I was driven over the line.' The distance covered, he said, 'gets longer every time I tell the story'.

A third Grand Slam in a row was widely expected in 1993. Geoff Cooke spoke of putting England on top of world rugby. 'It may be arrogant, we may be knocked off in the championship, but it is where we want to go,' he said, believing that 'we will have to shoot ourselves in the foot to stop being successful'. England reserve Stuart Barnes, the radical outside-half alternative to the more conservative – in rugby and politics – Andrew, a product of Welsh schools rugby but fated never to play against Wales, said: 'The Welshmen who recognised me would have taunted me unmercifully in 1973 but in 1993 wanted to know by how many points I thought England would win.'

Wales's captain Ieuan Evans caught a whiff of complacency. 'You always know when teams are smug,' he said. 'Certainly the English supporters that week wore smug, self-satisfied expressions . . . We were just there as so much cannon-fodder . . . it was certainly the impression we got, after reading all those England players in their various newspaper columns . . . They had not concentrated as ruthlessly on beating us as they ought to have done. They weren't, to coin a vogue word, focused.' That sense communicated itself to the crowd. 'The atmosphere that day was the best I have ever known at Cardiff,' said Evans. 'It made the blood tingle and the electricity crackle. The anthem was sung as I have never heard it sung before.'

While Wales started fierily, Paul Ackford in the *Sunday Telegraph* admitted to thinking: 'I've seen it all before . . . twenty minutes of huff and puff and then nothing for the rest of the game.' England led 9-3 shortly before half-time with two penalties by Webb and a drop-goal by Jeremy Guscott, the languidly elegant Bath centre and England's first player of West Indian descent since James Peters, to a Jenkins penalty. Then flank forward Emyr 'Tarw' Lewis kicked down the Welsh right. Ieuan Evans had hoped Lewis would pass, but instead found himself in an apparently hopeless chase against the fearsomely quick Underwood. The England wing 'wasn't exactly ambling back but nor was he running at full tilt,' said Evans. 'At that stage I was flying and I thought to myself: "He doesn't know I'm up this quickly." The roar of the crowd must have told him someone was coming, but it was obvious he didn't hear my footsteps. When Emyr kicked the ball behind him, he must have been ten yards ahead of me. By the time he had turned and gone five yards I was up to his shoulder . . . The ball bounced marginally beyond their ten-yard line and once I went past him within a yard of reaching the ball, he knew he wouldn't catch me.' Evans fly-hacked on and beat the English cover to the touchdown. Jenkins converted, later admitting: 'When I took the kick I had assumed we were in front, and that took all the pressure off. It was only afterwards that I realised we had only won by a point. I had been so caught up in the atmosphere and the drama of the game that the scoreboard never registered.'

Wales led 10-9 at the break. It was still 10-9 at the end of a second half dominated by England. The *Rothmans Rugby Union Yearbook* report said that England 'did everything but score'. Their main threat was Morris, who thinks that he played 'probably my best game for England. I did score in the first half. It was given as a double movement but I know I scored. Richard Webster told me afterwards: "I know you scored because I was walking behind the posts for the conversion." Then I made a break and Mike Rayer took my head off, which should have been a penalty try. Martin Bayfield went over and Neil Jenkins ripped the ball out of his hands. We should have won easily. It was one of those days.' England foundered on ill-luck, resolute defence in which Gibbs was outstanding, and the line-out lifeline given Wales by Neath lock Gareth Llewellyn, who was chaired off the field with 'fists clenched in a victory salute'. Carling spoke of desolation in the England dressing room. 'Rory was in tears,' he said, 'convinced he had cost England the match and it took Geoff Cooke to put it all into context. "Hang on," he told Rory. "You have scored more tries for England than anyone else. Does that mean you won all those games?" That brought Rory round.'

Not for the first time Wales went to Murrayfield full of hope and were unceremoniously deflated, losing 33-12. Wales did not win again, finished bottom and in April a Special General Meeting carried a vote of no-confidence in the WRU committee. For England, too, it was, by recent standards, a poor season as they also lost to Ireland on the last weekend. It would have taken uncanny perception to believe that the next time England and Wales would meet – the last match of the Cooke era, at Twickenham, in March 1994 – it would be to decide the championship. This was also the match that pitched border-crossers Dewi Morris and Rupert Moon directly against each other. Moon came from Walsall and had played for England at colts, under-21, student and B level, but wanted to be Welsh. Influenced as a schoolboy by the strong Welsh presence at Walsall, he joined Abertillery rather than a Midlands club and studied at the Polytechnic of Wales. 'The whole "English rugby experience" left me rather cold,' Moon said. 'I felt more at home and in tune with the Valley boys from Aber than I did with the public schoolboys of England.' In England teams, he said: 'I never felt I belonged and I never had the nerve to walk away.' Moving from Abertillery to Llanelli via an uncomfortable year with Neath, he became a Stradey fixture. In 1992, he declined an invitation to join England's development squad for the next World Cup, and was capped by Wales in 1993 after yet another defeat in which Robert Jones had taken a fearful beating behind a hopelessly outgunned pack.

The 1993–4 season started inauspiciously with defeat at the National Stadium by Canada. But, as Moon says, it was a different story in the Five Nations as 'Alan Davies's shrewd coaching methods, his focus on defence and consistency in selection' paid off. Davies, too, was a refugee from England. A native of Ynysybwl, he had coached the upwardly-mobile Nottingham club, striking Andrew during a brief stay as 'an innovator, a meticulous planner . . . constantly devising ways of getting the players to think for themselves'. He coached England in Australia in 1988 but, reckoned Brian Moore – another Nottingham player, who credited Davies for much of his own success – was squeezed out because he was 'very much a player's man' and his approach differed from Cooke's. Appointed by Wales in 1991, he restored stability, not least by his handling of players outside the team. Robert Jones was upset when he was dropped, not least because he regarded Moon as English, but 'at least Alan did it the right way, taking the trouble to explain the decision to me and making it clear I had a role to play'.

Wales came to Twickenham in 1994 with three wins. England had lost at home to Ireland, but could still take the new Five Nations trophy on points difference if they won by sixteen points. The Queen was there to mark the one hundredth England v Wales match and present the trophy. England scored early through Underwood and dominated. As Moore claimed: 'It was a match we could not envisage losing.' Their ascendancy was greatest in the line-out, where England's Cardiff-born Bath lock Nigel Redman dominated and a steal by Northampton's Army officer back-rower Tim Rodber produced a second try after half-time. Wales's title was in jeopardy until a late try by Nigel Walker, an Olympic hurdler turned winger, cut the gap to seven points. Clem Thomas said of England: 'If they had invested in imagination [they] would have carried off the big prize. They were the best-equipped team in every department except one – self-belief.'

This was in keeping with a transitional period dominated by the shift to open professionalism after 1995. Reality was so confused that England won easily at Cardiff in 1995 and 1997 but had to battle at home in 1994 and

1996. The change was not merely in structure and rewards but personnel as well, as major figures such as Andrew, Carling, Moore, Underwood and No. 8 Dean Richards departed. All played against Wales in 1995; none was left three years later. While falling short in the World Cup in 1995, blown away by Jonah Lomu's four semi-final tries, they went out as winners at home with three consecutive Triple Crowns, and a Grand Slam immediately before the World Cup. At the same time, significant figures such as backs Matt Dawson and Mike Catt and back-rowers Richard Hill and Lawrence Dallaglio made their first appearances. Continuity was provided by forwards of differing temperament but shared commitment, the cheerful Leonard and the glowering Johnson, whose standing was confirmed when he, rather than glossier figures, became one of the most sought-after players in the panic-stricken free-for-all that followed Newcastle's irruption into the market. He was reported to have turned down £350,000 from Northampton to stay with Leicester.

Cooke's successor as England manager was the towering Jack Rowell who, after taking Gosforth to unprecedented success in the 1970s, had moved south to pursue a business career that took in several major directorships and have an even greater impact in rugby as Bath's overlord. Rowell's England talked an excellent game, but would not always achieve it. In 1997, the *Telegraph* ran a mock apology: 'In previous editions of this newspaper we reported England's intention to play a sharper and more expansive game in keeping with the lessons of the World Cup. We acknowledge unreservedly that there was no truth in these suggestions and would like to apologise unreservedly for any embarrassment or distress caused.'

On the Welsh side Alan Davies joined the list of Welsh coaches to lose their job within a year of tangible success when he, manager Norster and assistant coach Gareth Jenkins quit after the 1995 whitewash. Cardiff's Australian coach Alec Evans took Wales to the World Cup, replaced the universally respected Ieuan Evans as captain with his own club skipper Mike Hall and failed to get Wales through the pool stages, losing a match against Ireland that plumbed depths comparable to the Brisbane quarter-final against England in 1987. His successor Kevin Bowring proclaimed 'a Welsh way of playing' based on traditions of instinctive invention, but operated in a context of limited forward talent, chaos at club level and inflated expectations. Professionalism brought little immediate benefit apart from the return of many players who had 'Gone North'. Jonathan Davies joined Cardiff after seven years at Widnes and Warrington, amid expectation generated by Wales's growing King Arthur complex – the belief that a single individual could reverse a decline with deep-rooted causes. If Davies's reappearance boosted morale, the more significant returns were those of younger players such as Bateman, Gibbs and Quinnell, who had much more rugby ahead of them.

Under Rowell, England won 23-9 in Cardiff in 1995 and 34-13 two years later. Farewells were said after both. The earlier match saw Rory Underwood's last visit to Wales – he played once more at Twickenham, completing a record fourteen appearances in the fixture – and a personal exorcism as he crossed twice, the first tries by an English back in Cardiff for a decade. It was Robert Jones's last appearance against England, discarded when not yet thirty. Prop John Davies made a still more premature and unwelcome departure, sent off for stamping on England back-rower Ben Clarke in the sixty-fifth minute, a ruling *Rothmans* considered 'marginal . . . but correct' but Ieuan Evans felt was 'beyond my comprehension'. Evans had to negotiate rapidly with Carling for a front row replacement, as there was still no provision for substitutions except in the case of injury. Dean Richards became the world's most capped No. 8 on his final appearance against Wales. A policeman son of a Treorchy-born father, his shambling, bucolic appearance was at odds with his modulated middle-class tones and his totemic importance to England. Morris, often the scrum-half behind Richards the No. 8, says of him: 'When you needed people to stand up, he was always there. He was the greatest guy I ever played with. If you needed more room you'd tell him, he'd move his backside and the North Stand would go with him. He had that much presence. And you knew that if he got two fingers on the ball in a maul the opposition would never see it again.' Mick Cleary spotted another departure, writing that: 'The trip to Cardiff is no longer a mental purgatory. If you need a benchmark of how far England have come in the Carling years, this observation is perhaps it. There are no more terrors, real or imaginary, to confront.'

It looked that way two years later. Carling, playing in his final international season under the captaincy of Bath centre Phil de Glanville, recalled: 'Even 1995 wasn't an easy match. However, 1997 was.' It was, wrote

Stephen Jones, 'a real contest for fifty minutes'. At about that time Guscott, marginalised by the Carling-De Glanville combination, replaced wing Jon Sleightholme. England went on to score four more tries, including a first in international rugby for Saracens flanker Richard Hill. Jones perceived 'an air almost of unreality' towards the end, with Jonathan Davies and Rob Andrew, who had played against each other twelve years previously and worked as television analysts the year before, in opposition for the final few minutes. Davies had started what was to be his last game, and tackled superbly. Andrew, director of rugby at Newcastle, was recalled as a replacement after a two-year absence – Martin Johnson said that many England players felt the Wasps tyro Alex King should have been given a chance – and came on for the last few minutes. Carling recounts: 'I turned round on the pitch to find Rob standing next to me. I said: "What the hell are you doing?" and he said: "I don't know. Jack has put me on." I thought it was taking the mickey and I didn't feel it was right.'

Many observers felt that Rowell's England needed a few more flights of fancy, their grinding plainness laid bare by Guscott's injection of flair, but Gerald Davies argued that: 'This team, like that of Geoff Cooke, is endowed with power and a sense of direction. These qualities are allied to organisation and control. These are the solid virtues of English rugby. To say as much is often interpreted as this is something to cavil about the style and as a sign of disapproval. Far from it. The team must be true to itself to exploit its own strengths.'

Carling, Andrew and Davies were not the only departures. The Arms Park hosted its final England v Wales match after 104 years, before its replacement by the Millennium Stadium. It was unmourned by Stephen Jones, who felt that its best days were long gone. 'The passions, the sense of community, the oneness of the team and the people were simply, utterly electrifying. Then the people were behind the team from the first kick. Now they cheer only when Wales attack. Then they sang the Welsh hymns in fervency. Now they mumble 'Delilah'. Then you couldn't hear yourself scream. Now you can hear the line-out signals being called. On all but the best days, the Cardiff crowd is a pastiche.'

Though Bowring aimed to restore a Welsh style, the sense of renewal at Twickenham in 1996 was not confined to Wales, with Wasps back-rower Lawrence Dallaglio and Northampton scrum-half Matt Dawson making their first appearances in the fixture. Frank Keating recorded Carling warning his team: 'We're not only bigger than them, but better than them. By far. But don't think they're cowards, the Welsh don't lie down easily . . . And they're clever with it. They are planning at this very moment somewhere to out-think us. It's in their psyche to do that. They'll be organising funny drop-outs, crazy line-outs, all sorts of plays. We must be switched on to every scheme.' Carling knew his enemy. After a few minutes, Wales were awarded a penalty twenty metres out. England's players retreated towards their posts assuming that Welsh outside-half Arwel Thomas would kick the goal. Thomas, a gamin figure with a dazzling side-step and a gift for straightening attacking lines with passes that obliged their recipient to make a break, realised that they were not paying attention. His quick tapped penalty was not brilliantly executed but England were so surprised by Thomas taking a calculated risk in the first few minutes of his Five Nations debut that the try was scored by flanker Hemi Taylor, the first of a modern succession of red-shirted Kiwis.

Carling was eventually proved right. Tries by Guscott, charging down a kick from Welsh full-back Justin Thomas, and Underwood, his forty-ninth and last in all internationals and sixth against Wales, ensured England a 21-15 win, but Keating reported 'a disappointing series of fits and starts against a Welsh team full of insecure promise and more spirit than likely achievement'. Debutant scrum-half Robert Howley, a whippet-like runner from Bridgend, provided Wales's second memorable moment with a late solo try of the sort that he was to make a habit of scoring, often as the sole leavening of Welsh misery. Even as losers, Wales were more cheerful. Their vast, gangling lock Derwyn Jones went to England's changing room to swap shirts and told them: 'Blimey, it's like a morgue in here. If we'd won we'd be drunk and singing already.'

Welsh optimism, raised by the style and vigour shown at Twickenham, was eroded by poor results over the next two seasons, then extinguished on their next trip to England in 1998. This was England's first Five Nations under Clive Woodward, appointed their first full-time professional coach the previous summer. The fall-guy of that 1981 match against Wales, Woodward was by no means the obvious choice. England had wanted either the Yorkshire-born Scot Ian McGeechan or Auckland's Graham Henry. Woodward's coaching credentials were sound but slim after spells with Henley, London Irish and Bath. It proved an inspired appointment. Driven, intense and relentlessly curious, Woodward applied lessons from Loughborough mentor Jim Greenwood's *Total Rugby*, 'the only rugby book I ever read', and a successful business career. He showed a predilection for the mantras and acronyms of management-speak, but this fitted him perfectly for his time and place. He was an enthusiast for the possibilities of professionalism, when most English opinion was somewhere between dubious and hostile, and showed himself to be in tune with the corporate RFU style introduced by former television executive Francis Baron from 1998. Woodward became 'a manager of change rather than the coach of a team'. He recruited top-quality specialists not only for rugby specifics like defence – flanker Richard Hill remembered the arrival of former England league coach Phil Larder meant that 'our training was changed to reflect the fact that fifty per cent of the game is about defence' – but for tasks such as video analysis and mental preparation. None of it – least of all the five-star training facilities and accommodation at Pennyhill Park in Surrey – came cheap.

Woodward was fortunate in having a union that could pay for his innovations and a group of players that included formidably tough and committed forwards. He showed perception and skill in building on both advantages. Previously England had seen only the size of Leicester flanker Neil Back. Woodward saw the scale of his talent and combined him with Hill and Dallaglio in the best home nation back row since Wales's Taylor, Morris and Davies. Matt Perry, a twenty-year-old Bath centre who had also played at outside-half, was recast at full-back and became England's best back for three seasons. Eighteen-year-old schoolboy Jonny Wilkinson was capped after fifty-eight minutes of senior rugby. Players appreciated the quality of their facilities and back-up – a favoured mantra of the management was 'give us superstar performances and you will be treated like superstars'. Dallaglio praised Woodward's 'ability to see the bigger picture', while Leonard found him 'very good at challenging preoccupations and making you think about the way you do things'. Previous England teams were powerful and resolute, but inflexible and unimaginative. Woodward's teams would develop, centre Will Greenwood remembers, 'four or five different ways of playing'.

Encouraging initiative in a previously risk-averse environment made England at times more vulnerable than Cooke's steamroller of a team, but it also made them capable of reaching heights beyond their predecessors. Both faces were shown in England's first two meetings with Wales under Woodward.

Wales travelled hopefully to Twickenham in 1998. Howley, by now captain, said: 'We've never felt better, we're going to Twickenham with an obvious chance of victory.' *Mail on Sunday* columnist Pat Collins detected English apprehension on the trains from Waterloo. 'Twickenham Man, usually a reliable pain in the Barbour, was a touch muted,' wrote Collins. 'The Welsh were patronised, of course. There were a few sophisticated jokes about sheep . . . but they were not delivered with the old leering glee, the Saxon certainty that success was just a couple of hours away.'

Early exchanges justified English apprehension. Perry remembers 'an absolute onslaught' and Wales led 12-6 after two tries by Bateman, the second from a length-of-the-field counter-attack. As Howley said, 'England were a shambles and we had them where we wanted them.' Yet, one Welsh fan told the *Sunday Times* a year later, 'deep down, we expected England to come back and thrash us.' They duly did, beginning before half-time when captain Dallaglio, after earlier misses by outside-half Paul Grayson, opted to kick a penalty to the corner. Wing David Rees crossed from the ensuing assault, then Back and Dallaglio scored in the next six minutes. It was 34-12 by half-time. Opinions on the second half depend on your allegiance. Perry looks back on 'one of the best attacking games of rugby ever'. For anyone Welsh, it was an unmitigated nightmare. Greenwood, Catt and the versatile back Austin Healey, who thought that England might have scored another thirty points, went over for their first international tries while Rees, whose Welsh father had sung both anthems beforehand, scored a second in a 60-26 victory which, as Stephen Jones said, 'tore Wales and the record books apart'. England were stronger and faster in mind and body, if not entirely gracious winners – Howley recalls Dallaglio shouting 'You've been dicked' outside the Wales dressing room. Perhaps the unhappiest Welshman was Neil Jenkins, who was playing at full-back to accommodate Arwel Thomas at outside-half. In his memoirs, Jenkins wrote that he would do everything again except 'playing against England at Twickenham at full-back'.

By 1999 he was back in his usual place, outside-half. Bowring had been replaced as coach by Graham Henry, who preferred Jenkins as the Welsh equivalent to his Auckland 'pilot of the ship' Grant Fox. Wales were in anything but their usual place, squatting at Wembley for two years while the Millennium Stadium was built in Cardiff, but were in all too familiar territory in the championship – last, with France and Ireland, on two points – after losing to Scotland and the Irish. England expected to win Triple Crown, Grand Slam and title playing away on a ground they had used as home against Canada seven years earlier. For football fans such as Dallaglio and Dawson playing at Wembley was a childhood dream fulfilled, but as Dawson pointed out: 'If someone mentions Wembley Stadium to us now I don't think of all those May Saturdays of my youth watching cup finals . . . I think of Scott bloody Gibbs running through us and breaking my heart.'

Wales should not have been anywhere near striking distance of England. As the impeccably fair-minded Gerald Davies wrote: 'This was in truth England's game.' Gibbs himself said: 'We didn't play particularly well.' England dominated, scoring three tries to two, the third by nineteen-year-old debutant Steve Hanley, a huge Sale winger hailed in some quarters as 'England's Jonah Lomu'. Yet, as Johnson lamented, 'Whenever they got within thirty or forty yards of our line we seemed to be penalised.' Just as invariably Jenkins, the red-haired idol of Pontypridd who was described by Wales back-rower Colin Charvis as 'an awesome thinker about the game, a back interested in things like where props place their feet', kicked the goal – six times in all before half-time. England led by six points with less than five minutes to go when they were awarded a kickable penalty. Dallaglio chose to kick to the corner rather than ask Wilkinson to land the goal. He admitted: 'The key mistake was my belief that, at that point in the game, Wales weren't going to go down to the other end of the field and score a try. I should have known better.' Wales kept England at bay, won a penalty of their own, and kicked deep into English territory as injury time ticked on. From the line-out the ball was passed to No. 8 Scott Quinnell. His fumble was, England back-rower Richard Hill reckoned, crucial. 'A few of us anticipated a knock-on and a loose ball but he held on and passed to Gibbs,' said Hill.

The centre, whose rugged build led Guscott to label him 'the world's fastest prop', had not had a great game, being bottled up by England's defence. Now, though, he made the vital incision between Hill and Rodber. Perry was in his way. 'He had a beautiful line and was going like a steam-train. I tried to tackle him, but nothing was going to stop him. If he'd been running with bulls he would still have won.' Jenkins still had to kick the conversion for a Welsh win, but nothing was ever more certain.

It was, Dawson said, 'like a bad dream, only I was awake'. Perry remembers that 'nobody said anything for about two hours afterwards. When we came out of the ground you could see Grand Slam T-shirts being packed back into white vans by people who had them printed in advance'. Almost as happy as the Welsh fans erupting in euphoric disbelief were Scotland, transformed by this turn of events into the last Five Nations champions after beating France in Paris the day before.

Three weeks later Wales elected its first National Assembly, created following a knife-edge referendum two years earlier. There is, though, little doubt which event in 1999 made the greatest impact in Wales. Pictures of Gibbs with his fist raised in triumph as he crossed the line are common in Welsh homes. How much the Assembly matters will be debated for years to come. The Wembley victory is easier to assess. It raised morale in Wales and contributed to Henry being hailed, for a few months at least, as the latest Arthurian saviour. Clive Rowlands joked that if the New Zealander and Gareth Edwards walked down opposite sides of the road in Cardiff, people would cross the road to shake hands with Henry. It was, though, the rugby equivalent of an FA Cup giant-killing – joyous for the winner and shattering to the recipient, yet ultimately changing nothing. Dallaglio's downfall as England captain a few months later was down to a tabloid 'sting', not his tactical gaffe at Wembley. England had begun a perverse triple crown – losing Grand Slams on the final day of consecutive seasons to Wales, Scotland and, in 2001, Ireland. But at least they were still playing for Grand Slams, while Wales won only six matches out of twenty – three against newcomers Italy – in the next four seasons of the new Six Nations Championship. The extent of the reaction was a backhanded compliment to England. Beating them had become so important to Wales, and so unlikely, that it triggered disproportionate celebration.

There was no repeat in the next four years, rather there were six England victories – most conclusive, some humiliating. By 2002, Rhodri

Morgan, First Minister of the Welsh Assembly and, unlike some politicians who pontificate on sport, a genuinely informed rugby fan, was warning that the WRU was 'drinking in the last chance saloon'. The Twickenham matches were routine executions. England won 46-12 in 2000 and 50-10 two years later. The first was a triumph for their back row, the smart and speedy Back, the physically and psychologically dominant Dallaglio – a consummate big-game player – and perhaps most important of all, Hill, this generation's version of Dai Morris as the exemplar of understated virtue. Scrum-half Kyran Bracken thought that Clive Woodward's vision of the perfect team could be realised only by fifteen Richard Hills, while Dallaglio jokily called him 'the most over-praised unsung hero'. All three scored, although Hill admitted that his try was 'of dubious legality'. Back said: 'In the dressing room at half-time we weren't even blowing, but as the Welsh lads trooped off they were knackered.' He cited Scott and Craig Quinnell as examples and argued that Wales were 'trading on former glories and the players don't want to buckle down and work'.

Two years later, Wales's chief persecutor was Wilkinson, by now the most prodigious points-scorer British rugby had seen, his kicking feats overshadowing his cool judgement and capacity for taking the right option. He scored thirty points, emulating Jerry Shea's feat of going through the card of scoring methods. Wales coach Steve Hansen had succeeded his fellow Kiwi Henry, who was exhausted by poor results, the alienation of some players who felt marginalised on the 2001 Lions tour of Australia, and, perhaps most of all, by the 'Grannygate' scandal. In that, two of the New Zealanders he had recruited for Wales, Shane Howarth and Brett Sinkinson, were shown to be in no way qualified. Hansen said: 'England played at a pace we could not sustain,' while Stuart Barnes reported that Welsh fans were 'resigned, not shocked'. Gerald Davies voiced resignation: 'There is only the mere hope that the result might not be as bad as the previous one and the one before that. It is just a question of trying to save some face', and he pointed to a 'muted, almost apologetic' performance of the Welsh anthem. Dawson admitted before the match that most English players were enjoying some form of payback for routine defeats by Wales as juniors – and as if to prove his point, the same paper reported Wales's fourth consecutive under-21 win over England – but English superiority was now so complete that crowds were no longer excited. Barnes wrote that 'never can so many Englishmen have been disappointed by so many points', while Rupert Bates in the *Sunday Telegraph* concluded that the match was 'plain boring'.

Among the scorers in 2002 was centre Will Greenwood, whose father Dick suffered at Welsh hands as England player and coach. 'He used as a joke to refuse to have Welsh pound coins in his pocket, but now he lives in Rhos on Sea and is an honorary Welshman,' says his son, who took copious revenge. With seven tries in six matches, he finally erased the mark set by Wade in the 1880s – which had since been equalled by such luminaries as Llewellyn, Bebb, Gerald Davies and Underwood – to become the most prolific try-scorer in the fixture's long history. As Perry says, 'Will was the brains of our back division, a real tactician and a terrific footballer with fantastic spatial awareness which gave him the ability to run very close to defenders.'

The first Millennium Stadium meeting, in 2001, marked his, and England's, peak in a dominant era. The psychological ploy of putting large cardboard cut-outs of Welsh players in the England dressing room produced differing reactions. Perry was amused. The spiky Dawson was furious, karate-kicked the Scott Quinnell replica, and scored two first-half tries in a 44-15 victory. He was outdone by Greenwood. For him, it was 'one of those days about which cricketers say, "I'm seeing it like a football," everything went right. I scored a lot of tries for England because I played in a terrific team – a lot of people scored a lot of tries, but this was a time when you could think "you pass it and I'll catch it", there was so much confidence.' He recalled the noise of the crowd pre-match and Johnson, whose five-week ban for violent play had concluded the day before, telling his team-mates: 'Let's silence it.' Wales started at a furious pace. 'The first five minutes were absolute carnage,' said Dawson, 'as if they had twenty men.' Greenwood, though, scored from England's first attack and completed his hat-trick a minute after half-time, by which time they led 37-8. It was the first English hat-trick against Wales since 1893. The only Welsh consolations were Jenkins becoming the first man to pass 1,000 points in international rugby and another flash of solo defiance from Howley. Henry reckoned it the best display he had ever seen from England, while French international

Thomas Castaignède hailed 'the best team in the world'. It had been a bad day all round for Wales, with substantial steel closures announced that very morning.

Greenwood continued his persecution of Wales two years later at the Millennium Stadium in one of the tougher matches of England's long awaited, hugely conclusive first Grand Slam under Woodward. Wales trailed by only 9-6 at the interval and scented a genuine chance when England's replacement threequarter Phil Christophers was sent to the sin-bin. England, though, had a well-practised routine for such situations. Greenwood says: 'That was typical of the Woodward era. We'd prepared for every eventuality. Later that year we played for a while against New Zealand with thirteen.' England not only survived, they scored while short-handed – Greenwood completing a long-range assault incorporating seven rucks and eleven passes to blast past Gareth Thomas and Steve Williams to the line. As Ackford wrote, 'Wales are not blessed with the behemoths that England can pick from, and in the modern game there is no substitute for size and speed.' Joe Worsley added a second score. Woodward commented: 'I never thought we'd lose the game. Maybe I'm just getting calmer in my old age.' *Guardian* writer Robert Kitson pointed out that 'England, as Wales used to in their heyday, now arouse such levels of expectation that some wins are no longer acceptable'.

Greenwood did not score when England travelled to the Millennium Stadium for a pre-World Cup friendly in August, because he was not playing. Nor was anyone else who had played in England's previous match, a comprehensive victory over Australia in Melbourne, or would start the World Cup final three months later. Some rugby writers thought the game was an opportunity for Wales, with a team reckoned to be close to their strongest, to end a nine-match losing run that included the whole of the 2003 Six Nations. Instead, it became a crowning humiliation. As Ackford wrote, 'Twenty years ago the joke was that England could not beat a Wales second team. Yesterday the reverse was true. Literally. Only it was no joke.' England kicked off, immediately stole possession back from Wales and continued in the same vein throughout the match. They had to make only forty-one tackles and were in Welsh territory for thirty-four minutes of the second half. If anything, their 43-9 winning margin, with the five try-scorers including the Wrexham-born,

Ynysybwl-raised replacement hooker Dorian West, understated their superiority. Welsh loose forward Martyn Williams spoke for a nation when he said: 'I've been through some low times with Wales, but my mood after that game was the lowest of the low. We'd lost by a record score at home to England, and it was basically their B side.' Not least of the reasons for Welsh misery was spelt out by Ackford. 'Heaven knows what will happen when a first-choice England meet Wales again in the quarter-final, as they are predicted to do,' he wrote. 'It could be carnage.'

They did indeed meet again. As with the only previous meeting on neutral ground twenty years earlier, it was in Brisbane, albeit with 45,000 spectators packed into the modernised Suncorp Stadium rather than a smattering at Ballymore. England had laboured in the pool stages, although they were seriously inconvenienced only by Samoa. Wales had been much worse, having been distinctly fortunate to scrape past Tonga and Canada, before what looked like a team of sacrificial victims thrown in against the All Blacks had rediscovered in extremis the old traditions of flair and calculated risk epitomised by the sensational side-stepping of Neath wing Shane Williams. He had been discarded by Henry as being too small and was in the squad only because he could also play scrum-half. New Zealand won 53-37, but not before being exhilaratingly scared.

The days before the quarter-final offered an echo of the 1987 Brisbane clash. Greenwood remembers that the England coaches, anxious about Wales, 'kept us out in the sun for long training sessions'. If that evoked memories of the previous game, so did the balance, although not the quality, of the first half at Suncorp. Wales, 'playing brilliantly' according to Greenwood, scored two tries to lead 10-3. The first came after Williams fielded a loose kick and went round England lock Ben Kay, in Greenwood's words, 'like a speedboat round an oil tanker'. Kay would later ask: 'How can I have missed a tackle when I didn't get within fifteen yards of him?' Johnson recalled feeling 'leg-tired and weary . . . leading to the boys making mistakes' and wondering 'whether we had the energy to come back'. Playmaker Wilkinson was, said one report, 'cramped and jittery'. Welsh fans shouted 'Rodney Trotter, you're going to win nothing' at Greenwood as he walked off at half-time. Decisions made during the break ensured that he would. Woodward took off wing Dan Luger and introduced veteran Mike Catt at inside centre to take the pressure off Wilkinson.

The decisive moment came four minutes into the second half with a searing break by England wing Jason Robinson, a former Wigan rugby league player who appeared to have ball-bearings where others have joints and whose transfer to Sale had been funded by the RFU. Greenwood, up in support, scored what he reckons was 'the most important try of my life. I was absolutely knackered and was taken off a few minutes later.' It was also his record-breaking seventh try against Wales. From that point, Johnson said, 'I didn't think we would lose'. English pressure exacted a toll and five penalties followed from the now fully relaxed Wilkinson. A late try by Martyn Williams meant that, though losing, Wales had scored three tries to England's one. As Simon Barnes wrote in *The Times*, 'The losers walked off looking like winners and the winners like losers.' Proving that the spirited display against New Zealand was no fluke, Wales's effort was, according to Stuart Barnes, 'the result of playing with their eyes open and their heads up', removing 'the shackle of playing by numbers'. Woodward said: 'We did not play well, but we are in the semi-final of the World Cup.' Two weeks later they were on top of the world as Wilkinson's extra-time drop-goal beat the hosts and holders Australia to take the trophy.

CHAPTER THIRTEEN
MODERN TIMES 2004 AND BEYOND

If England were playing the Third Reich, you'd be cheering on Hitler's boys.

Rob Brydon to friend, *Rob Brydon's Identity Crisis*, 2008

The English have learned to shy away from generalizations about West Indians or Asians, yet still feel free to make sweeping assertions about their immediate neighbours.

Jeremy Paxman, *The English*, 1999

If victory in Sydney on 22 November 2003 and the subsequent parading of the World Cup through the streets of London in front of hundreds of thousands of cheering supporters represented a previously unscaled peak for English rugby, it also ended an era. Descent from the heights was steep and abrupt, the closeness of the World Cup quarter-final was shown to be more than just a team liberated by having little to lose meeting one inhibited by the weight of expectation.

Some predicted long-term English hegemony over not just European but world rugby. Somewhat hubristically, the programme for one of England's first matches following their return carried a mock report of a repeat triumph in 2007. The reality proved very different. The team that won in Sydney rapidly unravelled. Johnson retired immediately from international rugby, Back was dropped and Leonard played only once more. Dallaglio retired in late 2004, changed his mind after a season, got injured with the Lions and was never again the same force for England. Indeed, injuries took a severe toll. Media obsession with Wilkinson meant that every advance and setback in his fitness was covered in minute detail. That resulted in an awful lot of coverage because he did not play for England again until 2007. Hill's disappearance after 2004 was no less important. Of the front row that started the final Trevor Woodman had to retire through injury, Phil Vickery suffered almost as many mishaps as Wilkinson and huge Northampton hooker Steve Thompson was perhaps the most conspicuous victim of the sense of anticlimax that can grip an achiever once he has achieved.

England dropped back into the ranks, consistent only in their mediocrity. Thirteen victories in five Six Nations seasons since 2003 – three years with three wins out of five, two with two – places them in the bottom half over that period. Yet in 2007 they hauled themselves to another World Cup final, succumbing only to opponents, South Africa, who could play, and beat, them at their own limited but appealingly bloody-minded game. The England of 2003 were characterised by the fearsome Johnson, the massively competent Wilkinson and the quicksilver league-schooled genius of Robinson. Johnson's leadership role fell after 2004 to his Leicester club-mate Martin Corry – perennially underrated but international class at lock, blind-side or No. 8, a battler whose subscription to the American ideal of 'taking one for the team' was routinely paid in blood, personifying all the best virtues associated with Englishness, but who was also partly Welsh. Wilkinson's place went to Charlie Hodgson, a sublimely gifted attacker but variable goal-kicker and decision-maker, and the butt of much criticism from a Twickenham crowd for whom his real crime was not being Jonny. Robinson was followed across the codes by his former Wigan team-mate Andy Farrell, an authentic rugby league legend, but whose conversion came too late in his career and was dogged by injury.

In one sense Wales's record looks similar. Wales won one more match, fourteen, in those five seasons. Ten of those victories were, though, concentrated into two Grand Slam years. Where England have been consistently not very good, Wales have veered between two magnificent years and three shockers – the last followed by ejection from the 2007 World Cup by Fiji. That failure precipitated the sacking, without the minimal dignity of returning home with his squad, of coach Gareth Jenkins, definitive proof that the 'so long as we beat the English we don't care' theory voiced by the Stereophonics is not only witless but wrong. Easily the best result of Jenkins' spell in charge, which was disfigured by a squalidly personalised press campaign against him, was the 2007 Six Nations victory over England.

Jenkins' fate, and its clumsy execution, typified an era of coaching upheavals. Both countries were, in late 2008, on their fourth national team chief since 2004 – the England manager Martin Johnson following Clive Woodward, Andy Robinson and Brian Ashton; and Warren Gatland standing in a Welsh line stretching back through Jenkins to Mike Ruddock and Steve Hansen. Each union contrived to supply a case history for the book of bad employment practice. Ruddock lost his job less than a year after taking Wales to a Grand Slam, Ashton still more rapidly after reaching a World Cup final. Both were shockingly let down by their employers.

The vigour of leading English clubs, who pulled in ever-larger crowds, was, from an England point of view, offset by their belief that they had legitimate interests that should not automatically be subordinated to the national team. The most spectacular victim of the conflict over player release that simmered, and occasionally blew up, from the beginnings of professionalism was Woodward. Knighted after the World Cup triumph, he quit with unbecoming (and untypical) petulance in October 2004. If his reputation suffered with the failure of his 2005 Lions team in New Zealand, caused in part by his over-attachment to the heroes of 2003, England's struggles after he left underline his achievements. Robinson, a superb coach of forwards, was unlucky – Wilkinson, his chosen captain, never played – but he was summed up in a verdict delivered by Dallaglio. 'Under Clive Woodward,' he said, 'we had a vision of where we wanted to go. With Andy, the focus was on the next game.' Ashton came in as a stopgap and the RFU never treated him as anything else.

For so long the great underlying strength of the Welsh game, its clubs were, by the early 2000s, seen as its besetting weakness. The WRU finally realised the futility of seeking Arthurian redeemers – the last, rugby league player Iestyn Harris, returned north in 2004, neither failing as a player nor remotely justifying the cost of signing him – and instead went in for genetic engineering. The clubs, who had neither the financial resources nor the recent playing record to resist, were corralled into five 'regional' franchises. The balance sheet so far is mixed. The Celtic Warriors were abruptly axed after a year, leaving a resentful vacuum in Bridgend – one of Wales's most fertile nurseries – to be filled by rugby league. Any improvement in Heineken Cup results has been minimal. At the same time Warren Gatland built the 2008

Grand Slam team around a gifted group already playing together for the Swansea-based Ospreys.

The head-to-head record since 2003 is three wins apiece, but Wales lead three to two in competitive meetings, including three of the last four, and have the only away win in that time – at Twickenham in 2008. That England had fallen from the high of 2003 was clear even before they played Wales at Twickenham the following spring. They had lost to Ireland in their third match of the Six Nations – their first home defeat in twenty-two matches. The line-out fell apart in a manner that had hooker Thompson, painfully concerned to take full responsibility, confessing that he could not have hit 'a cow's arse with a banjo'. Dallaglio's view was more considered. 'Mentally and physically we just didn't have it,' he said. He added that Woodward's coaching team 'were still doing a professional job, but no longer with the same conviction'. Wales could not take full advantage, but got closer at Twickenham than they had since 1988. England started well, a tidy early line-out winning ironic cheers and Ben Cohen, the powerful straight-running Northampton winger with the unique distinction of also being the nephew of a World Cup winner – his uncle George played full-back in the football team in 1966 – scored the first of his two tries after five minutes. England led 16-9 at the break, but two Wales tries – the first by full-back Gareth Thomas, the second set up by Shane Williams's superbly timed pass for durable centre Mark Taylor – gave them a 21-16 lead. Taylor also helped keep Greenwood scoreless for the only time in England v Wales matches. Welsh ascendancy was symbolised by a long break from Gareth Llewellyn – a second row so venerable that he had been chaired off as a hero as long ago as 1993. By virtue of his debut coming against New Zealand a few weeks before the Berlin Wall was breached in 1989, he was the last surviving Cold War rugby player.

England, Kevin Mitchell wrote in the *Observer*, were rattled. 'One move after another ran into the red brick wall.' It took until the sixty-seventh minute for Cohen to force a way through. Bath's Olly Barkley, making his home debut and goal-kicking with a routine remarkably reminiscent of the absent Wilkinson, landed the conversion. Joe Worsley, a rugged Wasps back-rower winning his thirty-third cap but who was not yet a regular first choice, nailed down victory with his third try in consecutive matches against Wales. It finished 31-21 but, wrote Mitchell, felt much closer. 'This was not a ten-point win,' he said.

England often started well — winning their opening two matches in three seasons out of five — before losing momentum. Rarely did optimism look better justified than in 2006 when a 47-13 win over Wales on the opening weekend suggested that the old order — and style — was returning. Wales flanker Martyn Williams told Chris Hewett, of the *Independent*: 'They're so strong up front. It seems to me that, although Charlie Hodgson pulls the strings and gives them more of a cutting edge, they still love doing what they do best.' Wales, with injuries depleting their 2005 Grand Slam team, were overwhelmed in the tight and the loose. England's second-half dominance allowed Wales only nine minutes of possession and was underlined by three tries from replacements — the most popular coming from Dallaglio, back from international retirement and serious injury, with a typical drive from the base of a scrum. Hewett, who is English and a connoisseur of forward play but no blind partisan, was not alone in believing that England were set for 'their strongest championship showing since 2003'. Victory a week later in Rome underlined that conviction, but England unravelled at Murrayfield. It proved the beginning of the end for Robinson, who was gone by the end of the year. His Welsh counterpart Mike Ruddock went earlier, in spite of this being his only defeat in seven Six Nations matches.

Wales's next visit to Twickenham brought a still more resounding, but less significant, hammering in a pre-World Cup friendly. Coach Gareth Jenkins chose a team with only three regulars, and one of them was played out of position. England, their fans and No. 8 Nick Easter, who scored four tries before giving way to Dallaglio, who claimed his last international score, enjoyed themselves in a 62-5 win. It seemed unlikely that there were any World Cup lessons to be learnt, although Hewett's 'suspicion that irreparable damage has been done' would be substantiated by Wales's abysmal campaign in the 2007 tournament.

For Jenkins it cancelled out the credit he gained four months earlier when England were beaten 27-18 at the Millennium Stadium. England arrived on one of their periodic surges of optimism after beating France for the first time since 2003. Wales had lost to Italy and were in danger of yet another whitewash and wooden spoon. Catt, recalled thirteen years after his first cap as captain/nursemaid of the tyros assembled by Brian Ashton, recalled: 'Our set-piece play was poor and tactically we were naïve. We played in the wrong parts of the pitch, especially in the second half. The real culprits were not the forwards, but us backs. We knew Wales would come at us hard in the first twenty minutes and we needed to take the steam out of their performance. Instead, we just fuelled the fire by handing them turnover ball.' Wales lock Ian Gough remembers: 'We had been losing narrowly throughout the Six Nations and felt we weren't far from producing a decent display. It happened against England – for once we had even better than parity up front and got off to a really good start.'

Within two minutes outside-half James Hook, a tall, angular twenty-one-year-old who so impressed Jenkins that he capped him in Argentina before his first start for the Ospreys, announced himself as the latest in that long line of players whose best moments came in this fixture. He charged down opposite number Toby Flood's clearance kick, touched down for the try, added the conversion and, a few minutes later, a penalty. Chris Horsman, an England-qualified prop born in Newport Pagnell – Hewett wrote that 'presumably he avoids mentioning the Pagnell bit these days' – playing in the English Premiership for Worcester and a cancer survivor, forced his way over for Wales and his side led 15-0.

England struck back with Catt chipping astutely for Harry Ellis, the scrum-half from Leicester, to score before Ellis turned creator with a break that sent Jason Robinson over for his fourteenth and last try in twenty-one Six Nations starts. As Eddie Butler wrote: 'When Wales lose concentration, they lose it totally.' The half-time gap was 18-15 and England were level soon after. That, though, was as far as they got, as Wales reasserted themselves. Two more penalties and a drop-goal from Hook – who matched Shea and Wilkinson's achievement of scoring in every possible way – sealed a victory accompanied in Wales by almost as much relief as delight. It was in many ways a throwback to the 1980s, a settling of scores of no great significance for other nations.

Wales's other wins were of far greater importance. In 2005 and 2008 they started the Six Nations in the once traditional manner, against England. Both times it proved the launch pad for an unexpected Grand Slam. The first was perhaps the least predictable clean sweep since England's in 1980. Only one national newspaper journalist, Tim Glover of the *Independent on*

Sunday, predicted a Welsh championship. Nor was it easy. Wales beat England 11-9, the lowest-scoring match since the last Cardiff victory over England in 1993. It should have been more comfortable, captain Gareth Thomas saying: 'We should have been out of sight.' Wales had threatened early on, Shane Williams crossing at the end of one of the combined passing moves with significant forward involvement – particularly by the dextrous No. 8 Michael Owen, whose pass to Williams was recalled by centre Gavin Henson as 'a lovely floated one that opened up enough space for Shane to dart over in the left corner' – that characterised Wales's season. Wales, though, failed to build on their lead and were trailing 9-8 in the last few minutes following three penalties by Hodgson and the belated introduction of Barkley as a second kicking option at centre. For Wales outside-half Stephen Jones, Barkley's arrival brought back unhappy memories of Brisbane in 2003. 'I thought to myself "oh no, it's Mike Catt all over again",' said Jones.

The decisive moment came with four minutes left. Wales were awarded a penalty forty-four metres out, close to the right-hand touchline. Centre Gavin Henson, the IRB's Young Player of the Year in 2001 but only now making his Six Nations debut, took the kick. His spiky haircut, silver boots, permanent suntan and shaved legs gave him the look of a pop star. He had already made two distinctive contributions. The better remembered was a tackle that lifted England's teenage centre Mathew Tait off his feet; the more significant was the ten-minute period with Gareth Thomas in the sin-bin when he filled in capably at full-back, fielding an evil bouncing ball with a slip fielder's aplomb. It was, though, the penalty that made him famous. Coach Mike Ruddock told Henson that he had been unable to watch. Henson said: 'Why not? I knew I was going to kick it.' He recalled: 'I had spent all week practising kicks from that kind of distance and when I concentrated, and got my preparation right, they had all gone over . . . From the moment I struck it, I knew I had scored. I turned away, threw the tee back to the touchline and raised my finger in the air.'

Welsh rugby and Henson have since followed parallel trajectories. He played the Grand Slam season then went on the Lions tour to New Zealand, struggled and featured in a press stunt imported from politics by Woodward's ill-chosen media chief Alastair Campbell. In 2006, a dispute over his autobiography, which upset several team-mates, exposed the internal tensions that precipitated Ruddock's departure. Injuries, suspension and variable form meant that he missed two complete Six Nations seasons. He may have been absent but was never remotely forgotten – to the visible exasperation of coach Gareth Jenkins, who was wont to ask if anybody was interested in players who were actually playing for Wales. One reason for Henson's prominence was his relationship with singer Charlotte Church, begun in 2005. Like footballer David Beckham's marriage to a singer, this almost certainly distracted journalists more than it did Henson. Even so, it seemed possible, when Jenkins left him out of the 2007 World Cup squad, that his might be an unfulfilled career with a single peak.

His return came following the arrival of New Zealander Warren Gatland. He had been hugely successful as coach of Wasps, alongside Shaun Edwards, one of many league men – and by far the greatest player – who crossed codes to become a defence coach in union. Edwards had been the ever-present in the Wigan team who dominated rugby league between 1988 and 1995. Lawrence Dallaglio, coached by Edwards at Wasps, reckoned him 'odd, but interestingly odd', writing that 'what he did on the training ground was relevant to what you would do on the Saturday'. Training sessions became shorter and sharper. Ian Gough, playing for his fifth head coach, says: 'They brought an intensity and a work ethic. You didn't want to upset them and wanted to do well for them.'

Gatland had had little time to work with Wales before his first match, against England at Twickenham, and sensibly downplayed expectations, saying that he was not interested in 'a quick fix and instant results' and that 'if I were them, I'd try to bully us'. The opening stages suggested that, after starting with thirteen Ospreys including new captain Ryan Jones, he was right. Wales were shambolic, losing possession at the breakdown six times in the first twenty-five minutes. As Graham Price told *Wales on Sunday*: 'We could have been twenty-five to thirty points down at half-time.' Instead it was only 16-6, England's try coming when vast wing Lesley Vainikolo, who had previously played rugby league for New Zealand, passed superbly out of contact to send centre Toby Flood over. England came desperately close immediately before the break, Wales hooker Huw Bennett getting underneath wing Paul Sackey to prevent him grounding the ball. Gough says: 'We were at breaking point, but going in at half-time we were able to think "it's only ten points, we're still in with a chance" and couldn't wait to get back out there.'

England were not helped by injuries, losing open-side Lewis Moody in the first few minutes then his replacement, Tom Rees, who had been playing extremely well, at the break. Lock Ben Kay had to play as a flanker after half-time. The tide turned as Shane Williams, destined for the season of his life and epitomising, in both stature and attitude, Welsh rugby's preferred self-image, took a quick tapped penalty to surge into the English half. A long, languid break by Henson followed, then Hook landed two penalties and centre Mike Tindall, one of few experienced players behind the England scrum, was hurt. From being in control, England were degenerating into disarray. Gough says: 'Their senior players were going off and you could see them looking around, asking what was going on and lacking somebody to give them a bit of leadership.' Wilkinson, perhaps the coolest head in international rugby, committed an error so uncharacteristic that, as Paul Rees wrote: 'You had to watch a replay to be sure that it was him.' He ballooned a pass yards over the head of replacement centre Danny Cipriani, whose first touch in international rugby was a desperate scramble to retrieve a loose ball.

Two Welsh tries completed the transformation. First Hook made the space for full-back Lee Byrne to score, then big, powerful scrum-half Mike Phillips – an Osprey who had played for Cardiff Blues and Llanelli Scarlets, and lacked only Newport-Gwent Dragons for a full set of Welsh regions – charged down a clearance from England full-back Iain Balshaw. Phillips linked with two former Blues team-mates, replacement prop Gethin Jenkins and open-side Martyn Williams, who had been persuaded out of a brief retirement by Gatland, before scoring himself. Hook converted both tries to complete a blitz of twenty points in thirteen minutes and Wales had their first win at Twickenham since 1988 – a run of defeats longer than the original 'Twickenham jinx'. Gatland said: 'I spoke to Brian Ashton after the game and he was wondering how they had lost, while I was trying to figure out how we had won.'

While Wales would not play another half as poor as their first forty minutes at Twickenham, they had laid down the template for their eventual Grand Slam – defending with such efficiency that the only subsequent try they conceded was from a mistake at a line-out against Italy, while making and taking chances, more often than not through the darting genius of Shane Williams, scorer of six championship tries. Henson, a winner in all ten of his Six Nations appearances so far, was recast from glamour boy to selfless grafter, Gatland played horses-for-courses with Hook and the reliable Stephen Jones, and the pack improved game by game. England concluded a spectacularly uneven season on a comparative high, beating Ireland for the first time since 2003 to steal second place, albeit four points behind Wales. Wilkinson, seen for so long – and particularly in his absence – as indispensable, was dropped in favour of the dashing Cipriani. It is possible that Ashton was not ideally cast as a head coach, but that in no way justified the off-hand manner in which he was treated by the RFU, who eventually placed their faith in iconic but totally untried Martin Johnson as manager.

Wales go into the next chapter of this saga on 14 February 2009 as reigning champions, with home advantage and knowing that victory will tie up the all-time series at 53 wins apiece. The 2008 Grand Slammers hope to emulate their predecessors of exactly a century before by doing it again the next year. A more realistic aspiration may be to keep Wales near the top of the table and avoid the catastrophic crashes that have followed success over the past twenty years. There are reasons for optimism. Dick Best, an England coach under Geoff Cooke, who warned that Wales's 2005 triumph was not sustainable, told Paul Rees that: 'Under their 2008 management team, I see them moving on.' Wasps and Lions coach Ian McGeechan said: 'I cannot see a repeat of what happened in 2005. I think this is a start for Wales, not an end. They will get stronger.' That ought to be the case as, though they were the most experienced team in the championship, Martyn Williams was the only true veteran in the Wales squad.

England are much more of an imponderable after taking a faith-based punt on character by appointing Martin Johnson. His presence is undimmed, and unconditional respect is a huge advantage for any authority figure. He has, though, no record as a coach and must show that a leadership style based on what he did can be adapted successfully into a role inevitably much more dependent on what he says. Going head-to-head with the astute Gatland will be a severe early test.

Looking beyond 2009, it is inherent in the relationship between England

and Wales, and has been since 1881, that Wales have to run faster and make better use of more limited resources if they are to compete with England. Sheer playing numbers have always been on England's side. Now, in a professional game, so is wealth — the money that funds a strong club structure and the support systems that underpin national teams. England are no more immune than any other rugby nation to poor selection, ill-luck and mismanagement. The systemic inefficiencies of old have, though, long gone.

It is a modern rugby truism that you cannot build success on passion alone. That is true insofar as teams relying solely on feverish commitment but lacking in structure, organisation and basic skills will not win very often. Passion in a different sense remains, however, Wales's great potential advantage. Rugby remains central to Welsh culture and national identity, wearing the red shirt is still an aspiration for a large, socially diverse cross-section of its athletic elite. Boys born into English families of similar occupation and income would dream only of football, but in Wales they still see rugby fame as the greatest prize. English elite rugby has, by contrast, seen a narrowing of its social base as demonstrated by Tony Collins's finding that the proportion of privately educated England players is rising steadily. The forty-one per cent of privately educated players in the 2003 World Cup squad rose to sixty-seven per cent four years later, and seventy-nine per cent in the 2008 elite squad. This does not make England uncompetitive — there are 223 English schools in the Headmasters' Conference, almost precisely the same number as there are state secondaries in Wales, and a significant private sector selling point is the quality of sports facilities and coaching. It does, though, help even the odds.

There are no guarantees that even the most hallowed of international fixtures will be played indefinitely. One possibility not discussed by Brian James in 1968 in his fine history of the England v Scotland football match — in terms of long-term competitive balance and significance to both parties, the nearest thing to England v Wales at rugby — was that it would cease to be played little more than twenty years later. England v Wales has a number of comparative advantages. It has never been considered a threat to public order, unlike its football equivalent. International rugby offers nothing like football's range of opponents capable of attracting crowds and providing a serious contest. It sits within the wider competitive context of the Six Nations Championship, which still works both as a sporting event and, increasingly important nowadays, a commercial one. So long as it remains a guaranteed money-maker, we are unlikely to hear a serious repetition of the English voices of the late 1990s advocating a break with the Celts.

Another sustained downturn in Welsh playing fortunes, particularly if Scotland and Ireland were weak at the same time, would, though, bring its dangers, not least because the cessation of regular cross-border club fixtures means that administrators and decision-makers are decreasingly likely to have the affinities once routinely formed by the exchange of punches and pints with regular opponents in their playing days. The relationship will be affected by politics. The Six Nations has coped seamlessly with Irish partition and the admission of separate nation states in France and Italy, so there is no reason to believe that it would be challenged or threatened by an independent Scotland. That would, though, increase the likelihood of Wales being ruled by governments it had not voted for, with a corresponding increase in tension and resentment.

Shared history and common memories – the 'magnets of remembrance' of Gwyn Thomas's affectionate, though less than enthusiastic, analysis of rugby's importance in South Wales – are, though, potent binding agents. Some are inevitably partisan. It will be some time before Englishmen contemplate the 2008 Twickenham match with equanimity, in the same way that the same fixture ten years earlier and the World Cup warm-up match of 2003 are still engraved on Welsh hearts. There is, though, a longer heritage that is shared – the recall of gripping matches and great players, of the journeys made to see them and the fair or foul weather, clear or clouded states of mind, in which they were watched. It can be shared more readily because of the long-term competitive balance of the fixture – that for every happy English memory, there is a Welsh one; for each Welsh disappointment, an English equivalent. We have much for which to thank Lennard Stokes and Richard Mullock, their heirs and successors, and, we must hope, those who are still to come.

RESULTS OF ENGLAND V WALES MATCHES

1881: England 7g 6t 1d–0 Wales   19 February, Richardson's Field, Blackheath
1882: Wales 0–2g 4t England   16 December, St Helen's, Swansea
1884: England 1g 2t–1g Wales   5 January, Cardigan Fields, Leeds
1885: Wales 1g 1t–1g 4t England   3 January, St Helen's, Swansea
1886: England 1g 2t–1g Wales   2 January, Rectory Field, Blackheath
1887: Wales 0–0 England   8 January, Stradey Park, Llanelli
1890: England 0–1 Wales   15 February, Crown Flatt, Dewsbury
1891: Wales 3–7 England   3 January, Rodney Parade, Newport
1892: England 17–0 Wales   2 January, Rectory Field, Blackheath
1893: Wales 12–11 England   7 January, Cardiff Arms Park
1894: England 24–3 Wales   6 January, Birkenhead Park
1895: Wales 6–14 England   5 January, St Helen's, Swansea
1896: England 25–0 Wales   4 January, Rectory Field, Blackheath
1897: Wales 11–0 England   9 January, Rodney Parade, Newport
1898: England 14–7 Wales   2 April, Rectory Field, Blackheath
1899: Wales 26–3 England   7 January, St Helen's, Swansea
1900: England 3–13 Wales   6 January, Kingsholm, Gloucester
1901: Wales 13–0 England   5 January, Cardiff Arms Park
1902: England 8–9 Wales   11 January, Rectory Field, Blackheath
1903: Wales 21–5 England   10 January, St Helen's, Swansea
1904: England 14–14 Wales   9 January, Welford Road, Leicester
1905: Wales 25–0 England   14 January, Cardiff Arms Park
1906: England 3–16 Wales   13 January, Richmond Athletic Ground
1907: Wales 22–0 England   12 January, St Helen's, Swansea
1908: England 18–28 Wales   18 January, Ashton Gate, Bristol
1909: Wales 8–0 England   16 January, Cardiff Arms Park
1910: England 11–6 Wales   15 January, Twickenham
1911: Wales 15–11 England   21 January, St Helen's, Swansea
1912: England 8–0 Wales   20 January, Twickenham
1913: Wales 0–12 England   18 January, Cardiff Arms Park

1914: England 10—9 Wales   *17 January, Twickenham*
1920: Wales 19—5 England   *17 January, St Helen's, Swansea*
1921: England 18—3 Wales   *15 January, Twickenham*
1922: Wales 28—6 England   *21 January, Cardiff Arms Park*
1923: England 7—3 Wales   *20 January, Twickenham*
1924: Wales 9—17 England   *19 January, St Helen's, Swansea*
1925: England 12—6 Wales   *17 January, Twickenham*
1926: Wales 3—3 England   *16 January, Cardiff Arms Park*
1927: England 11—9 Wales   *15 January, Twickenham*
1928: Wales 8—10 England   *21 January, St Helen's, Swansea*
1929: England 8—3 Wales   *19 January, Twickenham*
1930: Wales 3—11 England   *18 January, Cardiff Arms Park*
1931: England 11—11 Wales   *17 January, Twickenham*
1932: Wales 12—5 England   *16 January, St Helen's, Swansea*
1933: England 3—7 Wales   *21 January, Twickenham*
1934: Wales 0—9 England   *20 January, Cardiff Arms Park*
1935: England 3—3 Wales   *19 January, Twickenham*
1936: Wales 0—0 England   *18 January, St Helen's, Swansea*
1937: England 4—3 Wales   *16 January, Twickenham*
1938: Wales 14—8 England   *15 January, Cardiff Arms Park*
1939: England 3—0 Wales   *21 January, Twickenham*

Second World War: Red Cross Internationals

1940: Wales 9—18 England   *9 March, Cardiff Arms Park*
1940: England 17—3 Wales   *30 March, Kingsholm, Gloucester*

Service Internationals

1942: Wales 17—12 England   *7 March, St Helen's, Swansea*
1942: England 3—9 Wales   *28 March, Kingsholm, Gloucester*
1942: Wales 11—7 England   *7 November, St Helen's, Swansea*
1943: England 7—34 Wales   *20 March, Kingsholm, Gloucester*
1943: Wales 11—9 England   *20 November, St Helen's, Swansea*
1944: England 20—8 Wales   *8 April, Kingsholm, Gloucester*
1944: Wales 28—11 England   *25 November, St Helen's, Swansea*
1945: England 9—24 Wales   *7 April, Kingsholm, Gloucester*

Victory Internationals

1946: Wales 13–25 England   *19 January, Cardiff Arms Park*
1946: England 0–3 Wales   *23 February, Twickenham*

Resumed Peacetime Internationals

1947: Wales 6–9 England   *18 January, Cardiff Arms Park*
1948: England 3–3 Wales   *17 January, Twickenham*
1949: Wales 9–3 England   *15 January, Cardiff Arms Park*
1950: England 5–11 Wales   *21 January, Twickenham*
1951: Wales 23–5 England   *20 January, St Helen's, Swansea*
1952: England 6–8 Wales   *19 January, Twickenham*
1953: Wales 3–8 England   *17 January, Cardiff Arms Park*
1954: England 9–6 Wales   *16 January, Twickenham*
1955: Wales 3–0 England   *22 January, Cardiff Arms Park*
1956: England 3–8 Wales   *21 January, Twickenham*
1957: Wales 0–3 England   *19 January, Cardiff Arms Park*
1958: England 3–3 Wales   *18 January, Twickenham*
1959: Wales 5–0 England   *17 January, Cardiff Arms Park*
1960: England 14–6 Wales   *16 January, Twickenham*
1961: Wales 6–3 England   *21 January, Cardiff Arms Park*
1962: England 0–0 Wales   *20 January, Twickenham*
1963: Wales 6–13 England   *19 January, Cardiff Arms Park*
1964: England 6–6 Wales   *18 January, Twickenham*
1965: Wales 14–3 England   *16 January, Cardiff Arms Park*
1966: England 6–11 Wales   *15 January, Twickenham*
1967: Wales 34–21 England   *15 April, Cardiff Arms Park*
1968: England 11–11 Wales   *20 January, Twickenham*
1969: Wales 30–9 England   *12 April, Cardiff Arms Park*
1970: England 13–17 Wales   *28 February, Twickenham*
1971: Wales 22–6 England   *16 January, National Stadium, Cardiff*
1972: England 3–12 Wales   *15 January, Twickenham*
1973: Wales 25–9 England   *20 January, National Stadium, Cardiff*
1974: England 16–12 Wales   *6 March, Twickenham*
1975: Wales 20–4 England   *15 February, National Stadium, Cardiff*
1976: England 9–21 Wales   *17 January, Twickenham*
1977: Wales 14–9 England   *5 March, National Stadium, Cardiff*
1978: England 6–9 Wales   *4 February, Twickenham*

1979: Wales 27–3 England	*17 March, National Stadium, Cardiff*
1980: England 9–8 Wales	*16 February, Twickenham*
1981: Wales 21–19 England	*17 January, National Stadium, Cardiff*
1982: England 17–7 Wales	*6 March, Twickenham*
1983: Wales 13–13 England	*5 February, National Stadium, Cardiff*
1984: England 15–24 Wales	*17 March, Twickenham*
1985: Wales 24–15 England	*20 April, National Stadium, Cardiff*
1986: England 21–18 Wales	*18 January, Twickenham*
1987: Wales 19–12 England	*7 March, National Stadium, Cardiff*
1987: England 3–16 Wales	*8 June, Ballymore, Brisbane (World Cup)*
1988: England 3–11 Wales	*6 February, Twickenham*
1989: Wales 12–9 England	*18 March, National Stadium, Cardiff*
1990: England 34–6 Wales	*17 February, Twickenham*
1991: Wales 6–25 England	*19 January, National Stadium, Cardiff*
1992: England 24–0 Wales	*7 March, Twickenham*
1993: Wales 10–9 England	*6 February, National Stadium, Cardiff*
1994: England 15–8 Wales	*19 March, Twickenham*
1995: Wales 9–23 England	*18 February, National Stadium, Cardiff*
1996: England 21–15 Wales	*3 February, Twickenham*
1997: Wales 13–34 England	*15 March, National Stadium, Cardiff*
1998: England 60–26 Wales	*21 February, Twickenham*
1999: Wales 32–31 England	*11 April, Wembley Stadium*
2000: England 46–12 Wales	*4 March, Twickenham*
2001: Wales 15–44 England	*3 February, Millennium Stadium, Cardiff*
2002: England 50–10 Wales	*23 March, Twickenham*
2003: Wales 9–26 England	*22 February, Millennium Stadium (friendly)*
2003: England 28–17 Wales	*9 November, Suncorp Stadium, Brisbane (World Cup)*
2004: England 31–21 Wales	*20 March, Twickenham*
2005: Wales 11–9 England	*5 February, Millennium Stadium, Cardiff*
2006: England 47–13 Wales	*4 February, Twickenham*
2007: Wales 27–18 England	*17 March, Millennium Stadium, Cardiff*
2007: England 62–5 Wales	*4 August, Twickenham (friendly)*
2008: England 19–26 Wales	*2 February, Twickenham*

ACKNOWLEDGEMENTS

The original idea for this book came from Peter Charles, who thereby added the role of literary adviser to those of fellow supporter of Swansea City, chauffeur to many away matches, occasional unofficial financial counsellor and all-round good friend that he and his wife Bethan have fulfilled since I had the good fortune to get to know them. In thanks for this, the book is dedicated to their new son Gethin Rhys John, qualified by birth for England and parentage for Wales, and their daughter Carys, along with my godson Matthew Finn 'Finny' Wittstock McDonald, a force of nature qualified for England, Ireland, Canada and the United States.

One reason why I recognised that the rivalry between two international teams could be made into a decent book was having read and enjoyed Brian James's history of the England v Scotland football match as a child. Discovering that he was living only a couple of miles away, I was treated by him to a thoroughly enjoyable afternoon that mixed good advice on how to go about the project with some wonderful stories from his life as a Fleet Street feature writer.

Once research was under way, help was received from numerous people. Thanks in particular are due to the former and current players who agreed to be interviewed – John Taylor, Clive Rowlands, Bleddyn Williams, Jack Matthews, Dewi Morris, Eddie Butler, Peter Ford, Don Rutherford, Micky Steele-Bodger, Mike Burton, Geoff Windsor Lewis, Ian Gough, Keith Jarrett, Alastair Hignell, Matt Perry and Dick Jeeps gave face-to-face interviews while Bev Risman, Ray French, Will Greenwood and Maurice Richards spoke over the phone. All were unfailingly friendly, helpful, receptive and generous with their time. Most of the secondary research was done in the library of the World Rugby Museum at Twickenham. This has changed both name and curator in the past year, but not its ethos and style of operation, with Michael Rowe maintaining the warmth, friendliness and openness to researchers of his predecessor Jed Smith. Thanks are due to Michael, Jed and all the team at the museum, and also to staff at the National Newspaper Library, Colindale, the British Library and Swansea Central Library.

Ideally tranquil environments were provided for the planning stage of the book by Peter Berlin, who allowed me to stay in his flat in Paris, and for writing by Alejandro Molins Alcala and his family at Apartamentos Sevilla. The outcome of that process was scrutinised by Gareth Williams, Adrian Smith and Rob Steen. Their contribution went way beyond the reasonable demands of friendship, reading each chapter and drawing on their own knowledge and expertise to offer critique, correction, questioning and encouragement. Thanks are also due to Gwyn Prescott and John Jenkins for helping untangle some of the minutiae of early Welsh teams and Tony Collins for permission to borrow the analysis of the changing social composition of England teams presented at a British Society of Sports History conference.

Graham Coster, of Aurum Press, commissioned the book and once the manuscript was received showed himself to be a thorough, thoughtful and sympathetic editor. Thanks also to David Edwards, Dan Steward and Lydia Harley.

None of this would have been possible without the assistance and advice of John Pawsey, who continues to prove that it is possible to be both a gent and an astute literary agent.

Further thanks should be made to long-suffering commissioning editors – Charles Morris, of the *Financial Times*, Peter Berlin, of the *International Herald Tribune*, Stephen Penman and Jonathan Jobson, of the *Sunday Herald,* and Graham Jenkins, of scrum.com – for their toleration of the ill-temper, forgetfulness and unreliability endemic among contributors who are attempting to complete large writing projects.

Assistance of various sorts – contacts, suggestions, encouragement and moral support – was also provided by Hugh Godwin, Alan Evans, David Hands, Sally Price, Rachel McKibbin, David Llewellyn, Tim Glover, Simon Rimmer, Brendan Gallagher, Helen Hollick, Dave Fox, Phil Atkinson, Huw Bowen, Peter Stead, Mike Marqusee, Steve Pinder, John Richards, Paul Melly, Ruth Melly, Ian Lewis, Eva Melly, Kate and Andrew Green, Mark McDonald, Melinda Wittstock, Stan and Sheila Richards, Paul McFarland, Michael Fitzpatrick, Marti Stewart, Paul Geradine and Bill Dinning. My heartfelt thanks to all of them, and apologies to anyone inadvertently omitted.

Huw Richards
Seville and Walthamstow, November 2008

SOURCES AND BIBLIOGRAPHY

Interviews

Face to face: John Taylor, Clive Rowlands, Bleddyn Williams and Jack Matthews, Eddie Butler, Dewi Morris, Micky Steele-Bodger , Geoff Windsor Lewis, Mike Burton, Ian Gough, Peter Ford and Don Rutherford, Keith Jarrett, Alastair Hignell, Matt Perry, Dickie Jeeps.

Telephone: Bev Risman, Ray French, Maurice Richards, Will Greenwood.

Archives

Rugby Football Union Committee minutes, Museum of Rugby library, Twickenham.
Daniell, John: Personal record of English rugby football 1931-2 to 1936-7, notebook in Twickenham archives.

Published Sources

Rugby Annuals

The Football Annual, IRB Yearbook, Leng's Rugby Handbook, Pall Mall Gazette Rugby Football Annual, Playfair Rugby Football Annual, Rothmans Rugby Union Yearbook, Rugby Football Annual, Rugby Guide Française et International, Standing's Rugby Football Annual, Wisden Rugby Almanack

Match programmes

1954—date

Newspapers and Magazines

Badminton Magazine, Bristol Evening World, Cambrian Daily News, Daily Express, Daily Graphic, Daily Mail, Daily Mirror, Dewsbury Chronicle, Evening Standard, Illustrated Sporting and Dramatic News, Leicester Mercury, Manchester Guardian / The Guardian, News of the World, South Wales Daily Post/Evening Post, South Wales News, The Daily Telegraph, The Field, The Illustrated London News, The Mail on Sunday, The Observer, The Sketch, The Sportsman, The Sunday Times, The Sunday Telegraph, The Times, Western Daily Press, Western Mail

Books and articles

Ackford, Paul (ed). *125 years of the RFU*, Rugby Journal, 1996.
Andrew, Rob. *A Game and a Half*, Hodder and Stoughton, 1994.
Andrew, Rob and Richards, Dean. *England's Grand Slam 1991*, Stanley Paul, 1991.
Archer, Dennis (ed). *They're Off, a Journalistic Record of British Sports*, 1934.
Back, Neil. *Size Doesn't Matter*, Milo, 2000.
Barker-Davies, J.R. (ed). *One Hundred Years of Coventry Blue: CRFC*, 1974.
Barrett, Ted (ed). *English Rugby, A Celebration*, Mainstream, Edinburgh, 1991.
Bateman, Allan with Rees, Paul. *There and Back Again*, Mainstream, 2001.
Bennett, Phil. *Everywhere for Wales*, Stanley Paul, 1981.
Beaumont, Bill. *Thanks To Rugby*, Stanley Paul, 1982.
Billot, John. *History of Welsh International Rugby*, Ron Jones, Ferndale, 1970.
Birnie, Richard. 'Like an angel and probably better, the story of Ronnie Poulton-Palmer', Sporting Globe, 1979.

Blair, Michael. *Life at 100 miles per hour, A Biography of Peter Robbins*, G and A, Ludlow, 1987.

Blackheath RFC, A Record 1875–1898, Southwark Boys Home, 1898.

Blakeway, Phil. *Rubbing Shoulders*, Stanley Paul, 1985.

Bracken, Kyran. *Behind the Scrum*, Orion, 2004.

Bragg, Billy. *The Progressive Patriot*, Black Swan, 2007.

Burton, Mike. *Never Stay Down*, Queen Anne's Press, 1982.

Carling, Will. *Captain's Diary 1989–91*, Chatto and Windus, 1991.

— *My Autobiography*, Coronet, 1998.

Catt, Mike. *Landing on My Feet*, Hodder and Stoughton, 2007.

Cleary, Mick. *The Carling Years 1988-96*, Victor Gollancz, 1996.

Collins, Tony. *Dickie Lockwood, a Victorian Working-Class Hero*, Association of Sports Historians, 1997.

— 'The Gentleman Amateur in Rugby', paper at British Society of Sports Historians conference, 2008

Collins, W.J.T. *Rugby Recollections*, R.H. Johns, Newport, 1948.

Colls, Robert. *Identity of England*, Oxford University Press, 2002.

Colls, Robert and Dodd, Philip (eds). *Englishness: Politics and Culture 1880–1920*, Croom Helm, London, 1986

Cotton, Fran. *Fran, An Autobiography*, Queen Anne Press, 1981.

Crichton-Miller D. *Man of a Stout Countenance, The Life of Major R.A. Gerrard DSO, RE*, DP Publications, Abertillery, 1976,

Dallaglio, Lawrence. *It's In The Blood, My Life*, Headline, 2007.

Davies, Gareth. *Standing Off*, Queen Anne Press, 1986.

Davies, Gerald. *An Autobiography*, Unwin, 1973.

— *Tries*, Harrap, 1984.

Davies, Mervyn with Parry-Jones, David. *Mervyn Davies, No 8*, Pelham, 1977.

Davies, W.J.H. *Rugby Football*, 1923.

Dawson, Matt. *Nine Lives*, Collins Willow, 2004.

Day, H.L.V. *Rugby Union Football*, Nicholson and Watson, 1952.

De Glanville, Phil. *A Whole New Ball Game*, Mainstream, 1991.

Dooley, Wade. *The Tower and the Glory*, Mainstream, 1992.

Duckham, David. *Dai for England*, Pelham, 1980.

Durham County Rugby 1876–1936, Reid, Newcastle, 1936.

Edwards, Gareth. *Gareth, An Autobiography*, Stanley Paul, 1978.

Evans, Howard. *Welsh International Rugby Players 1881–2000*, Mainstream, 1999.

Evans, Ieuan and Jackson, Peter. *Bread of Heaven*, Mainstream, 1995.

Fairall, Barrie (ed). *Year of the Rose, England's Grand Slam 1991*, Mainstream, 1991.

Farmer, Stuart. *The Official England Rugby Union Miscellany*, Vision Sport, 2006.

Farmer, Stuart; Morgan, Paul; Lodge, Nick and Hathaway, Adam. *English Rugby Player by Player*, Marks & Spencer, 2007.

Fishlock, Trevor. *Talking of Wales*, Cassell, 1976.

Foster, Simon; Gate, Robert and Lush, Peter. *Trevor Foster, Life of a Rugby League Legend*, London League Publications, 2006.

Fraser, Alasdair and Horan, Frank. *A History of St Mary's Hospital Rugby 1965–1997*, F and H Publications, Plumpton, East Sussex, 2003.

French, Ray. *My Kind of Rugby*, Faber and Faber, 1979.

Frith, David. *My Dear Victorious Stod*, self-published, Guildford, 1970.

Frost, David. *The Bowring Story of the Varsity Match*, Queen Anne Press, 1988.

Gent, Dai. *Rugby Football*, Eyre & Spottiswoode, 1932.

Godwin, Terry. *Complete Who's Who of International Rugby*, Blandford Press, Poole, 1987.

Goodyear, David. *'Tiz All Accordin', The Life of Peter Cranmer*, Brewin, Studley, 1999.

Greenwood, J.E. *A Cap for Boots*, Hutchinson Benham, 1977.

Greenwood, Will. *Will*, Arrow, 2005.

Griffiths, John. *The Book of English International Rugby*, Collins Willow, 1982.

— *The Phoenix Book of International Rugby Records*, Phoenix House, 1987.

Guiney, David. *Dunlop Book of Rugby Union*, Eastland Press, Lavenham, 1974.

Guscott, Jeremy. *The Autobiography*, Headline, 2000.

Gwilliam, John. *Rugby Football Tactics*, Stanley Paul, 1958.

Hands, David. *The Five Nations Story*, Tempus, Stroud, 2000.

Hare, Dusty with Norrie, David. *Dusty*, Queen Anne Press, 1985.

Harding, Rowe. *Rugby Reminiscences and Opinions*, Pilot Press, 1929.

Harris, Ed. *Twickenham, A History of the Cathedral of Rugby*, Sports Books, Cheltenham, 2005.

Harrison, Miles. *Grand Slam*, Aurum, 1999.

Hearn, Danny. *Crash Tackle*, Arthur Barker, 1972.

Henson, Gavin. *My Grand Slam Year*, Harper Sport, 2005.

Hignell, Andrew. *Turnbull, A Welsh Sporting Hero*, Tempus, 2001.

Hill, Richard. *The Autobiography*, Orion, 2007.

Holmes, Terry. *My Life in Rugby*, MacMillan, 1988.

Howley, Robert with Clutton, Graham. *Number Nine Dream*, Mainstream, 1999.

Jackson, Peter. *Lions of Wales*, Mainstream, 1998.

— *Lions of England*, Mainstream, 2005.

Jenkins, John M.; Pierce, Duncan and Auty, Timothy. *Who's Who of Welsh International Rugby Players*, Bridge Books, Wrexham, 1991.

Jenkins, Neil and Rees, Paul. *Life at Number Ten*, Mainstream, 1998.

John, Barry. *The Barry John Story*, Collins, 1974.

Johnes, Martin. *A History of Sport in Wales*, University of Wales Press, Cardiff, 2005.

Johnson, Martin. *The Autobiography*, Headline, 2004.

Jones, Lewis. *King of Rugger*, Stanley Paul, 1958.

Jones, Robert with Richards, Huw. *Raising the Dragon*, Virgin, 2001.

Keating, Frank. *Gents and Players*, Robson, 1986.

— *The Great Number Tens*, Partridge, 1993.

— *Band of Brothers, A Celebration of the England Rugby Squad*, RFU, 1999.

Kilburn, James. *In Search of Rugby Football*, Arthur Barker, 1938.

Leonard, Jason. *The Autobiography*, Collins Willow, 2001.

Lewis, Steve. *The Priceless Gift*, Mainstream, 2005.

Lister, Fred. *Hartlepool Rovers FC 1879–1979*, HRFC, 1979.

McLean, Terry. *Red Dragons of Rugby*, Reed, Wellington, New Zealand, 1969.

Malin, Ian and Griffiths, John. *The Essential History of Rugby Union, England*, Headline, 2003.

Mallalieu, J.P.W. *Sporting Days*, Sportsmans Book Club, Newton Abbot, 1957.

Marshall, The Rev. F (ed). *Football, the Rugby Union Game*, Cassell, 1894.

Marshall, The Rev. F and Tosswill, L.R. *Football, the Rugby Union Game*, Cassell, 1925.

Marshall, Howard (ed). *Rugger Stories*, Putnam, 1932.

Marshall, John. *Headingley*, Pelham, 1970.

Moon, Rupert and Roach, David. *Full Moon*, Mainstream, 2002.

Moore, Brian with Jones, Stephen. *The Autobiography*, Corgi, 1996.

Morgan, Kenneth O. *Birth of a Nation, Wales 1880–1980*, Oxford University Press, 1982.

Morgan, W. John. *John Morgan's Wales*, Christopher Davies, Swansea, 1993.

Morgan, W. John and Nicholson, Geoffrey. *Report on Rugby*, Heinemann, 1959.

Mortimer, Gavin. *Fields of Glory*, Andre Deutsch, 2001.

Newcombe, Barry. *Carling's England*, Harper Collins, 1991.

Nicholls, Gwyn. *The Modern Rugby Game and How to Play It*. Health and Strength, 1908.

Nicholson, Geoffrey with Morgan, Cliff and Frost, David. *Touchdown and Other Moves in the Game*, Rugby Football Union, 1971.

Owen, O.L. *History of the Rugby Football Union*, Playfair, 1955.

Parry-Jones, David. *Out of the Ruck*, Pelham, 1986.

— *Rugby Remembered*, Partridge, 1988.

— *Prince Gwyn*, Seren, Bridgend, 1999.

— *The Gwilliam Seasons*, Seren, 2002.

Paxman, Jeremy. *The English*, Penguin, 1999.

Poulton, Edward Bagnall. *Ronald Poulton*, Sidgwick and Jackson, 1919.

Price, Graham. *Price of Wales*, Willow, 1984.

Probyn, Jeff. *Upfront, the Jeff Probyn Story*, Mainstream, 1993.

Raphael, J.E. *Modern Rugby Football*, Grafton, 1918.

Rees, Paul. *Resurrection Men, Wales's Grand Slam 2008*, Mainstream, 2008.

Reyburn, Wallace. *Men in White, The Story of English Rugby*, Pelham, 1975.

— *Twickenham*, G Allen and Unwin, 1976.

Richards, Alun. *A Touch of Glory*, Michael Joseph, 1980.

Richards, Huw. *Dragons and All Blacks*, Mainstream, 2004.

Richards, Huw; Stead, Peter and Williams, Gareth (eds). *More Heart and Soul*, University of Wales Press, 1999.

Ring, Mark with Parfitt, Delme. *The Ring Master*, Mainstream, 2006.

Robinson, Jason. *Finding My Feet, My Autobiography*, Hodder and Stoughton, 2007.

Rowlands, Clive and Evans, John. *Top Cat*, Mainstream, 2002.

Russell, A (ed). *100 Cherry and White Years*, British Publishing, Gloucester, 1973.

Salmon, Jamie (ed). *Rory, The Official Tribute*, Grandstand Media, 1997.

Sewell, E.H.D. *Rugby Football Internationals Roll of Honour*, T.C. and E.C. Jackson, 1919.

— *Rugby Football Up To Date*, Hodder, 1921.

— *Rugby, The Man's Game*, Hollis and Carter, 1944.

Sharp, Richard. *Winning Rugby*, Pelham, 1968.

Smith, Dai. *Wales, A Question for History*, Seren, 1999.

Smith, David and Williams, Gareth. *Fields of Praise*, University of Wales Press, Cardiff, 1980.

Smith, Steve. *The Scrum Half of my Life*, Stanley Paul, 1984.

Sowden, Sq Ldr D. *Our Tribute to Air Chief Marshall Sir Augustus Walker*, Yorkshire Air Museum and Allied Air Forces Memorial, York, 1998.

Stephens, Meic. *Wales in Quotation*, University of Wales Press, 1999.

Taylor, John. *Decade of the Dragon*, Hodder and Stoughton, 1980.

Team England. *World Cup 2003*, Orion, 2003.

Thomas, Clem and Nicholson, Geoffrey. *Welsh Rugby, The Crowning Years*, Collins, 1980.

Thomas, Gareth with Parfitt, Delme. *Alfie! The Gareth Thomas Story*, Mainstream, 2007.

Thomas, Gwyn. *A Welsh Eye*, Hutchinson, 1964.

Thomas, J.B.G. *Great Rugger Players*, Stanley Paul, 1955.

— *Great Rugby Matches*, Stanley Paul, 1959.

— *Great Contemporary Rugby Players*, Stanley Paul, 1963.

— *52 Famous Tries*, Stanley Paul, 1966.

— *Rugby – Men, Matches and Moments*, Pelham, 1970.

Thomas, Watcyn. *Rugby Playing Man*, Pelham, 1977.

Thomas, Wayne. *A Century of Welsh Rugby Players*, WRU, 1980.

Thomson, A.A. *Rugger My Pleasure*, Sportsmans Book Club, 1957.

Trevor, Col Philip. *Rugby Union Football*, Heinemann, 1922.

Underwood, Rory. *Flying Wing*, Stanley Paul, 1992.

Uttley, Roger. *Pride in England*, Stanley Paul, 1981.

Wakefield, W.W. and Marshall, Howard. *Rugger*, Longmans, 1930.

Wakelam, H.B.T. *The Game Goes On*, Sportsmans Book Club, 1954.

Watkins, Alan. *Sportswriters' Eye*, Queen Anne Press, 1989.

Watkins, David. *An Autobiography*, Cassell, 1980.

Weight, Richard. *Patriots, National Identity in Britain 1940–2000*, MacMillan, 2002.

West, P. *The Harlequins, 125 years of Rugby Football*, Breedon, 1991.

Wheeler, Peter. *Rugby from the Front*, Granada, 1984.

Williams, Bleddyn. *Rugger My Life*. Stanley Paul, 1956.

Williams, Gareth. *1905 and All That*, Gomer, Llandyssul, 1991.

Williams, Gwyn Alf. *When Was Wales?*, Pelican, 1985.

Williams, J.P.R. *Given The Breaks, My Life in Rugby*, Hodder and Stoughton, 2006.

Williams, Martyn with Thomas, Simon. *The Magnificent Seven*, John Blake, 2008.

Woodward, Clive. *Winning!*, Hodder and Stoughton, 2004.

Woolgar, Jason. *England, The Official RFU History*, Virgin, 2004.

Wolrige Gordon, Anne (ed). *Peter Howard, Life and Letters*, Hodder and Stoughton, 1969.

Wynne-Jones, G.V. *Sports Commentary*, Hutchinson, 1951.

Films

A Run For Your Money, Ealing Studios, 1949.

More than Just a Game; An Official History of Wales v England, Empire Media Productions for the WRU, 2005.

Rob Brydon's Identity Crisis, BBC Four, 2008.

INDEX

Aarvold, Carl 99
Aberavon RFC 77, 159
Abertillery RFC 8, 154, 156, 219
Ackford, Paul 203, 206, 212, 215, 218, 231–2
Acts of Union (1536–43) 4
Adkins, Stan 128
Agar, Albert 132
Allen, Charles 25
Allen, Dave 116
Allison, Fenwick 136–7
Andrew, Rob 192–4, 199–200, 214–5, 217, 220–1, 223
Andrews, George 80, 87
Angouleme 185
ap Cedifor, Peryf 148
Armstrong, Robert 201
Armthorpe Rovers 201
Ashcroft, Alan 137
Ashton, Brian 266, 239, 242–3
Asquith, H.H. 32
Atkinson, Phil 158

Back, Neil 225–6, 229
Badger, Owen 41
Bale, Steve 216
Ballantine, E.W. 69
Balshaw, Iain 242
Bancroft, Bill 29, 33, 35, 37, 40–1, 44, 48, 54, 67–8, 110
Bancroft, Jack 67–8, 88, 157
Bancroft, Reg 110
Bangor RFC 15
Barbarians RFC 142
Bark-Jones, Raymond 98
Barnes, Simon 233
Barnes, Stuart 203, 217, 229–30, 233
Barnstaple RFC 37
Baron, Francis 225
Barrow RLFC 158
Bartlett, Ricky 127, 136–7
Barton, John 158
Bassett, Jack 92, 94, 97
Bateman, Allan 217, 222, 226
Bates, Rupert 230
Bath RFC 88–9, 91, 129, 131, 185, 191, 199, 209–10, 220–2, 225, 237
Baxter, James 57, 75
Bayfield, Martin 219
Beaumaris RFC 25
Beaumont, Bill 3, 182, 184–6, 191, 195–6
Bebb, Ambrose 144

Bebb, Dewi 144, 147–9, 152, 158, 165, 230
Beckham, David 241
Bedford RFC 50, 63, 68–9, 105, 123, 155
Bekker 74
Benedict XV, Pope 5
Bennett, Billy 119
Bennett, Huw 241
Bennett, Phil 146, 168–9, 175, 178–80, 182
Bennetts, Barzillai Beckerleg 56
Berry, Tom 143
Best, Dick 243
Bevan, James 16
Bevan, John 181, 190
Beynon, Ben 72, 80
Biggs, Norman 38, 40, 54
Biggs, Selwyn 44
Bingley RFC 35
Birkenhead Park 37, 72
Birkett, John 2, 51, 60, 62, 82
Black, Brian 89, 92, 99–100, 109
Blackheath
  (Rectory Field) 17, 26, 34, 37, 41, 43–4, 58, 63, 196
  (Richardson's Field) 2, 12, 16–7, 21–2, 26
  (RFC) 12–14, 17, 19, 26, 33, 34, 37, 40–1, 53, 57, 63–4, 71, 88, 124
Blakeway, Phil 185
Blyth, Len 132
Blyth, Roger 178
Bolton, Reg 99–100
Bolton, Wilfred 23, 25
Boon, Ronnie 94, 98–100, 102, 147
Borges, Jorge Luis 192
Botting, Ian 115
Boucher, Arthur 44
Boughton, Harold 105
Bowcott, Harry 97
Bowen, Bleddyn 194–5
Bowen, Harry 24, 26
Bowes, Stan 114
Bowring, Kevin 221, 223, 226
Boyce, Max 9, 160, 167, 179, 207
Bracken, Kyran 209, 229
Bradford Northern RLFC 111, 155, 194
Bradford RFC (pre 1895) 35, 36
  (modern) 155
Bradshaw, Harry 35, 38
Bradshaw, Keith 149

Bragg, Billy 4
Bramley RFC 35
Brecon
  (Christ's College) 14
  (RFC) 15
Brettargh, Arthur 59
Bridgend RFC 16, 62, 81, 98, 105, 148–9, 177, 196, 224
Brisbane
  (Ballymore) 199, 232
  (Suncorp Stadium) 232, 240
Bristol
  (Ashton Gate) 53, 60, 64
  (RFC) 50, 63, 65, 86, 89, 91–2, 99, 137, 155, 159, 169–70, 173, 191, 202, 209, 215
Broadley, Tom 35
Broadstreet RFC 123
Bromet, W.E. 35, 42
Brooke, Rupert 69
Brougham, Henry 68
Broughton Rangers RLFC 55
Brown, Bruno 71, 73–4
Brown, Ivor 82
Brown, Tom 99–100
Brownlie, Cyril 187
Bryce, James 4
Brydon, Rob 234
Budd, Arthur 13, 21–3, 25, 27, 29–30, 33–4, 37
Burland, Don 92, 98–9
Burnett, David 187
Burnett, Roy 129, 133
Burton, George 13, 17, 19
Burton, Mike 151, 164, 166, 170–1, 174, 177–8
Burton, Richard 113
Bush, Percy 49, 53, 60
Butcher, Walter 48
Butterfield, Jeff 2, 127, 138, 143, 152
Butler, Eddie 186–7, 189–90, 192, 194–5, 197, 198, 202, 214, 239
Bynea 132, 135
Byrne, Lee 242

Cale, Ray 122
Calmet, Robert 175
Calon Lan 207
Cambrian, The 21, 22, 23
Cambria Daily Leader 26, 28, 30, 54–6
Cambridge University RFC 14, 16, 21, 23, 30, 41, 55, 65, 89, 92, 96–7, 148, 151, 181, 194

Campbell, Alastair 240
Candler, Peter 102
Cannell, Lewis 133, 137
Cardiff
(Arms Park) 9, 21, 35, 38, 48, 53,
55, 56, 66, 71, 73, 85, 87, 89, 96,
102, 104, 109–110, 113, 119, 123,
126–7, 129–30, 135, 137, 145–7, 151,
155, 160–1, 163, 168, 177
(Blues) 242
(Millennium Stadium) 1, 3,
207–8, 223, 230–1, 238
(National Stadium) 161, 163, 168,
192, 195–99, 202, 205, 207, 215–8,
222–3
(RFC) 21, 32, 34, 39, 49, 53, 56, 67,
72, 81, 98, 114, 116–7, 119, 136, 148,
161, 167, 173, 181, 183, 185, 194, 197,
202, 209–10, 221–2
Carleton, John 185, 193, 197
Carling, Will 2, 3, 202–4, 210–5, 217,
219, 221–4
Cartwright, Vincent 65–6
Castaignede, Thomas 230
Castleford RLFC 41, 43
Catcheside, Carson 86–7, 136, 143,
146
Catt, Mike 221, 226, 232, 238–40
Cattell, Richard 41, 57
Celtic Warriors RFC 236
Chadwick, Owen 114
Challis, Bob 137
Chantrill, Bevan Stanislaus 186
Chapman, Fred 62–4, 71
Charvis, Colin 227
Chepstow RFC 15
Cherry, Rupert 105, 180
Chilcott, Gareth 199
Christopher, John 123
Christophers, Phil 231
Church, Charlotte 241
Cipriani, Danny 242–3
Clapp, Tom 21
Clarke, Ben 222
Clarke, Simon 151
Cleary, Mick 214, 222
Cleaver, Billy 117–120
Clement, Tony 201
Cobner, Terry 182
Cohen, Ben 237
Cohen, George 237
Colclough, Maurice 185, 194
Collins, Pat 226
Collins, Tony 35, 38, 80, 211, 244
Collins, W.J. Townsend 24, 32–3,
35, 38, 40–2, 49, 51, 65, 72, 80, 86,
101, 117
Colls, Robert 4
Cooke, Geoff 201, 203, 210, 212–3, 215,
217, 219, 223, 226, 243

Cooke, Paul 108–9
Cooper, Terry 120, 213
Coopper, Sydney 57–8
Copsey, Tony 217
Corbett, Len 91–2
Cornwell, Bernard 153
Corrigan, Peter 203–4
Corry, Martin 9, 235
Coslett, Kel 153
Cotton, Fran 170, 185, 187–9, 191, 195,
217
Coventry RFC 7, 50, 112–3, 123, 128,
136–7, 142, 153, 155, 158, 168–9,
172, 177, 191
Cowbridge Grammar School 14,
101
Cranmer, Peter 103
Craven, Michael 34
Crosland, T.W.H. 4, 58
Cross Keys RFC 74
Crystal Palace 63
Cumberlege, Barry 76–7
Currie, John 136, 148
Cusworth, Les 192–3
Cwm Rhondda 207
Cynan 96, 121

Dacey, Malcolm 195
Dai for England 170, 179
Daily Chronicle 46
Daily Express 89
Daily Graphic 55
Daily Herald 83
Daily Mail 77, 137
Daily Telegraph 17, 23, 43, 59, 70, 89,
180, 193–4, 200, 221
Dallaglio, Lawrence 205, 221, 223,
225–9, 234, 236–8, 241
Darbishire, Godfrey 16, 18
Darwin, Bernard 96
Davey, Claude 98–101
Davey, 'Maffer' 56
Davies, Alan 211, 220–1
Davies, Alban 65
Davies, Cecil 105
Davies, Cliff 118, 122
Davies, Cyril 148
Davies, D John 114
Davies, Dai 119, 135
Davies, Gareth 183, 188–190, 195,
198
Davies, Gerald 6, 147, 158–9, 164,
166–9, 173, 181–2, 223, 227, 229–30
Davies, George 56
Davies, Glyn 113–4, 119–20, 123
Davies, Howard 115
Davies, John 222
Davies, Jonathan 194, 198–9, 201–2,
222–3
Davies, Lynn 'Cowboy' 136

Davies, Mervyn 114, 165–70, 178, 181,
225
Davies, Phil (England centre) 2,
127, 152
Davies, Phil (Wales forward)
198–9
Davies, Terry 132, 135, 138, 148
Davies, Victor 73, 105
Davies, Willie 111
Davies, W.J.A. 6, 69–7–, 72–7, 82, 86,
91
Davies, Wynford 113–4
Dawe, Graham 199
Dawes, John 163–5, 171
Dawson, Matt 221, 223, 227–30
Day, Harold 72–4, 176
De Glanville, Phil 222–3
Delahay, Bobby 81, 87
Delilah 207, 223
De Lotbiniere, Seymour 131
Devereux, Don 138
Devereux, John 194, 200
De Winton, Robert 39, 41
Dewsbury
(Chronicle) 30
(Crown Flatt) 29–30, 32
(RFC) 28–30
Dillon, Edward 51, 59–60
Dixon, Peter 170, 178
Dobson, Denys 53–4, 58
Dodge, Paul 185
Donnelly, Martin 115
Dooley, Wade 194, 198–200, 203, 215,
217
Duckham, David 169–171, 175–7, 179
Dylan, Bob 140, 146

East, David 211
Easter, Nick 238
Ebbw Vale RFC 151
Eddison, John 68
Edward, Prince of Wales (later
Edward VIII) 5, 94, 103
Edwards, Alan 112
Edwards, Arthur 135, 137
Edwards, Gareth 2–3, 100, 146,
158–9, 162, 164–5, 168–78, 182–3,
198, 228
Edwards, Reg 74
Edwards, Shaun 241
Elliot, Charles 26, 59
Elliot, Edgar 59
Elliot, Jack 44
Elliot, Walter 98, 100
Ellis, Harry 239
Encyclopaedia Britannica 4
England, Tommy 29
Evans, Alec 210, 221
Evans, Bill 20
Evans, Bob 114, 122

Evans, Bryn 97—99
Evans, Dai 43—4
Evans, Eric 127—8, 137, 186
Evans, Gwyn 118
Evans, Ieuan 201, 206, 211, 216—8, 221—2
Evans, John 105
Evans, Stuart 198—9, 203
Evanson, Arthur 8, 16, 22—3
Evanson, Wyndham 8
Evening Standard 107

Farrell, Andrew 235
Faulkner, Charlie 167, 174
Fenwick, Steve 181, 196
Fernandes, Charles Walker Luis 13
Field, The 17
Fielding, Keith 178
Fields of Praise 95
Findlay, Crawford 53, 59
Flood, Toby 239, 241
Fluellen 4
Fookes, Ernest 41, 44—5
Foot, Michael 89
Football Annual 14, 25—8, 86
Ford, Peter 142—3
Forrest, Reg 53
Foster, Trevor 111—2
Fox, Grant 227
Freakes, Hubert 107
French, Ray 145—6, 148—9
Frost, David 151

Gabe, Rhys 47, 49, 56, 58—60
Gadney, Bernard 102—3
Gallagher, Brendan 180
Gamlin, Herbert 2, 51—2, 55—6, 58—9
Gardner, Ernest 74
Gatland, Warren 236, 241—3
Gent, Dai 33, 47—9, 51—2, 62, 65, 82, 85, 87, 94, 98, 104—5, 107, 110
Gerrard, Ronnie 99, 109
Gibbs, Reggie 56, 64
Gibbs, Scott 3, 98, 210—11, 216, 219, 222, 227—8
Gibson, Alan 186
Girling, Barry 18
Gladstone, William Ewart 12
Gloucester
  (Kingsholm) 37, 110, 111
  (RFC) 44, 63, 93—4, 105, 128, 137, 142, 170, 181, 185, 191, 203, 215—6
Glover, Tim 239
Goebbels, Joseph 75
Gosforth RFC 173, 221
Gough, Ian 239, 241—2
Gould, Arthur 19, 26—8, 30, 23—3, 35, 37—8, 40—4, 47
Gourdon, Jean-Francois 178

Grace, W.G. 32, 42
Graham, Tom 55
Gravell, Ray 181—2, 189
Gray, Tony 201—2
Grayson, Paul 226
Green, Martin 198—201
Green, Michael 184
Greenwood, Dick 198, 230
Greenwood, Jim 225
Greenwood, John 'Jenny' 65, 72, 82
Greenwood, Will 2, 225—6, 230—3, 237
Gregory, Jack 118
Griffiths, Clive 183
Griffiths, Gareth 127, 133
Griffiths, Jim 144
Griffiths, Vincent 121
Grimsdell, Alan 201
Gronow, Ben 62
Guardian, The 151, 182, 194, 197, 201, 231
Guest, Dickie 115
Guillemard, Arthur 12—13, 17
Guilty Men 89
Gurdon, Charles 13, 23, 35
Gurdon, Temple 13, 19, 21—3, 25, 35, 38
Guscott, Jeremy 2, 218, 223—4, 227
Gwendreath Grammar School 183
Gwilliam, John 24, 64, 112, 121—3, 129, 131—2
Gwynn, Bill 24, 33
Gwynn, Dai 21

Hadley, Adrian 195, 202
Halifax
  (RFC) 93
  (RLFC) 111
Hall, John 199
Hall, Mike 203, 221
Hall, Nim 113, 118—9, 121, 133, 135
Hamilton-Fazey, Ian 103
Hamilton-Wickes, Henry 92
Hammett, Ernest 74
Hancock, Frank 24
Hanley, Steve 227
Hannaford, Charlie 181
Hannan, Tom 38, 40
Hansen, Steve 229, 237
Harding, Rowe 74, 81—4, 92
Harlequins RFC 38, 63—4, 83, 91, 127, 136—7, 145, 169, 193
Harris, Danny 149
Harris, Iestyn 236
Harrison, Miles 106
Haslett F.W. 104
Hastings, George 127—8, 137
Haverfordwest RFC 15
Hayward, Dai 152
Hayward, Don 119

Hazeldine, Rex 201
Headingley RFC 65, 68, 115, 138
Healey, Austin 226
Heaton, Jack 103
Heckmondwike RFC 29, 38
Heineken Cup 208—9, 236
Hellings, Dick 43, 53, 57
Hendrix, Jimi 146
Henley RFC 225
Henley, H.J. 91
Hennessy, Peter 125
Henry V 4
Henry VIII 4
Henry, Graham 224—6, 228—30, 232
Henson, Gavin 2, 240—1, 242—3
Herbert, A.J. 141
Hereford 14, 15
Hewett, Chris 238—9
Hiddleston, Dai 73, 154
Higgins, Reg 138
Hignell, Alastair 2, 166, 169—71, 173, 75, 178, 181—3, 185—6, 215
Hill, Frank 38
Hill, Richard (flanker) 166, 221, 223, 225, 227, 229, 234—5
Hill, Richard (scrum-half) 165, 199, 215
Hiller, Bob 9, 159, 161—2, 169, 176—7
Hirst, George 70
Hoare, W.J. 96
Hobsbawm, Eric 5
Hodges, Jehoida 53, 56, 58, 162
Hodgkinson, Simon 213, 216
Hodgson, Charlie 235, 238
Hodgson, Grahame 149—50, 153
Hofmeyr, Murray 122
Hollis, Gerry 114
Holmes, Barry 115, 117, 121
Holmes, Bill 127
Holmes, Terry 183, 188—9, 193—4, 198
Hook, James 239, 242—3
Hopkins, Ray 'Chico' 175—6
Horrocks-Taylor, Phil 149
Horsman, Chris 239
Horton, John 185, 187
Horton, Nigel 181, 191—2
Hosen, Roger 155, 158
Houghton, Sam 43
Howard, Peter 89, 202
Howarth, Shane 229
Howe, John 203
Howells, Bryn 105
Howley, Robert 211, 224, 226, 230
Huddersfield RLFC 80
Hudson, George 58
Hughes, Brigadier Glyn 142
Hunslet RLFC 120
Hunt, Robert 17
Hymns and Arias 10, 207

Identity of England 4
Illustrated London News 107, 110, 122
Independent, The 238
Independent on Sunday 239–40
Irvine, David 182

Jackett, Edward 51–2, 57
Jackson, Peter 136, 141, 147–8, 152, 169, 177
Jacob, Hal 86–7
Jacobs, Ron 142
James, Brian 244
James, Carwyn 182–3, 188, 195, 197
James, David 36–7, 54–5, 58
James, Evan 36–7, 54–5, 58
James, Mal 149
Jarrett, Keith 155–60, 163, 176, 187
Jeeps, Dickie 118, 128, 136–8, 141–3, 148, 150–1
Jeffares, Robert 58
Jenkins, Albert 72, 81, 88
Jenkins, Brice 129
Jenkins, Dai 80
Jenkins, Gareth 221, 235–6, 238–9, 241
Jenkins, Gethin 242
Jenkins, Jack 77
Jenkins, Katherine 207
Jenkins, Neil 211, 216, 218–9, 226–8, 230
Jenkins, Vivian 92, 98–100, 102–3, 105–7, 145
John, Arthur 88
John, Barry 159, 162–3, 168, 174–8, 183
John, Dai 88
John, Glyn 133–4, 155
John, Roy 119, 135
Johnes, Martin 85
Johnson, Arthur Tysilio 58
Johnson, Bill 65, 70
Johnson, Johnny 175
Johnson, Martin 3, 167, 210, 221, 223, 227, 232–6, 243
Jones, Chris 212
Jones, Cliff 100–1, 107, 113, 144, 156, 168
Jones, Dai (Wales forward, 1920s) 92–3
Jones, Dai 'Tarw' (Wales forward, 1900s) 53
Jones, Derwyn 224
Jones, Dick 49, 56, 64
Jones, Edgar 98
Jones, Elwyn 81, 179–80
Jones, Idris 81
Jones, Ivor 81, 134
Jones, Jack 77
Jones, Ken 117–9, 124, 126–7, 132–3, 135

Jones, Lewis 121–2, 124, 131–2
Jones, Robert 2, 146, 194, 200, 202–4, 207, 211–2, 214–5, 220, 222
Jones, Ryan 241
Jones, Stephen (journalist) 186, 200, 204, 214, 223, 226
Jones, Stephen (player) 240, 243
Jones, Tom 207
Jones, Willie 110
Jordan, Martyn 25
Jordan, Philip 23
Joseph, Will 46, 59

Kay, Ben 232, 242
Keating, Frank 194, 197–8, 214, 223–4
Kemp, Tommy 110, 114
Kendall-Carpenter, John 134
Kendrew, Douglas 89, 102
Kershaw, Cyril 74–7, 86
Kewney, Alf 67
Keynes, John Maynard 58
Kilburn, Jim 76
King, Alex 223
King, John 65, 71
Kitson, Robert 231
Kittermaster, Harold 93
Knight O.W. 112
Knight, Robert 16
Krige, Jannie 74
Kyle, Jack 116

Laird, Colin 88, 93
Lampeter College 14
Lampkowski, Mike 178
Lao-Tzu 12
Lapworth, Charles 83
Larder, Phil 225
Lawrenson, Johnny 112
Leeds
  (Cardigan Fields) 25
  (RFC) 13
  (University RFC) 148–9
Leicester
  (*Mercury*) 58
  (RFC) 50–1, 67, 72, 170, 185, 210, 210, 221, 225, 235, 239
  (Welford Road) 53, 58, 74, 184
Leleu, John 148
Leonard, Jason 216, 221, 234
Lewis, Alec 131
Lewis, Charles 21, 25
Lewis, Edward 16
Lewis, Emyr 218
Lewis, Geoff Windson 8, 150
Lewis, Gerry 137
Lewis, J.A. 16
Lewis, Ted 'Kid' 72
Lewis, Tony 167

Leyland, Ray 103
Liverpool RFC 132, 191
Livesay, Richard 50, 54
Llandovery
  (College) 14, 156
  (RFC) 21
Llanelli
  (RFC) 8, 15, 21, 24, 41, 70, 72, 81, 88–9, 97–8, 115, 165, 167, 179, 182, 217, 219
  (Scarlets) 242
  (Stradey Park) 21, 27, 40
Llansoy 8, 16
Llewellyn, Gareth 219, 237
Llewellyn, Willie 49, 55, 58–9, 162–3, 230
Lloyd, John 177
Lloyd-Davies, Hugh 114
Lloyd George, David 52–3, 58
Llwynypia RFC 43, 55
Lomu, Jonah 131, 221, 227
London Irish RFC 225
London Welsh RFC 6, 81, 135, 164–5, 167
Long, Eddie 102
Longland, Ray 104, 112
Loughborough University 127, 143–4, 149, 201, 225
Lowe, Cyril 65, 76–7, 82, 86, 141, 214
Lowry, Wilfred 72
Luger, Dan 232
Luya, Humphrey 115, 117
Lyne, Horace 101, 113

McCarley, Alan 102, 117
McFadyean, Colin 143, 157
McGeechan, Ian 172, 224, 243
MacIllwaine, Alfred 68
McKelvie, Roy 157
MacLaren, Archie 52
McLaren, Bill 160
McLean, Terry 119, 163
MacLennan, Roderick 75
MacMillan, Harold 125
McNab, Tom 201, 213
Maddocks, Keith 137
Maesteg RFC 175
Mail on Sunday 226
Mann, Bathyust Bellers 16–18
Mantle, John 150
Marques, David 136
Marshall, Rev. Frank 25, 29, 32–3, 35, 40
Marshall, Howard (player) 40–1
Marshall, Howard (journalist) 76, 105, 107
Marshall, Robert 108–9
Martin, Chris 198
Mason, John 89, 194, 200, 216

MATCHES between England and
Wales 1881 2, 12—19, 1882 20—3,
1884 25, 1885 25—6, 1886 26, 1887
27—8, 1890 29—30, 32—4, 1891
36—7, 1892 37, 1893 33, 38—41,
1894 37—8, 1895 36—7, 1896 41,
1897 43—4, 1898 44, 1899 50,
54—5, 1900 53, 57, 1901 53, 1902
58, 1903 53—4, 56, 1904 53, 1905
19, 52, 55—6, 1906 57, 1907 51,
56—7, 63, 1908 53, 1909 56, 1910
62—4, 1911 65—6, 1912 67—8, 1913
66, 69—70, 1914 65, 70—1, 1920
71—2, 1921 74, 77—8, 1922 71,
73—4, 1923 91—2, 1924 81—2,
86—7, 1925 92—3, 1926 87, 1927
92, 1928 87—8, 1929 93, 1930
89—91, 1931 91—2, 1932 94—5,
1933 97—100, 1934 101—2, 104—5,
1935 102, 104, 1936 101—2, 104—5,
1937 102, 106—7, 1938 102, 107,
1939 102, 107—8, (Red Cross
Internationals) 1940
(Cardiff) 110, (Gloucester)
110, (Forces internationals)
1942 (Swansea, March) 110,
(Gloucester) 110—1,
(Swansea, Nov) 110, 1943
(Gloucester) 112, (Swansea)
112, 1944 (Gloucester) 111,
(Swansea) 112, 1945
(Gloucester) 113, (Victory
internationals) 1946
(Cardiff) 113—4,
(Twickenham) 114,
(Resumed peacetime
Championship matches)
1947 114—5, 119, 1948 115—6, 120,
1949 120—1, 1950 116—7, 121—2.,
1951 122—4, 1952 128, 130—2, 1953
132, 1954 130, 133—5, 1955 135,
1956 128, 136, 1957 136—7, 1958
137—8, 1959 141, 147—8, 1960
150—1, 1961 148, 1962 140, 153,
1963 141, 151—3, 1964 149—50,
1965 141, 153, 1966 145, 155, 1967
155—9, 1968 159, 1969 161, 1970
169, 175—6, 1971 181, 1972 176—8,
1973 181, 1974 178, 1975 181—2,
1976 178, 1977 182, 1978 171—5,
1979 182—3, 1980 184—90, 1981
192, 195—6, 1982 192—3, 1983 192,
197, 1984 194—5, 1985 198, 1986
192—3, 1987 (Cardiff) 198—9,
(Brisbane, World Cup) 192,
199—200, 1988 201—2, 1989 192,
202—4, 1990 213—4, 1991 141,
215—6, 1992 217, 1993 205, 217—9,
1994 206, 220, 1995 222, 1996
223—4, 1997 222—3, 1998 210, 224,
226, 1999 9, 205, 226, 2000 229,
2001 3, 230, 2002 229—30, 2003
(Cardiff, championship) 208,
231, (Cardiff, friendly) 208,
231—2, (Brisbane, World Cup)
232—3, 2004 237—8, 2005 239—40,
2006 238, 2007 (Cardiff) 238—9,
(Twickenham, friendly) 238,
2008 241, 2009 243

Matthews, Jack 98, 110, 188—20,
123—4, 127, 129
Matthews, Norman 91
Matthews, Stanley 76
Maynard, Alfred 71
Megson, Ray 199
Meikle, Graham 104—5
Meikle, Steve 105
Mellish, Frank 74—5
Melly, Ruth 109
Meredith, Bryn 127, 138
Meredith, Courtenay 137
Michaelson, Roger 152
Miles, Jack 50
Milton, John 59
Milton, William 59
Mirabeau, Honore 184
Mitchell, Frank 41
Mitchell, Kevin 237—8
Mobbs, Edgar 71
Monmouth School 14, 21, 155, 187
Moody, Frank 72
Moon, Rupert 8, 219—220
Moore, Brian 171—2, 194, 199—200,
207, 213, 215—6, 220—1
Moore, Philip 124
Moran, Lord 113
Mordell, Bob 175
Morgan, Cliff 126—9, 132, 136—8, 141,
168
Morgan, Haydn 150, 154
Morgan, Ivor 65, 67
Morgan, Kenneth 79
Morgan, Rhodri 228—9
Morgan, Robert 152
Morgan, Teddy 59, 56, 58—9
Moriarty, Richard 195, 197
Morning Leader 39, 54, 56
Morning Post 76, 89
Morris, Dai 159, 166—8, 176, 225, 229
Morris, Dewi 8, 202—3, 213, 216—7, 219
Morris, Steve 74
Moseley RFC 143, 155
Mosley, Oswald 89
Mullock, Richard 15—17, 19, 27, 30,
245
Munro, Leo 75, 85, 88—9, 92
Murdoch, Keith 180
Mycock, Joe 115
Myers, Edward 73—4, 76—7, 86

Narberth RFC 16
Nash, David 144, 159, 164
Neary, Tony 170, 185, 191
Neath RFC 4, 17, 73, 110, 119, 127,
137—8, 151, 198, 210, 216, 219, 232
Newbridge RFC 119, 156
Newcastle RFC 208, 221, 223
Newcombe, Barry 179, 188
Newman, Charles 16, 20—21
Newman, Syd 115, 120
Newport
(— Gwent Dragons) 242
(RFC) 14, 21, 27, 29, 32—4, 38, 42,
44, 56, 67, 70, 74, 80, 102, 105, 116,
118, 122, 136, 154, 156, 194
(Rodney Parade) 19—21, 36, 43,
133, 152, 156
Newsome, Mark 30
Newton, Isaac 2
Newton, Philip 21
Newton Abbot RFC 53
Nicholl, Charles 39
Nicholls, Gwyn 3, 8, 32, 44—4,
46—50, 57—8, 63, 72
Nicholson, Geoffrey 138, 147—8, 164,
169, 181, 187
Norster, Bob 1, 193—5, 197—8, 200—1,
203, 221
Northampton RFC 50, 104, 118, 127,
137, 142, 144—5, 155, 220—1, 223,
235, 237
Nottingham RFC 199, 220
Novak, Tony 175

Oakley, Lionel 123
Obolensky, Alexander 103, 105—6,
109
Observer, The 36—7, 41, 44, 58, 64—5,
67—70, 85, 93, 114, 140, 163, 174,
187, 203, 214, 237
O'Connor, Terry 170
Offa, King of Mercia 4
Old, Alan 170, 180
Old, Chris 170
Old Merchant Taylors RFC 75
Old Milhillians RFC 150
Orwell, George 9
Orwin, John 198
Oti, Chris 206
Oughtred, Bernard 56, 58
Owen, Dickie 2—3, 48—9, 56, 58—9,
63—5, 67—8, 76, 100, 135, 146,
196
Owen, John 153
Owen, Michael 240
Owen, O.L. 94
Owen-Smith, H.L. 'Tuppy' 107
Oxford University RFC 8, 13, 16,
21—3, 39, 89, 92, 97—8, 120, 128,
136, 195

Palmer, Frank 73
Parker, Tom 74
Parry-Jones, David 48, 113
Pask, Alun 152, 154—5
Pathe Newsreel 115—6
Paxman, Jeremy 4, 234
Payne, John 26
Peake, Edward 16, 18
Pearson, Tom 33, 44, 53, 56
Penarth RFC 94
Penygraig RFC 43
Percy Park RFC 54, 142
Perfidious Welshman, The 58
Periton, Henry 83
Perkins, John 167
Perkins, W.J. 79
Perry, David 149
Perry, Matt 225—6, 228, 230
Phillips, Alan 189
Phillips, Malcolm 152—3
Phillips, Mike 242
Phillips, Percy 37
Phillips, William 18, 20
Pickering, Roger 155
Pillman, Charles 'Cherry' 64, 68, 70—1
Pillman, Robert 71
Plaid Cymru 5, 144
Playfair Rugby Football Annual 115, 128, 153—6, 181
Plummer, Ken 163
Pontypool RFC 77, 122, 138, 167, 173, 182, 190
Pontypridd
   (Grammar School) 113
   (RFC) 136, 216, 227
Poulton (later Poulton-Palmer), Ronnie 2, 62, 64, 69—71
Powell, David 145
Powell, Wick (scrum-half) 81, 92
Powell, Wickham (wing) 72
Preece, Ivor 123
Prescott, Robin 106, 112
Preston Grasshoppers RFC 194
Price, Brian 164
Price, Graham 167, 187, 190, 241
Price, Leo 91
Price, Terry 154—6
Probyn, Jeff 213—4
Pugh report 209
Pugh, Vernon 211
Pugsley, Joe 67
Pullin, John 155, 161, 170, 177
Pullin, W.E. 'Old Ebor' 43—4
Purdon, Frank 20—1
Pym, John 68

Quinnell, Craig 229
Quinnell, Derek 189, 202
Quinnell, Scott 211, 222, 227, 229—30

Rafter, Mike 188
Ralston, Chris 171
Rankin, R. 112
Ranson, John 149
Raphael, John 33, 47—9, 51—2, 70—1
Rayer, Mike 219
Reason, John 161—2, 186, 193, 214
Redman, Nigel 220
Redruth RFC 63
Redwood, Bill 159
Rees, Aneurin 18
Rees, Arthur 102, 104, 107
Rees, David 226
Rees, Elgan 183, 189
Rees, Enoch 129
Rees, Idwal 101—2, 107
Rees, Joe 77
Rees, Paul 242
Rees, Tom 242
Rees, Walter 66, 97, 101
Rees-Jones, Geoffrey 101
Reeve, Jim 91
Referee, The 67
Regan, Martin 132—3
Rendell, Paul 200
Renier, G.J. 79
Report on Rugby 138
Rew, Henry 89, 91
Rhapps, Jack 43—4
Rhodes, Cecil 8, 59
Richards, Alun 119, 122
Richards, Ken 148—9
Richards, Maurice 161—3, 165
Richards, Stephen 155
Richmond
   (Athletic Ground) 57, 63, 142
   (RFC) 13—14, 63, 107, 155, 208
Rimmer, Gordon 118, 123, 131, 135
Ring, John 77, 80
Ring, Mark 197
Ringer, Paul 187, 189
Ripley, Andy 170, 173, 178, 180
Ripley's Rugby Rubbish 180
Risman, Bev 8, 111—2, 148—50
Risman, Gus 80, 111
Rives, Jean-Pierre 185
Robbins, Peter 126, 136—8, 141, 150, 186
Roberts, Bill 96—7
Roberts, Evan 52
Roberts, Gareth 200
Roberts, Geoffrey 60
Roberts, Jim 150, 152
Roberts, Mike 182—3
Roberts, Sam 28
Robertson-Glasgow, R.C. 114
Robins, John 8, 112, 119, 122
Robinson, Andy 237—8
Robinson, Jason 233, 235, 239
Robinson, John 58

Robinson, Tot 54
Rodber, Tim 220, 228
Rogers, Budge 153, 192
Rose, Marcus 199
Ross, Gordon 155
Rosslyn Park RFC 134, 143, 170
Rotherham, Alan 23, 26—7
Rotherham, Arthur 50, 54
Rothmans Rugby Union Yearbook 219, 222
Rowell, Jack 210, 221, 223
Rowlands, Clive 141, 144, 146—7, 149—52, 154—5, 164—5, 180, 189—90, 197, 200, 210, 228
Rowlands, Gwyn 8, 115—6, 134—5
Rowles, George 37
Royds, Percy 50
Ruddock, Mike 236, 238, 240—1
Rugby Football Annual 86, 91, 94, 97, 99, 101
Rugby Football Union 7, 12—13, 15, 19—20, 24—6, 28—30, 33—4, 36, 38—9, 42—4, 50, 57, 61, 63, 67, 69, 74, 82, 107, 111, 115—6, 121, 130—1, 133, 144, 152, 172, 177, 179, 199, 200—1, 208, 225, 233, 236, 243
Run For Your Money, A 10, 109, 116, 121
Runcorn RFC 43
Runyon, Damon 205
Rutherford, Don 142—3, 147, 151, 153—4, 172, 191, 201
Ryan, John 214

Sackey, Paul 241
St Bart's Hospital 16
St Helens
   (Recs RLFC) 97
   (RFC, modern) 145, 149, 191
   (RFC, pre-1895) 36
   (RLFC) 153
St Luke's College 133
St Mary's Hospital 113, 118—9
Sale RFC 98, 103, 170, 227, 233
Salford RLFC 43, 80, 93, 163
Saracens RFC 223
Savage, Keith 157
Saxby, Les 94
Schwarz, Reg 51
Scott, Bob 118
Scott, Eric 119
Scott, John 173, 185, 188, 195, 197
Seddon, Bob 28
Sedbergh School 212
Sellar, Kenneth 'Monkey' 87—8
Sellicks, F.J. 77
Sever, Hal 103, 106—7
Sewell, E.H.D. 48, 51, 58—9, 72, 75—6, 81, 83, 177
Shakespeare, William 4
Sharp, Richard 142, 147, 149—51, 153,

186

Shaw, Glyn 190
Shea, Jerry 71, 74, 77, 80, 157, 229, 239
Shepherd, Bill 39
Sinkinson, Brett 229
Skinner, Mick 201
Skym, Archie 98
Slattery, Fergus 185
Sleightholme, Jon 212
Slemen, Mike 185, 193
Slocock, Noel 51, 71
Smallwood, Alastair 74, 91—2
Smith, Adrian 7, 168—9
Smith, Dai 1, 44, 48—9, 94—5, 146, 173
Smith, J.V. 121
Smith, M.J.K. 128, 136
Smith, Stephen (1950s scrum-
    half) 148
Smith, Steve (1970s, 1980s scrum-
    half) 170—1, 174, 185, 188—9,
    192—3, 196—7
Solomon, Bert 62—5
South Wales Football Union 15, 17
Sowerby Bridge RFC 41
Sparks, Brian 136
Sparks, Ron 89
Spencer, Jeremy 145
Spencer, John 169—70, 212
Spooner, Bob 51
Sportsman, The 17, 25, 63—4
Squire, Jeff 167, 188, 197
Stadden, William 'Buller' 26, 29,
    30—1
Stafford, Dick 68—9
Steele-Bodger, Micky 109—11, 113—5,
    117—9, 141, 179
Steffens, Lincoln 78
Stephens, Rees 127, 134, 135
Stereophonics 235
Stoddart, Andrew 26, 30, 35, 39
Stokes, Frederick 12
Stokes, Lennard 12—14, 17, 19, 21, 245
Stoop, Adrian 62—4, 76
Stout, Frank 44, 59
Stout, Percy 44—5
Strand-Jones, John 58—9
Sullivan, Jim 80
Summers, Richard 16—17
Sunday Closing Act (1881) 15
Sunday Express 77, 153
Sunday Telegraph 218, 230
Sunday Times 67, 204, 226
Sunderland RFC 26
Sutton, Ernest 66
Sutton, Steve 198—9
Swansea
    (Cricket and Football (Rugby)
      Club) 14, 15, 21, 29, 34, 46, 48—9,
      73—4, 102, 144, 167, 184, 194—5, 199
    (Daily Post) 48, 65—7, 72, 86—8, 93,

95, 104
(Evening Post) 112, 123
(Mackworth Hotel) 23
(Ospreys) 237, 239, 241—2
(St Helen's) 4, 20—1, 24—5, 27, 33,
    50—1, 53—4, 66, 71—2, 74, 85—8,
    94, 101—2, 104, 106, 110—3, 123, 177
(Town FC) 72, 95
(White Rock Works) 54
Swanton, E.W. 107
Swing Low Sweet Chariot 206
Swinton RFC 28, 43

Taffy was a Welshman 58
Tait, Mathew 240
Tanner, Haydn 2, 100—1, 107, 111,
    114—5, 118, 120—1, 131—2, 146
Taylor, Arthur 22
Taylor, Bob 155
Taylor, Charles 25, 71
Taylor, Ernest 41, 43
Taylor, Hemi 223
Taylor, John (England back) 54
Taylor, John (Wales forward) 155,
    158—9, 162, 164—7, 169—70, 173,
    175, 178, 180—1, 185, 225
Taylor, Mark 237
Taylor, William 69
Teague, Mike 203, 216
Teden, Derek 108—110
Temple, William 68
Templeton, Bob 200
Tennyson, Alfred Lord 153
Thatcher, Denis 191
Thatcher, Margaret 187, 190—1
Thomas, Alun 128—9
Thomas, Arwel 224, 226
Thomas, Brian 150—1
Thomas, Charles (England) 37
Thomas, Charles (Wales) 29
Thomas, Clem 123, 126—7, 136, 138,
    143—4, 147—8, 151, 164, 167, 178,
    183—4, 186, 195, 198—9, 201, 220
Thomas, Delme 164—5, 167
Thomas, Gareth 231, 237, 240
Thomas, Gwyn 35, 79, 125, 245
Thomas, J.B.G. 40, 90, 106, 115, 143,
    179
Thomas, Jenkin 52
Thomas, Justin 224
Thomas, Malcolm 124, 132—3, 136
Thomas, T.H. 46
Thomas, Watcyn 83, 97, 99—101
Thompson, Daley 214
Thompson, Francis 153
Thompson, Joe 80
Thompson, Peter 138
Thompson, Steve 235, 237
Thomson, A.A. 48, 51, 65, 70, 117, 126
Thomson, W.B 37

Thorburn, Paul 201, 204, 211, 215
Times, The 99, 104, 107, 113, 116, 119,
    132, 134—6, 148, 151, 177, 191, 233
Tindall, Mike 242
Toft, Bert 102, 107, 109—110, 112, 140
Toothill, Jack 35
Tosswill, Leonard 77
Total Rugby 225
Travers, George 'Twyber' 49, 91
Travers, William 'Bunner' 102, 107,
    108, 121
Trebanos 194
Treharne, Edward 16, 20—21
Treharne, Gwilym 210
Treherbert RFC 53
Treorchy 8, 194
Trew, Billy 48—9, 56—7, 65, 67
Trinity College, Carmarthen 147
Tucker, Sam 82, 89—92
Turnbull, Lou 83
Turnbull, Maurice 98, 109
Turner, Paul 203
Twickenham 1, 3, 17, 34, 62—4, 66—8,
    70—1, 74, 77—8, 80, 82—3, 91,
    93—107, 109—10, 114, 116—8, 120—2,
    127—31, 133—4, 136, 138, 140, 143,
    145—7, 149, 150, 153, 155, 159—60,
    169, 171, 173—81, 184, 187—8,
    192—5, 197—8, 201—2, 206—10,
    213—4, 217, 219—20, 222—4, 226,
    229, 235, 237—8, 241—2
Twynam, Henry 25

Underwood, Rory 199, 203, 205,
    213—4, 217—22, 224, 230
United Services RFC 68
Uren, Richard 114
Uttley, Roger 170—1, 173, 185, 187—8,
    191, 213

Vainikolo, Lesley 241
Valentine, Jim 43
Vassall, Harry 13, 17, 21, 23
van Ryneveld, Clive 115, 120
Vaughan-Jones, Arthur 97—8
Vaux, Terry 210
Vickery, Phil 235
Viera, Ondino 5
Voyce, Tom 2, 82, 87, 93
Vivyan, Elliott 59

Wade, Gregory 21—3, 25—7, 230
Wakefield, Wavell 3, 72—3, 76, 79,
    82, 85—7, 93, 98, 153—4, 212
Wakefield Trinity
    (RFC) 36, 43
    (RLFC) 99
Wakelam, Teddy 84—4, 88, 123
Waldron, Ron 210
Wales on Sunday 241

Walford, Micky 114
Walker, Nigel 220
Warbrick, Joe 29
Ward, Ernest (journalist) 76
Ward, Ernest (player) 112
Ward, John 43
Waring, Eddie 29
Warrington RLFC 181, 222
Wasps RFC 131, 141, 213, 223, 237, 241
Waterloo RFC 97, 103–4, 191
Waters, David 194
Watkins, Alan 7, 112, 114, 117, 145
Watkins, David 149–52, 156–7
Watkins, Leonard 18
Watkins, Stuart 154–5, 162
Watts, Davie 70–1
Watts, Willie 70–1
Waugh, Evelyn 160
Webb, Jon 202–3, 218
Webster, Jan 170, 177, 180
Webster, Richard 219
Wedge, Tom 56
Weighill, Bob 111, 179
Wells, Cyril 38
Welsh Assembly 218
Welsh Language Act 144
Welsh Rugby Union 17, 19–21, 23,
    42, 66–7, 74, 80, 95, 97, 101, 121,
    144, 152, 172–3, 183, 202, 207–8,
    211, 219, 229, 236
Wembley Stadium 9, 205, 227
West, Dorian 9, 231
West, John 179
West, Peter 177
West Hartlepool RFC 54
Westoe RFC 63
Weston, Mike 152, 201
Western Daily Press 60–1
Western Mail 17, 21, 34, 36–7, 39, 41,
    44, 52, 57, 59–60, 69–70, 73–4,

85, 87, 179, 190, 235
Wetter, Jack 73, 77
Wheel, Geoff 167, 188
Wheeler, Peter 170, 182–5, 189
White, Don 118–9, 127, 132, 142, 172
Widnes RLFC 222
Wigan RLFC 80, 235, 241
Wilde, Oscar 160
Wilkinson, Harry 93
Wilkinson, Jonny 225, 227, 229,
    232–7, 239, 242–3
Williams, Billy (RFU
    committeeman) 63
Williams, Billy (Wales scrum-
    half) 129, 133
Williams, Bleddyn 111–3, 115, 117,
    118–21, 126–8, 133, 135, 141, 168
Williams, Brynmor 196
Williams, Gareth 6, 8, 15, 43, 48, 62,
    79, 94–6, 126, 146, 173
Williams, Gerwyn 133–5
Williams, Gwyn 111
Williams, Gwyn Alf 191
Williams, John (bandleader) 197–8
Williams, John (England scrum-
    half) 128, 154
Williams, John (Wales winger
    1910s) 56–7, 71
Williams, John 'J.J.' (Wales
    winger 1970s) 169, 179–81
Williams, John 'J.P.R.' (Wales
    full-back) 3, 8–9, 163, 165–6,
    168–9, 173, 175–183, 190
Williams, Les 120
Williams, Martyn 232–3, 238, 242–3
Williams, Ray 144, 172
Williams, Richard Garnons 71
Williams, Rhys 2, 127, 147, 210
Williams, Shane 232, 237, 240, 242–3
Williams, Stanley 67

Williams, Steve 231
Williams, Syd 108, 111
Williams, W.O. 'Stoker' 127, 134
Williamson, Rupert 60–1
Willis, Rex 129, 132, 134
Wilson, Harold 144
Windsor, Bobby 167
Winfield, Bert 46–7, 59–60
Winmill, Steve 100–1
Winterbottom, Peter 193, 217
Wisden Rugby Almanack 80, 92
Wodehouse, Norman 69–70, 109
Wodehouse, P.G. 70, 76, 107
Woodford RFC 89
Woodman, Trevor 235
Woods, Sammy 31, 35–7, 39–40, 52
Woodward, Clive 185, 192, 196, 198,
    207, 210, 224, 226, 229, 231–3, 236,
    240
Woodward, Ted 131–3
Worcester RFC 239
Wordsworth, Christopher 3
Worsley, Joe 231, 237–8
Wright, James 30
Wyatt, Derek 199–200
Wyatt, Mark 199
Wyman, Alf 172

Yarranton, Peter 133–5
Y Faner 24–5
Ynysybwl 9, 220, 231
Yorkshire Post 28, 35, 38, 43, 53
Young, Arthur 86
Young, Dai 200
Young, Jeff 176

Zuleika Dobson 7